D1286203

WEST GA REG LIB SYS
Neva Lomason
Memorial Library

The Fundamentals of Wind-Driven Water Pumpers

The Fundamentals
of Wind-Driven
Water Pumpers

J. A. C. Kentfield

University of Calgary
Alberta, Canada

Gordon and Breach Science Publishers

Australia Canada China France Germany India Japan
Luxembourg Malaysia The Netherlands Russia Singapore
Switzerland Thailand United Kingdom

Copyright © 1996 OPA (Overseas Publishers Association) Amsterdam B.V.
Published in The Netherlands under license by Gordon and Breach Science
Publishers.

All rights reserved.

No part of this book may be reproduced or utilized in any form or by any
means, electronic or mechanical, including photocopying and recording, or
by any information storage or retrieval system, without permission in writing
from the publisher. Printed in Canada.

Amsteldijk 166
1st Floor
1079 LH Amsterdam
The Netherlands

British Library Cataloguing in Publication Data

Kentfield, John A. C.
  The fundamentals of wind-driven water pumpers
  1.Wind pumps   2.Wind turbines   3.Pumping machinery
  4.Hydraulic turbines   5.Pump turbines
  I.Title
  621.4'5

ISBN 2-88449-239-9

CONTENTS

PREFACE

The prime intent of this book is to offer guidance to engineers charged with the task of designing new, or improving existing, wind-driven water pumpers. Emphasis has been given to material of specific interest in the wind water-pumping field not covered by most engineers during their formal engineering education. It has also been assumed that the reader has no detailed prior knowledge of, or practical experience with, wind-energy conversion equipment in general or wind-driven water pumpers in particular. The assumption is made, however, that the reader is familiar with basic fluid mechanics, machine dynamics, simple stress analysis, and machine design as covered in most undergraduate courses in mechanical engineering. If the reader's knowledge in these areas is a little rusty, appropriate reference to suitable mechanical engineering undergraduate course texts should repair any shortcomings with regard to background material. While the designer of a wind water pumper can be shielded, by using suitable existing computer software packages, from becoming heavily involved in some of the more complex and tedious aspects of the design process, the possession of a sound basic engineering knowledge is virtually indispensable.

Because of the large, almost infinite, number of machine specifications possible, no attempt has been made to provide complete designs ready for fabrication but rather to concentrate on consideration of the factors that must be taken into account when designing a suitable machine to satisfy the requirements of a particular specification. The designer is therefore left to select whichever combination of component types can best be used to achieve the desired result. To aid in this task, fundamental-level knowledge specific to the wind water-pumper field, such as component performances, is included in the material presented.

The content of the volume has been organised in what, it is hoped, the reader will find to be a logical sequence. It is not, unfortunately, possible to cover every detail in a work of this size but an effort has been made to target the main concerns. Chapter 1 introduces the topic and reviews, very briefly, the historical background of wind water-pumping. Chapters 2 and 3 present essential theoretical background material in sufficient detail for the reader to understand, and become familiar with, ideal turbine performances, practical considerations that conspire to impose restrictions on the performances of real turbines, commonly used turbine performance presentation formats, and so on. Chapter 4 is devoted to a brief overview of wind characteristics, including the influence of various obstructions upwind of a turbine, the importance of siting, and commonly used statistically based techniques for describing and quantifying winds.

The presentation of material related exclusively to water-pumping wind-turbine components commences with chapter 5, in which experimentally derived performance characteristics are presented for many types of wind-turbine rotors used on water-pumping machines. Chapter 6 deals with the overall conceptual aspects of the design of horizontal-axis wind-driven water pumpers. The three subsequent chapters deal in more detail with specific aspects of the topics touched upon in chapter 6. For example, chapter 7 covers provisions for furling to provide storm protection. The types of pump that can be employed and their performances are dealt with in chapter 8. The influence on machine performance of variable-delivery pumps is explained in chapter 9. Chapter 10 covers simplified systems, not of the horizontal-axis type, and the expected performance penalties associated with these. Finally, the advantages and disadvantages of various fabricational techniques available to machine builders are discussed in chapter 11.

I am grateful to the Renewable Energy Group of ECN, The Netherlands Energy Research Foundation, Petten, for making space available for me to work on this book during sabbatical leave from my home university. Thanks are due to Paul Smulders of the Technical University of Eindhoven, The Netherlands, for providing information relating to the work of the Dutch CWD organisation. I am indebted to Dutch Industries Ltd., Regina, Saskatchewan, Canada, and the former Calgary, Canada-based company Abax Energy Services Ltd. for implementing in practice some of my concepts. Thanks also to certain of my former project and graduate students, acknowledged appropriately in the References section of the volume, who assisted in carrying out some of the work described. Lastly, the typing on disc of the text was handled, very ably, by Karen Undseth, to whom I express my gratitude.

NOMENCLATURE

a	Axial flow induction, or inflow, factor (a' = tangential induction factor)
a'	Shaft diameter of Savonius rotor (see Figs. 10.7 and 10.9)
A	Cross-sectional area normal to flow (or c.s.a. of water column)
A_{PUMP}	Area of face of pump plunger
A_R	Airfoil, or turbine blade, aspect ratio
A'	Height of a tilt-up tower (Fig. 11.1)
b	Blade, or airfoil, span
B	Length of gin pole of a tilt-up tower (Fig. 11.1)
$\bar{c}$	Average chord of a blade
C	Weibull scale parameter (e.g., m/s)
C_D	Drag coefficient (local)
C_{DD}	Drag coefficient of an isolated blade, moving downwind, of a drag-type turbine
C_{DU}	Drag coefficient of an isolated blade, moving upwind, of a drag-type turbine
C_L	Lift coefficient (local)
$C_{L(EFF)}$	Effective lift coefficient, referred to mainplane projected area, of a canard-equipped flapping-vane pumper
C_P	Power coefficient $\equiv$ Actual Power Produced / $[(\rho_\infty U_\infty^3 S)/2]$
$\bar{C}_P$	Average power coefficient with gusting based on average prevailing wind speed U_∞ (see equation (4.6))
C_{PO}	Overall system power coefficient
$C_{(r)}$	Blade chord ($\bar{c}$ is the average chord)
C_t	Thrust coefficient
C_T	Torque coefficient $\equiv$ Actual Rotor Torque / $[(1/2)\rho_\infty U_\infty^2 S (D/2)]$
C'_T	Torque coefficient referred to a geared-down output shaft
C_W	Water flow-rate coefficient $\equiv C_{T(\lambda=0)} \lambda_{MAX}$

d	General representative dimension of a body
D	Rotor overall diameter
D_i	Induced drag
D'	Mainplane chord of flapping-vane pumper
$D*$	Diameter of a hypothetical reference turbine for which $\sigma' = 1.0$
f	Frequency of operation of a reciprocating pump (cycles/min)
F	Force required to raise load W in self-erecting systems
F_T	Tangential (reactive) thrust force
g	Acceleration due to gravity
h	Head, or lift
H	Ratio: $r_{(eff)}/r_{(MAX)}$
I	Polar moment of turbine rotor about the axis of spin
k	Constant
K	Weibull shape parameter (dimensionless)
l	Stroke of pump
L	Lift (aerodynamic)
$\overline{L}$	Distance from yaw axis to centre-of-pressure of tailvane
m	Gust-strength parameter
$\dot{m}$	Mass flow
M	Diameter ratio D_p/D_c
M'	Mass ratio factor of flapping-vane pumper component $\equiv$ Mass (full scale) / (Mass (model) $\times S'^3$)
n	Number of blades
n_G	Ratio of speed-reduction gear
N	Rotor speed
p	Savonius rotor dimension (see Fig. 10.7)
P	Pressure

q	Savonius rotor dimension (see Fig. 10.7)
Q	Volumetric flow rate of pumped liquid
Q_T	Ideal flow rate of pump
r	General radial station (of rotor)
R	Characteristic gas constant for air
S	Turbine rotor, or actuator surface, projected area
S_B	Air-lift pump submergence
S'	Linear dimensional scale-up factor from model to full-scale flapping-vane pumper
T	Temperature
U	Flow velocity
U_{BLADE}	Velocity of (moving) blade
$\overline{U}_\infty$	Time-averaged site wind speed
w	Downwash velocity
W	Dead load raised by force F
W_u	Useful work
W	Work rate
x	Blade span (see Fig. 5.31)
x'	Horizontal dimension of saddle of an inclined-plane tower (Figs. 11.3 and 11.4)
y	Coordinate normal to a surface
y_a	Extension of y' (Fig. 11.4)
y'	Vertical dimension of saddle of an inclined-plane tower (Figs. 11.3 and 11.4)
Y	Distance above the terrain
z	Vertically upward directed coordinate
Z	Maximum value of z

Greek Symbols

α Blade (local) angle of incidence

β Blade (local) pitch angle

γ Exponent of Prandtl's boundary layer power law

γ' Included angle between U_{TAIL} and tailvane surface

δ Angle of slope of an inclined plane (Fig. 11.3)

ΔE Change of kinetic energy

ΔP Pressure differential corresponding to h

ε Downwash angle

η Water pump energy utilisation efficiency

η_{BETZ} Betz efficiency $\equiv$

$$\text{Actual Power Produced} \Big/ \frac{16}{27}\left(\frac{\rho_\infty U_\infty^3}{2} S\right)$$

η_V Volumetric efficiency of a positive displacement water pump

θ Flow deflection angle

λ Tip-speed ratio $\equiv (\pi DN)/U_\infty = (\omega r_{MAX})/U_\infty$

$\bar{\lambda}$ Average tip-speed ratio with gusting based on average prevailing wind-speed U_∞

Λ Value of λ at $C_{P(MAX)}$

μ Absolute viscosity

ρ Density

ρ_M Effective density of air/water mixture in air-lift pump

σ Integrated solidity, i.e.,

$$= \frac{4n}{\pi D^2} \int_0^{D/2} C(r)\, dr \text{ for a horizontal axis rotor}$$

σ' Solidity based on flat generation of cambered sails or thin sheet blades (see Section 5.1)

σ'_L Local (or line) rotor solidity based on flat generation of cambered sails or thin sheet blades

ϕ Sail setting parameter for Cretian rotors (see Section 5.1)

ψ Angle of inclination of a tilt-up tower

ω Angular velocity of turbine rotor (radian/s)

ω_P Precessional, or yaw, angular velocity

Subscripts

1, 2, etc.	Stations in the flow or operating points
(ABS)	Absolute (i.e., relative to a stationary point)
c	Conventional
(eff)	Effective
i	Induced
$IDEAL$	Ideal value (i.e., without irreversibilities)
IN	Inflow (to rotor)
L	Liquid
MAX	Maximum value
O	Overall
OUT	Outflow (from rotor)
p	Perimeter-bladed
$PUMP$	Piston, or plunger, of a reciprocating pump
REL	Relative (to moving blades)
S	At location of actuator surface
T	Tangential or whirl component (of absolute velocity)
$TAIL$	Approaching tailvane
ω	Peripheral
∞	Undisturbed free-stream value

Abbreviations

ARETS	Alberta Renewable Energy Test Site
CWD	Consulting Services, Wind Energy, Developing Countries
KE	Kinetic energy
PDF	Probability Density Function (see equations (4.4) and (4.5))
WD	Work done

CHAPTER 1

Introduction

Most, but not all, wind-driven water pumpers incorporate wind-turbines to convert the kinetic energy of the wind into the rotary motion of a shaft which, in turn, provides the power input to a water pump. In most cases the turbine employed is of the horizontal-axis type; hence the turbine shaft is horizontal although in some machines the shaft is inclined, slightly, to the horizontal. In a few cases turbines are employed in which the axis of rotation is vertical. The commonly used term "windmill" to describe a wind-turbine driving a water pump, or for that matter an electric power generator, is strictly incorrect since a windmill is literally a wind-driven machine for milling grain or some other substance. Thus a "water-pumping windmill" is better identified as a water-pumping wind-turbine or a wind-turbine-driven water pumper.

The kinds of water pumps employed in wind-turbine-driven water pumpers range from simple reciprocating lift pumps to rotary positive-displacement pumps, often of the so-called progressive-cavity type. In some cases rotor-dynamic pumps are employed, usually of the centrifugal type. In yet other circumstances the wind-turbine drives an air compressor, the output from which serves to operate a remote pneumatically driven water pump often of the bubble, or air-lift, type.

The connection between the wind-turbine and the water pump, or air compressor, can be either direct, with or without speed-reducing or speed-increasing gearing, or an electric transmission can be employed. The inherent advantage of an electric transmission relates to the possibility of installing the wind-turbine, or turbines, remotely from the well site. This can be an important consideration when the well site is located in a sheltered position which does not constitute a good location for the wind-turbine. It is also possible, with an electric transmission, to divert the power output of the wind-turbine to other tasks when pumping is not required. Similar comments can be made with respect to air-lift pumping systems: the wind-turbine-driven air compressor can be located remotely from the well site and, if need be, the compressed air supply can be diverted to provide power for tasks other than water pumping.

Water pumpers have also been developed that do not employ wind-turbines but, instead, operate a reciprocating, lift-type pump by means of an oscillating airfoil or flapping vane. Machines of this type are sometimes termed aeolian pump jacks. They tend to have a relatively low-energy conversion efficiency compared with most turbine-driven water pumpers but are generally much easier to fabricate, especially if the airfoil is of the flat-plate type.

It can be appreciated that in order to cover the wide range of disciplines relating to wind-driven water pumpers in a concise and systematic manner it is desirable to organize the material under various subject headings. These are identified in detail in §1.1, which sets forth the objectives of the present work. The background material leading to the current level of knowledge and experience is described somewhat briefly in §1.2, which deals with the history of wind-driven water pumping. It is, perhaps, worth noting that technology developed specifically for pumping water can also be applied to the pumping of, say, oil provided appropriate allowances are made for differences in density and viscosity between oil and water. Wind-driven oil pumping may well be viable in some particular circumstances although the writer is not aware of any commercial applications.

1.1. Objectives

An objective of this work is to bring together, under a sound scientific umbrella, various aspects of the application of wind energy to water pumping. It is also an objective to present the scientific material as simply and as concisely as possible consistent with clarity. Yet another objective is to illustrate, where possible, the material presented with corresponding quantitative, experimentally obtained data.

It is also intended to concentrate on proven, demonstrated technology rather than speculative aspects of the field, although some speculative topics are touched upon in various places. The material covered includes some basic theory as it relates to defining the performance parameters of wind-driven water pumpers; aerodynamic theory relevant, in particular, to the operation of wind-turbine rotors; wind characteristics; the properties of various types of horizontal-axis turbine rotors; the configuration of horizontal-axis machines; various types of pumps in use and their properties including those involving variable delivery capabilities due, for example, to the application to reciprocating pumps of variable stroke mechanisms; furling systems for horizontal-axis machines; flapping-vane, Savonius and drag-type machines; structural-design considerations.

1.2. Historical Background

Earlier application of wind energy to operate water pumps appears to have occurred in Holland, now called The Netherlands. The incentive for this development was the need to drain the low-lying, and often water-logged, land areas to render them more suitable for agriculture and to prevent flooding. The use of wind-driven water pumpers in Holland appears to have been initiated approximately four to five hundred years ago. Generally the pumping was of the low-head type with a total lift of about 1 m to 5 m depending upon details of specific sites. For lifts of, say, 2 m to 5 m it was customary to employ multiple wind-turbine-driven water pumpers operating in series.

The type of water pump employed was usually of either the scoop wheel or Archimedean-screw type. A scoop wheel is, in essence, a reversed water wheel. An Archimedean-screw pump consists of a large-diameter screw thread built up on a central shaft, usually of wood, running in a tubular casing. The axes of the screw and casing are inclined with the lower end of the pump submerged in the water source. A pump of this type can justifiably be classified, in modern terminology, as a progressive cavity rotary pump. The essentially horizontal-axis wind-turbine rotors of the Dutch drainage pumpers appeared to remain virtually unchanged over a period of several hundred years. The rotor design featured four, essentially flat-plate, constant chord blades each with a removable sail-cloth covering on the pressure surface. An interesting feature was the provision of blade twist with the blade-pitch angle greatest at the root and least, sometimes negative, at the tips. A well-illustrated brief history of the early development of wind energy applications in Holland is available (Braay and Tersteeg, 1990). The classical Dutch type machines did not incorporate automatic control; the sail-cloth blade covering and, in most cases, the yaw setting were adjusted manually.

Construction of new machines of the classical Dutch type ceased towards the end of the nineteenth century since most of the major pumping duties had by that time been taken over by steam, internal-combustion engines or electrically driven pumps the operation of which was, of course, independent of the wind. The rotor diameter of the classical Dutch type machines, which were also reproduced in many other countries, ranged from about 4 m to more than 20 m. The (integrated) rotor solidity, σ, was

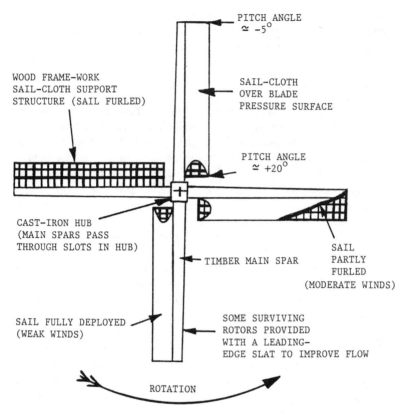

Figure 1.1. Geometry of a typical, classical, Dutch type, four-bladed, wind-turbine rotor.

typically in the region of 0.25. Figure 1.1 shows, diagrammatically, the geometry of a typical, classical, Dutch type turbine.

Whilst the Dutch water pumpers were gradually being replaced by engine, or electric-motor, driven pumps, an entirely different form of wind-driven water pumping equipment was under development in the United States. The perceived need was for small, self-regulating, wind-driven water pumpers to serve the fresh water requirements of individual farms, their primary duties being to provide drinking water for both the farmer and his family and the farm livestock. For most applications the water had to be pumped from a considerable depth, the water table being, in some cases, 100 m or more below ground level. It was equipment of this type that greatly helped the westward spread of agriculture in the United States during the latter part of the nineteenth century.

One of the pioneers in the development of small, self-regulating wind-turbine-driven water pumpers in the United States was Daniel Halladay. His earliest machines, dating from the 1850s, employed horizontal-axis rotors with variable pitch blading controlled by a centrifugal governor. The rotors of these early machines had solidities in the region of about 0.5 with from four to eight flat-plate blades. The face of the upwind rotor of the Halladay machine was maintained in a direction normal to the oncoming wind, automatically, by means of a yaw-control, downwind-mounted tailvane fixed to the rotor-support structure. In a later stage of development Halladay replaced his variable-pitch rotor design with a rotor featuring numerous, thin, slat-like, flat, wooden blades. The solidity of this type of rotor was in the region of 0.85. Prevention of overspeeding was by means of tilting the rotor blading, in sections, about chordwise-mounted pivots as shown in Fig. 1.2. Crank-operated, reciprocating, lift-type pumps were employed by Halladay and other pioneers and have, in effect, become standardised equipment in virtually all subsequent developments in the small, self-regulating, wind-driven water pumper field. In some cases the pump is driven directly from the turbine shaft; in other cases a reduction gear is provided between the turbine shaft and the crank operating the pump.

Rotors similar to that depicted in Fig. 1.2 were also used in small water-pumping wind-turbines in which the rotor was mounted downwind of the support tower. This configuration eliminated the need for a tailvane since the rotor quite naturally, and automatically, takes up a downwind position relative to the oncoming wind. Some upwind rotors of the slatted type were not arranged to fold in the manner shown in Fig. 1.2 and an alternative form of overspeed control was applied in which the rotor was contrived to turn, as a rigid structure, edgewise to the oncoming wind. A more detailed recounting of the early development in the United States of small, self-regulating wind-driven water pumpers has been given by T. Lindsay Baker (Baker, 1985).

What can probably be thought of as the final major step in the development of the small, self-regulating, wind-driven water pumper concept in the United States was the substitution, by T.O. Perry in the latter part of the nineteenth century, of cambered sheet-metal blades for the slatted wood blades of earlier rotors. The change from flat wood-slats to cambered sheet-metal blades was a result of tests carried out by Perry to measure the relative performance of both flat wood-slat blades and cambered sheet-metal blades. Perry's tests were carried out by moving a large-scale, dynamometer-equipped model rotor through nominally still

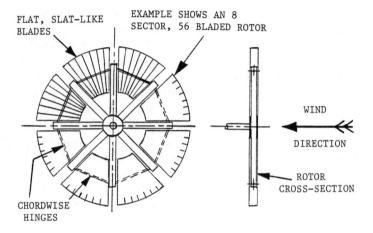

ROTOR IN NORMAL OPERATING CONFIGURATION

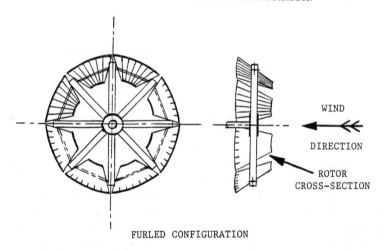

FURLED CONFIGURATION

Figure 1.2. Geometrical arrangement of a typical Halladay type sectional, furling, rotor employing slat-type blades.

air with the model rotor mounted on the outer end of an engine-driven radial arm rotating about a vertical axis (Perry, 1899).

It was the notably superior performance of cambered sheet-metal blades relative to that of wood-slat blading that led to the almost universal subsequent use of blades of the former type. Small, self-regulating, wind-driven water pumpers with cambered sheet-metal blades constitute a classical design usually now identified as the American type multibladed water pumper concept. The support towers of these machines are usually of the light space-frame type in contrast to the column-like wood, or masonry, towers of the former, classical, Dutch wind-driven water pumpers.

An additional development in the wind-driven water-pumping area has been the application of classical Cretian type sail-blade turbines, traditionally used for milling applications, to driving water pumps for irrigation purposes on the plain of Lassithi in Crete. Another specialised application of wind power to water pumping occurred in The Netherlands, where a small, four-bladed turbine was developed to drive a low head centrifugal pump with a lift of no more than 1 m. Many such units were produced, and some are still in use, for the local draining of flat reclaimed land, or polders.

More recently much research and development has been undertaken in The Netherlands directed at producing a light, low-cost, relatively high-speed water pumper for use primarily in developing countries. The organisation formerly undertaking this work was identified as Consultancy Services, Wind Energy, Developing Countries (CWD). Much progress was made, and this has been reported in the technical literature (Meel et al., 1986).

A recent development, originated in Canada, has been the application of turbines for wind-driven water pumpers featuring delta-wing planform blades. This development has advanced in two directions: one featuring moderate-speed rotors, the other leading to low rotor speeds. The aim, in both cases, has been to produce rotors capable of making the most effective use of the rotor-blade area provided in combination with realising special aerodynamic benefits due to the use of delta-wing planform blades. These turbines, in common with the turbines of many dedicated water pumpers, are designed to provide their maximum rotor torque, for a prescribed wind speed, at zero rotational speed. This characteristic is of particular use when starting a direct-coupled, lift-type, reciprocating water pump under loaded conditions. The version of the concept featuring the low-speed rotor has achieved production status. Technical literature is available describing both rotor concepts (Kentfield, 1992(a); Kentfield and Cruson, 1989).

A question that can be asked concerning large-scale water pumping applications relates to the use of pumped-storage systems for wind-electric machines. Pumped storage would, in principle, make it possible to deliver, via a hydroturbine, electrical power on demand instead of only when the wind is blowing. Several studies have been made of this concept and, up to the present time, such schemes have not been found to be viable from the cost-effectiveness viewpoint. Hence this topic remains speculative and will not be discussed here any further.

It should be appreciated that this brief review omits reference to many projects; for example, the recent development of a successful, small-scale, commercial air-lift pumping system in the United States. However, the matters touched upon are those which in the writer's opinion should help the reader formulate a relatively balanced view of the wind-driven water-pumping field. A review of the historical background of wind-driven water pumping by another author serves to both augment much of the material of this section and to present a view of the subject from a somewhat different perspective (Fraenkel, 1994). A photograph of an example of most models of wind-driven water pumper, plus a brief specification of each design, in production in the early 1990s is available (Fraenkel et al., 1993).

CHAPTER 2

Basic Theory

The theoretical considerations dealt with in this chapter are those of a fundamental nature which do not require any prior, detailed, knowledge of the wind-energy extraction device employed; usually, but not in every case, a wind-turbine. The matters considered relate, for example, to assessing the maximum possible work extraction in ideal circumstances; establishing parameters in terms of which machine performance can be expressed; establishing conditions consistent with maximising wind-turbine starting torque, etc.

2.1. Maximum Ideal Work

It is an important tenet of the science of wind-energy utilisation that to obtain a useful work output the wind must be slowed, but not brought to rest, by the wind-energy utilisation device. For example, an impervious wall, normal to the flow, will bring to rest all the flow that would otherwise have passed through the area occupied by the wall had it not been there. However the wall does not produce any work output. Replacing the impervious wall with a pervious wall will allow some flow to pass through the wall, although depending upon the porosity, and hence the pressure loss involved, the flow will be slowed. This still does not permit a useful work output to be obtained unless the pervious wall is replaced by specially designed moving surfaces to extract, and convert to a useful, usable form the kinetic energy of the flow. If the device involved slows the flow substantially it allows more energy to be extracted from the flow passing through the energy conversion system but reduces the flow rate relative to an alternative energy conversion device that permits a greater flow but therefore extracts, per unit mass flow, less energy. Clearly on the proviso of an ideal technology that allows the kinetic energy of the flow passing through the energy utilisation device to be converted into a useful form without losses, that is reversibly, there is likely to be an optimum reduction of wind speed through such an energy utilisation device.

Figure 2.1(a) depicts an unspecified form of (reversible) wind-energy extraction device of projected area S normal to the oncoming wind of velocity U_1. It is noteworthy that an implication of Fig. 2.1(a) is that the device, which is assumed to be of infinitesimal thickness, causes the flow passing through it to slow down both upwind and downwind of the plane occupied by, what can be termed, the actuator surface S. When a consideration of this type is applied to a horizontal-axis turbine of, essentially, infinitesimal thickness, as indicated in Fig. 2.1(b), the infinitesimally thin, hypothetical, ideal turbine is usually identified as an actuator disc. However, the concept is equally applicable to vertical-axis turbines, as suggested in Fig. 2.1(c), or other wind-energy utilisation devices. Hence, in the most general sense, it is better to refer to the actuator surface shown in Fig. 2.1(a). The static pressures at stations 1 and 2, which are well upwind and well downwind of S, respectively, are each equal to the surroundings pressure P_∞.

On the basis of what appears to be a reasonable assumption that the velocity through the actuator surface is the mean of the upwind and downwind velocity U_1 and U_2, respectively, an assumption that will, in Chapter 3, be proven to be valid:

The mean flow velocity $= (U_1 + U_2)/2$ and hence the mass flow, $\dot{m}$, passing through S is given, assuming incompressible flow, by:

$$\dot{m} = \rho_\infty (U_1 + U_2)S/2 \tag{2.1}$$

The ideal work obtained from the actuator surface $S = KE_1 - KE_2$ ($\equiv \Delta E$) and thus:

$$\Delta E = \frac{\dot{m}}{2}(U_1^2 - U_2^2) \tag{2.2}$$

or substituting for $\dot{m}$:

$$\Delta E = \frac{\rho_\infty S}{4}(U_1 + U_2)(U_1^2 - U_2^2)$$
$$= \frac{\rho_\infty S U_1^3}{4}\left(1 + \frac{U_2}{U_1}\right)\left(1 - \left(\frac{U_2}{U_1}\right)^2\right) \tag{2.3}$$

ie., for given U_1 and ρ_∞, the maximum or minimum of ΔE is given by:

$$\frac{d(\Delta E)}{d\left(\dfrac{U_2}{U_1}\right)} = 0$$

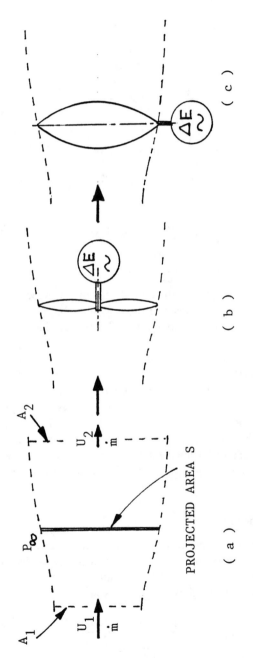

Figure 2.1. An actuator surface of area S in a stream-tube: a) fundamental situation; b) applied to a horizontal-axis turbine (diagrammatic); c) applied to a vertical-axis turbine (diagrammatic).

Performing the implied differentiation, it can be shown that:

$$3 \left(\frac{U_2}{U_1}\right)^2 + 2 \left(\frac{U_2}{U_1}\right) - 1 = 0$$

Thus:

$$\frac{U_2}{U_1} = +\frac{1}{3} \text{ or } -1$$

ie.,

$$\frac{U_2}{U_1} = \frac{1}{3} \text{ for maximum power}$$

and substituting $U_2/U_1 = 1/3$ in the previous expression for ΔE and simplifying gives:

$$\Delta E_{MAX} = \frac{8}{27} \rho_\infty S U_1^3 = \frac{16}{27} \left(\frac{\rho_\infty S U_1^3}{2}\right) = 0.593 \left(\frac{\rho_\infty S U_1^3}{2}\right) \tag{2.4}$$

This result is known as the Betz expression for the maximum power of an ideal, reversible, wind-energy extraction device of projected area S. The derivation presented here is, however, less rigorous, because of the initial assumption relating to the velocity through S, than that due to Betz (Betz, 1920).

A greater value of ΔE_{MAX} than that corresponding to the Betz expression can be obtained when the wind-energy extraction device, usually a turbine, is mounted at the throat of a suitable venturi-like shroud duct. Such a duct, normally identified as an augmenter, is seldom employed since it is usually heavy and expensive. Caution should be exercised if the foregoing analysis is applied to an augmented turbine since the flow-inlet and outlet areas of an augmenter duct are not necessarily equal, a situation that does not apply to a turbine represented as a simple actuator surface S.

2.2. Power Coefficient

A criterion of merit for the conversion of wind energy into a useable output in a wind-energy conversion device is the actual power produced divided by the Betz ideal power. Hence from equation (2.4) the expression for what is termed the Betz efficiency, η_{BETZ}, is given by:

$$\eta_{BETZ} \equiv \frac{\text{Actual Power Produced}}{\dfrac{16}{27}\left(\dfrac{\rho_\infty U_1^3 S}{2}\right)} \tag{2.5}$$

However the Betz efficiency is rarely employed in practice and a more commonly used expression is termed the power coefficient C_P. This is the ratio of the numerator of the right-hand side of equation (2.5) divided by the work done per unit time, due to the wind kinetic energy, passing through the flow area S of the wind-turbine when the turbine is removed. Hence:

$$C_P \equiv \frac{\text{Actual Power Produced}}{\left(\dfrac{\rho_\infty U_1^3 S}{2}\right)} \tag{2.6}$$

It can be seen that for a hypothetical perfect, or ideal, turbine the maximum value of η_{BETZ} is unity (or 100%) whilst the corresponding maximum value of C_P is 16/27 (ie., 0.593) or 59.3%.

A question that can be asked in relation to the analysis presented in §2.1 is how sensitive is the performance of a hypothetical, ideal, wind-energy conversion device to maintaining the optimum value of U_2/U_1 at 1/3? The power coefficient, as a function of U_2/U_1, has been evaluated from equation (2.3) and is presented graphically in Fig. 2.2. The corresponding area ratios S/A_1 and S/A_2 were also evaluated from application of continuity relationships between area A_1, at station 1, and area S and also between area A_2, at station 2, and area S. It can be seen from Fig. 2.2 that variation of U_2/U_1 within the range $0.2 \le U_2/U_1 \le 0.45$ has but a minor influence of $C_{P(IDEAL)}$. A reduction of U_2/U_1 much below 0.3 results in a rapid escalation in the exit cross-sectional area A_2 resulting for $U_2/U_1 = 0$ in an infinite exit area, an obviously very unrealistic situation. The flow entry cross-sectional area is half of the area S when $U_2/U_1 = 0$ and, of course, equals area S when $U_2/U_1 = 1.0$.

It is more usual to denote wind speed by means of the subscript ∞ rather than the subscript 1 employed, for convenience, in the previous analytical work. Hence definitions (2.5) and (2.6) are better written in the following forms:

$$\eta_{BETZ} \equiv \frac{\text{Actual Power Produced}}{\dfrac{16}{27}\left(\dfrac{\rho_\infty U_\infty^3 S}{2}\right)} \tag{2.7}$$

and

$$C_P \equiv \frac{\text{Actual Power Produced}}{\left(\dfrac{\rho_\infty U_\infty^3 S}{2}\right)} \tag{2.8}$$

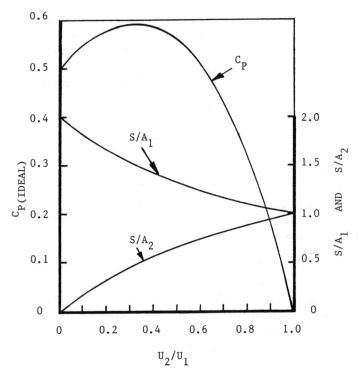

Figure 2.2. Ideal power coefficient and stream-tube area ratios as functions of U_2/U_1.

2.3. Torque Coefficient

Another parameter useful for describing the performance of wind-turbines in particular, especially those used for water pumping where the rotor torque must, for direct drive systems, equal the pump-load torque, is the dimensionless rotor torque termed the torque coefficient. The normalising term in the expression for torque coefficient, C_T, is the product of the dynamic pressure due to the wind, $(1/2)\rho U_\infty^2$, the rotor projected area S and a linear dimension representative of the system. The latter term is usually chosen, by most workers, to be the maximum radius, $D/2$, of the rotor although, in the past, the writer has, in other publications, elected to use the *average* radius $D/4$. Using, here, the conventional $D/2$ basis:

$$C_T \equiv \frac{\text{Actual Rotor Torque}}{(1/2)\rho_\infty U_\infty^2 S(D/2)} \qquad (2.9)$$

The torque coefficient can also be expressed in terms of the power coefficient, C_P, and the rotor tip-speed ratio λ. The rotor tip-speed ratio is the rotor peripheral speed divided by the wind speed U_∞. Thus

$$\lambda \equiv \frac{\pi DN}{U_\infty} \tag{2.10}$$

where N is the rotor speed, in revolutions per unit time, with the time unit cancelling with that of U_∞ to yield a dimensionless expression for λ. Thus expressing the rotor power in terms of C_T and also C_P and equating:

$$\omega \text{ (Actual Rotor Torque)} = C_P(1/2)\rho_\infty U_\infty^3 S$$

or since $\omega = 2\pi N$ and also invoking equation (2.9):

$$2\pi N C_T(1/2)\rho_\infty U_\infty^2 S(D/2) = C_P(1/2)\rho_\infty U_\infty^3 S \tag{2.11}$$

Simplifying equation (2.11) and introducing the definition of λ from (2.10) gives the following result:

$$C_T = C_P/\lambda \tag{2.12}$$

2.4. Maximum Ideal Torque Coefficient

A parameter of particular interest in the application of wind-turbines to water pumping is, for direct drive systems, the torque coefficient at zero rotor speed. This value of the torque coefficient is of special interest since it defines the ability of the turbine rotor to start the water pump under load.

A simple extension of the analysis presented in §2.1 allows, in the notation of that section, the optimum value of U_2/U_1 to be established corresponding to the maximum value of torque coefficient for a stationary rotor and, subsequently, a quantitative evaluation of $C_{T(MAX,IDEAL)}$ for a horizontal-axis rotor configuration.

With no losses and, due to a stationary rotor, zero power production, the flow through area S (Fig. 2.1(a)) will be deflected to produce a tangential component of velocity at station 2. This situation is illustrated in Fig. 2.3 which shows the velocity component, U_2, in the windward direction and the tangential velocity component U_T. The vector sum of U_T and U_2 must, for a loss-free system, yield a velocity equal to the inflow velocity U_1 as indicated in Fig. 2.3. The change of momentum associated with the

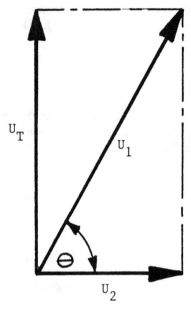

Figure 2.3. Velocity diagram at the stream-tube exit station with a stationary, reversible-flow rotor.

implied change of flow direction results in forces acting on the stationary turbine rotor. The thrust, F_T, generated due to the tangential component of the flow corresponds to the rate of change of momentum involved and hence is given by:

$$F_T = \dot{m}U_T \tag{2.13}$$

The mass flow can, conveniently, be referred to that through area S; hence from equations (2.13) and (2.1):

$$\dot{m}U_T = \frac{\rho_\infty S}{2}(U_1 + U_2)U_T \tag{2.14}$$

where, from Fig. 2.3:

$$U_T^2 = (U_1^2 - U_2^2) \tag{2.15}$$

Hence from equations (2.14) and (2.15) the expression for the thrust force F_T becomes:

$$F_T = \frac{\rho_\infty S U_1^2}{2}\left(1 + \frac{U_2}{U_1}\right)\left(1 - \left[\frac{U_2}{U_1}\right]^2\right)^{1/2} \tag{2.16}$$

Differentiating equation (2.16) with respect to U_2/U_1 and equating to zero leads to the result that the condition for maximum F_T, for a prescribed U_1, corresponds to the ratio:

$$\frac{U_2}{U_1} = 1/2 \tag{2.17}$$

It should be noted that this value is slightly greater than the value of $U_2/U_1 = 1/3$ previously shown to be the condition for maximum turbine output with zero residual whirl in the wake. Substituting $U_2/U_1 = 1/2$ in equation (2.16) leads to the result:

$$F_{T(MAX,IDEAL)} = \frac{\rho_\infty S U_1^2}{2} \left(\frac{3\sqrt{3}}{4} \right) \tag{2.18}$$

Restricting the discussion to the case of a horizontal-axis rotor, the consequence of F_T is the generation of a whirl in the turbine wake at station 2. Hence for a zero radial pressure gradient condition at station 2 the corresponding velocity diagram, at any radial station in the (expanding) wake, is that shown in Fig. 2.3. The resultant reactive torque generated on a horizontal-axis rotor of diameter D, and area $S = \frac{\pi}{4}D^2$, is, therefore, given by:

$$\text{Torque} = \frac{\rho_\infty U_1^2}{2} \left(\frac{3\sqrt{3}}{4} \right) 2\pi \int\limits_{0}^{D/2} r^2 \, dr \tag{2.19}$$

where r is a general radial station of the turbine. Carrying out the implied integration in equation (2.19), replacing U_1 with the more general U_∞ and expressing the result in the form of a torque coefficient in the manner of equation (2.9) gives the result:

$$C_{T(MAX,IDEAL)} = \sqrt{3}/2 = 0.866 \tag{2.20}$$

This, therefore, represents the maximum value of the torque coefficient corresponding to zero angular velocity of an ideal, loss free, horizontal-axis turbine. The flow deflection angle, θ, at station 2 (Fig. 2.3) corresponding to $C_{T(MAX,IDEAL)}$ is given, from equation (2.17), by:

$$\theta = \cos^{-1}\left(\frac{U_2}{U_1} \right) = \cos^{-1}(0.5)$$

hence:

$$\theta = 60° \tag{2.21}$$

2.5. Thrust Coefficient

Another parameter, in this case indicative of the downwind thrust on the wind-energy conversion device, is the thrust coefficient C_t. Referring to Fig. 2.1(a) the downwind thrust is defined by the magnitude of the momentum defect resulting from U_2 being less than U_1. The pressure terms have no net influence since the surroundings pressure, P_∞, is assumed to be active at station 1, station 2 and along the stream boundary surfaces shown dotted. Thus the rate of change of momentum in the windward direction $= \dot{m}(U_1 - U_2)$. Hence, expressing $\dot{m}$ as in equation (2.1) and multiplying by $(U_1 - U_2)$:

$$\text{Rate of change of momentum} = (1/2)\rho_\infty S(U_1 + U_2)(U_1 - U_2)$$

Thus simplifying and rearranging:

$$\text{Rate of change of momentum} = (1/2)\rho_\infty S U_1^2 \left[1 - \left(\frac{U_2}{U_1}\right)^2\right] \quad (2.22)$$

and expressing as the thrust coefficient by dividing by the dynamic pressure of the oncoming flow active on area S, ie., $(1/2)P_\infty U_\infty^2 S$:

$$C_t = \left[1 - \left(\frac{U_2}{U_1}\right)^2\right] \quad (2.23)$$

Equation (23) is presented graphically in Fig. 2.4. In the interests of simplicity with respect to evaluating aerodynamic loads it is common practice to make the conservative assumption that C_t has an invariant value of unity.

2.6. Typical Turbine Performance Presentation

The parameter commonly used for presenting the performances of the rotors of wind-turbines are the power coefficient C_P (equation (2.8)), torque coefficient C_T (equation (2.9)) and the rotor tip-speed ratio λ (equation (2.10)). Since C_P and C_T are not independent parameters there is a relationship between them involving λ (equation 2.12).

Experience shows that, in practice, due to various losses, for example surface friction, in turbine rotors the maximum achievable values of power coefficient and torque coefficient are, for water pumpers, in the region of 50 to 65% of the ideal maximum values. That is, peak power coefficients are typically in the region of about 0.3 to 0.4 and peak torque coefficients,

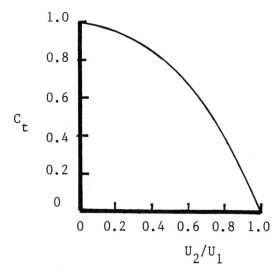

Figure 2.4. Thrust coefficient of an ideal rotor as a function of U_2/U_1.

at zero rotor speed, are in the region of 0.6 to 0.7. It is usually the case that the achievement of a high starting torque coefficient mitigates against the achievement of a high power coefficient in the same rotor or vice-versa.

The style of the C_P and C_T versus λ characteristics for a typical direct-drive water pumper rotor are presented in Fig. 2.5(a) and for a representative wind-electric turbine in Fig. 2.5(b). The characteristics of Fig. 2.5 are not intended to portray those of particular units. The principal differences relate to the high torque coefficient for $\lambda = 0$, and the relatively low maximum λ, of the water pumper compared with the low starting torque coefficient of the wind-electric machine coupled with a much higher running speed and the achievement of a somewhat higher peak power coefficient. The latter is, as will be shown later in Chapter 3, largely a consequence of the relatively low torque coefficient.

The higher running speed of the wind electric unit is helpful in matching the speed of the turbine rotor to that of the alternator with, in most cases, an intervening speed-increase gear-box. The attainment of a high peak power coefficient in the water pumper is sacrificed for a high torque coefficient at the $\lambda = 0$ condition. A high starting torque coefficient is not necessary for the wind-electric unit since machines of this type start-up under no-load.

When presenting wind-turbine-rotor test data, such as those depicted in Fig. 2.5, obtained, for example, by wind-tunnel testing it is often helpful

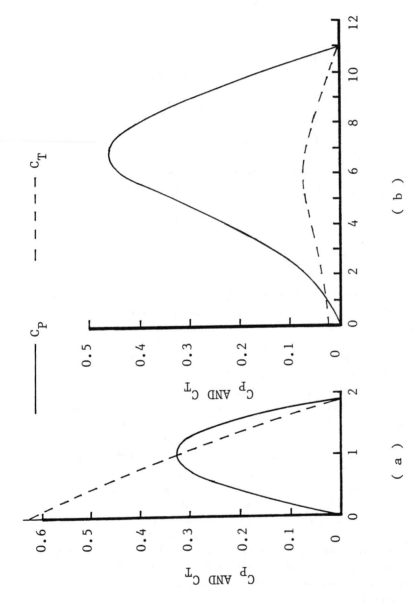

Figure 2.5. Turbine-rotor performances on the C_P and C_T vs. λ planes: a) water-pumping turbine (diagrammatic); b) wind-electric turbine (diagrammatic).

to employ additional, auxiliary, expressions that assist in the correlation of C_P and C_T. These are derived from differentiation of equation (2.12). Thus since:

$$C_T = C_P/\lambda$$

rearranging and differentiating gives:

$$\frac{dC_P}{d\lambda} = \lambda \frac{dC_T}{d\lambda} + C_T$$

Hence when $\lambda = 0$:

$$C_T = \left(\frac{dC_P}{d\lambda}\right)_{(\lambda=0)} \qquad (2.24)$$

and also when $dC_P/d\lambda = 0$ (ie., the condition for maximum power coefficient) then:

$$\frac{dC_T}{d\lambda} = -\frac{C_T}{\Lambda} \qquad (2.25)$$

where Λ is the value of λ corresponding to the maximum power coefficient.

2.7. Overall System Power Coefficient

The overall power coefficient, C_{PO}, expresses the ratio of the useful work performed by a wind water pumper as a fraction of the work done per unit time, due to the wind kinetic energy, passing through flow area, S, without the presence of the wind-turbine. The useful work performed by the pumper reflects the flow rate, $\dot{Q}$, of liquid, usually water, pumped by the machine, the lift or head, h, over which the liquid is raised and the density, ρ_L, of the liquid. It can thus be shown that the useful work, W_u, is given by:

$$W_u = \rho_L g \dot{Q} h$$

and hence expressing this as a coefficient:

$$C_{PO} \equiv \frac{\rho_L g \dot{Q} h}{(1/2)\rho_\infty U_\infty^3 S} \qquad (2.26)$$

or expressing ρ_∞ in terms of an ideal gas and substituting in equation (2.26) $\rho_\infty = P_\infty/RT_\infty$:

$$C_{PO} = \frac{RT_\infty \rho_L g \dot{Q} h}{(1/2)P_\infty U_\infty^3 S} \qquad (2.27)$$

It is found for most simple reciprocating lift-type pumps that, for all but very low head situations, $0.7 \leq C_{PO}/C_P \leq 0.8$. For other types of pump C_{PO}/C_P tends to be smaller and may also be a strong function λ.

A less fundamentally derived coefficient that has been found to be of use in reflecting the pumping potential of direct drive water pumpers, with positive-displacement pumps, is what has been termed the water flow-rate coefficient C_W. The coefficient C_W is represented by the value of C_T for $\lambda = 0$ multiplied by the value of λ at the runaway condition, that is, when $\lambda = \lambda_{(MAX)}$, and hence also $C_T = 0$. A detailed justification for considering C_W as an indicative, meaningful parameter has been presented elsewhere (Kentfield, 1988(a)).

CHAPTER 3

Aerodynamic Theory

The theoretical considerations dealt with in the previous chapter took but little account of the details of turbine operation. In fact in §2.1 of Chapter 2 the material was treated without reference to wind-turbines specifically although the application of the actuator surface concept to horizontal and vertical-axis turbines was at least alluded to in Fig. 2.1(b) and (c), respectively. In fact when more attention is paid to details of turbine flow fields some workers have, for example, chosen to model vertical-axis turbines, those of the Darrieus type in particular, as two actuator surfaces in series (Freris, 1990). In contrast in §2.1 of Chapter 2 a simple single-surface model was suggested, Fig. 2.1(c), as representative of all vertical-axis machines in general. The Darrieus turbine is rarely applied to water pumping duties and is never used in a stand-alone capacity because it is inherently non self-starting.

Here attention is paid to the operating principle of a turbine and also turbine geometries, primarily those of machines of the horizontal-axis type since these are of greatest practical importance in the wind-driven water pumper field. Consideration is also given to rotor aerodynamics with more attention paid to the reasons for the inherent differences in performance between water-pumping and wind-electric units touched upon, previously, in §2.6 of Chapter 2. A brief study is also included of rotor wakes since these generally constrain the minimum acceptable downwind spacing of machines in clustered installations. The basic aerodynamics of drag-type turbines and turbines of the Savonius rotor type, both normally configured with vertical axes, are also studied briefly since both of these types of machine are employed, occasionally, for water pumping. The essential purpose of the material of this chapter is to provide an extended descriptive background to turbine rotor design rather than to set-up analytical design tools.

3.1. Principle of a Turbine

The aerodynamic surfaces, or blades, of a turbine serve to deflect the incoming flow thereby generating forces on the blades which, in turn, exert a torque to cause rotation of the turbine rotor. The blades can generally be arranged close together as shown diagrammatically in Fig. 3.1(a), or in the other extreme, spaced well apart as implied in Fig. 3.1(b) such that they function, in large measure, as isolated aerodynamic surfaces or airfoils.

Even with only a single blade, some turbines of both the horizontal- and vertical-axis type have been built with a counterbalanced one-bladed rotor, the blade tends to be moving continuously into the wake it has, itself, generated. This situation is, therefore, somewhat analogous to that of a tandem-wing aircraft in which the second, or downstream, surface flies, constantly, in the wake of the upwind wing and, consequently, has a relatively high induced drag as a result of the downwash due to the upwind wing in addition to a self-induced downwash. It is, in large measure, to avoid this problem that tandem wings have, so rarely, been applied to aircraft. Clearly, in the case of a wind-turbine, it is not possible to have less than one blade in order to eliminate the blade-wake interference problem totally.

The analogy between aircraft wings and the blades of turbines with widely spaced blades is reasonable. Such a blade effectively "flies" in the manner of an aircraft wing. The blade pitch angle is chosen, as indicated in Fig. 3.1(b), to provide a suitable angle of incidence. Considering a radial element of the blade of a horizontal-axis machine, the tangential component of the lift vector, δL, acting in the direction of blade rotation less the opposing tangential component of the drag vector, δD, generates the net tangential force acting on the blade element. This net force multiplied by the radius, r, of the element constitutes the net torque generated by the element. The lift and drag fores acting on a blade element are illustrated, vectorially, in Fig. 3.1(b). The addition of the downwind components of δL and δD yields the thrust force, due to the blade element, acting on the rotor.

It should be noted that flow enters the rotor at a lower axial velocity than that of the wind. This feature is consistent with that represented in the stream-tubes pictured in Fig. 2.1. The flow entry velocity at the rotor face is conventionally expressed as $U_\infty(1 - a)$, where a is identified as the axial flow induction, or inflow, factor.

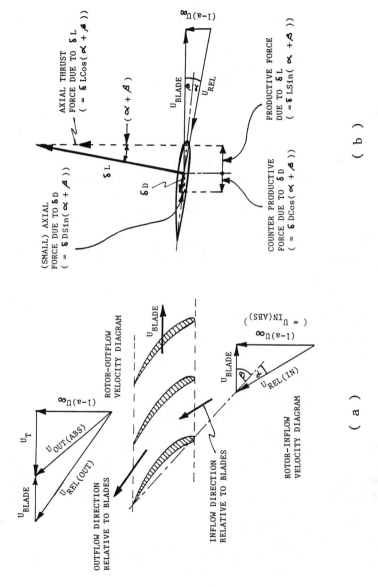

Figure 3.1. Representative velocity diagrams for wind-turbines: a) low-tip-speed ratio case; b) high-tip-speed ratio case.

A similar flow picture applied to the more closely packed blading is shown in Fig. 3.1(a). Here the blades are usually thought of as functioning, collectively, more as a cascade. Generally configurations of the type shown in Fig. 3.1(a) are used in low-tip-speed-ratio machines such as water pumpers. Cascaded blading is also widely used in steam- and gas-turbines, axial flow compressors, etc. The arrangement depicted in Fig. 3.1(b) is more applicable to the high-tip-speed-ratio turbines of most wind-electric machines. Because of their geometrical similarity to aircraft propellers such turbines are generally identified as "propeller type turbines" although, functionally, they operate in the reverse manner to aircraft propellers.

For a rotor blading geometry between the two rather extreme configurations shown in Fig. 3.1 interference between adjacent blades can play in a role. Such rotors typically have tip-speed ratios between those applicable to the two configurations of Fig. 3.1. The proximity of the blades can lead to mutual interference, relative to the performance of an individual airfoil, of the type that occurs in multi-plane aircraft configurations, such as biplanes, where the circulations around each airfoil interfere mutually, thereby reducing airfoil lift, compared with the magnitude of the circulation around a corresponding isolated airfoil (Glauert, 1948). On the other hand, each airfoil tends to serve, due to the stagger involved, partially as a leading edge slat for the blade downwind and, partially, as a trailing edge flap for the blade upwind although these beneficial influences will tend to be weaker than for the closely packed blading of Fig. 3.1(a). Figure 3.2 is an attempt to illustrate, notionally, the cause of the mutual interference that can be expected in the circulation around each airfoil.

Generally, to obtain the best performance over a range of tip-speed ratios turbine blade pitch angles should be adjusted as a function of operating conditions, in particular the tip-speed ratio itself. This form of complication is, in many cases, incorporated in wind-electric turbines but is very rarely applied to water pumper turbine rotors. Inlet guide vanes, or nozzles, and downwind flow straightening vanes, or a second counter-rotating rotor stage, are hardly ever used in wind-turbines. Their cost tends to be very high with only a relatively small benefit in terms of improved turbine performance. They tend, therefore, to reduce the overall cost effectiveness of the turbine.

The fraction of the rotor disc area occupied by blading is termed the solidity or more specifically the integrated solidity identified, here, by the symbol σ. The area of one blade is based on the integral of c, which may

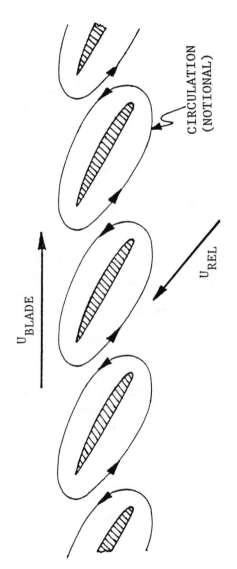

Figure 3.2. Mutual circulation interference with closely spaced individual airfoil blades.

be a function of radius r, from the rotor axis to the blade tip. Thus for a horizontal-axis type rotor with n blades:

$$\sigma \equiv \frac{4n}{\pi D^2} = \int_0^{D/2} c_{(r)} \, dr$$

Hence where $\bar{c}$ is the average chord of a blade:

$$\sigma = \frac{2n\bar{c}}{\pi D} \tag{3.1}$$

Typically the solidity of the rotor of a classical water-pumping wind-turbine of the American multi-bladed type is in the region of 0.8 whilst that of a high-tip-speed-ratio wind-electric unit is about 10% of that value or even less.

3.2. Induced Velocity

The assumption was made in Chapter 2, §2.1, that the location of the actuator surface, S, of Fig. 2.1(a) corresponded to the station at which $U_s = (U_1 + U_2)/2$. This assumption can be validated, quite readily, if account is taken of the pressure drop across the actuator surface, S, of Fig. 2.1(a).

The pressure differential acting across the disc area is equatable to the momentum defect occurring between stations 1 and 2 of the stream-tube since the surroundings pressure, P_∞, is assumed to act across both these stations and over the outer surface of the stream-tube. Thus since the flow slows down, reversibly, approaching S, leading to a positive pressure increment ΔP^+ acting on the upstream face of S, and recovers reversibly to P_∞ from a negative pressure increment, ΔP^-, active on the downstream face of S then:

$$(\Delta P^+ + \Delta P^-)S = \dot{m}(U_1 - U_2) \tag{3.2}$$

Also applying Bernoulli's equation independently to the flows upstream and downstream of S and omitting the potential energy terms since the flow is assumed to be horizontal:

$$P_\infty + \Delta P^+ + \rho_\infty U_s^2/2 = P_\infty + \rho_\infty U_1^2/2 \tag{3.3}$$

and:

$$P_\infty - \Delta P^- + \rho_\infty U_s^2/2 = P_\infty + \rho_\infty U_2^2/2 \tag{3.4}$$

Subtracting equation (3.4) from (3.3):

$$(\Delta P^+ + \Delta P^-) = \frac{\rho_\infty}{2}(U_1^2 - U_2^2) \tag{3.5}$$

substituting for $(\Delta P^+ + \Delta P^-)$ in equation (3.3) from equation (3.5) gives the result:

$$\frac{\rho_\infty S}{2}(U_1^2 - U_2^2) = \dot{m}(U_1 - U_2)$$

or since $\dot{m} = \rho_\infty S U_s$:

$$U_s = (U_1 - U_2)/2 \tag{3.6}$$

Equation (3.6) corresponds, therefore, to the initial, crucial assumption of §2.1. Furthermore, writing $U_1 = U_\infty$ and expressing the velocity U_s at the actuator surface as:

$$U_s = U_\infty(1 - a) \tag{3.7}$$

where a is, as noted in §3.1, the axial flow-induction, or inflow, factor; then substituting from equations (3.7) in equation (3.6) leads to the result:

$$U_2 = U_\infty(1 - 2a) \tag{3.8}$$

Equations (3.7) and (3.8) prove what was implied previously, namely that half of the slowing down of the flow due to S occurs upstream of S and the remainder downstream.

Substituting U_∞ for U_1 in equation (2.3) and for U_2 from equation (3.8) the expression for the power coefficient of a loss-free rotor becomes, after invoking equation (2.8):

$$C_P = 4a(1 - a)^2 \tag{3.9}$$

and similarly the expression for the thrust coefficient, equation (2.23), can also be expressed in terms of a:

$$C_t = 4a(1 - a) \tag{3.10}$$

Since equations (3.9) and (3.10) apply only to perfect, loss-free rotors they have no physical significance for values of a greater than 0.5. This value of a corresponds to $U_2 = 0$, where U_2 is the axial, or streamwise, component of the velocity of the flow leaving station 2. Higher values of a imply negative values of U_2 which are not physically reasonable for a model in which uniform flow conditions are assumed to prevail across stations 1 and 2. It can be seen that U_s remains positive within the range

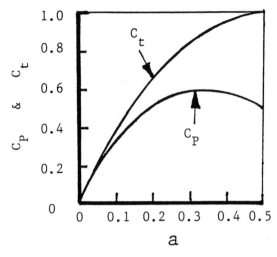

Figure 3.3. Power and thrust coefficients of idealised rotors as a function of the rotor inflow factor a.

$0.5 \leq a \leq 1.0$ whereas U_2 is negative within this same range. However equations (3.9) and (3.10) do give at least an indication of the behaviour of C_P and C_t in terms of a. These relationships are presented graphically in Fig. 3.3.

The simple actuator surface concept (Fig. 2.1(a)) has been extended, for horizontal-axis turbines where the actuator surface becomes an actuator disc, by other workers (Wilson et al., 1976; Freris, 1990) to allow for the modelling of rotors for which the inflow factor, a, need no longer be taken to be uniform across the actuator disc. In these circumstances a series of coaxial annuli is assumed. Also a tangential induction factor, a', is introduced and also a tip loss factor. With these additions it has been found to be possible to model, fairly realistically, the performances of high-tip-speed-ratio rotors of the propeller type on the basis of known lift coefficient, C_L, versus incidence angle, α, curves together with the corresponding drag coefficient, C_D, versus α relationships. Such mathematical modelling does not yet appear to have developed to the stage where it can be applied successfully to the relatively high solidity, low tip-speed ratio, rotors of typical water-pumping turbines. Hence it will not be discussed here any further.

3.3. Significance of Reynolds Number

A parameter serving as an indicator of the effectiveness of an airfoil is the Reynolds number, R_e, at which it operates. The Reynolds number, a concept due to Osborne Reynolds, is, fundamentally, the ratio of the local inertia stresses in a fluid passing over a surface to the corresponding local shear stress. Thus on a local basis an elementary formulation gives:

$$\text{Ratio}: \frac{\text{Inertia stress}}{\text{Shear stress}} = \frac{\rho U^2}{\mu \dfrac{\partial U}{\partial y}} \qquad (3.11)$$

where y is a coordinate normal to the surface over which the fluid flows. The shear stress, as it appears in equation (3.11), is for a laminar-flow situation; that is, for a case in which the fluid passes smoothly, in a laminar manner, over the surface. However the Reynolds number concept is not restricted to laminar flow situations only.

Normally the Reynolds number concept is treated, with respect to airfoils, as if it can be applied to an entire airfoil section as a whole employing representative values applicable to the airfoil. In reality the flow velocity and static pressure vary over the airfoil surfaces between the leading and trailing edges. Thus expressing the derivative, $\partial U / \partial y$, in the denominator of equation (3.11) in an approximate form:

$$\frac{\partial U}{\partial y} \simeq \frac{U}{kd} \qquad (3.12)$$

where d is a representative dimension of the body and k is a constant the value of which is selected such that equation (3.12) is valid. Thus from equations (3.11) and (3.12):

$$\text{Ratio} = \frac{\rho U k d}{\mu}$$

Normally, since the constant k serves only as a multiplier it is ignored in the expression for Reynolds number. Thus:

$$R_e = \frac{\rho U d}{\mu} \qquad (3.13)$$

where, for an airfoil, d is generally chosen to be the chord c and the other representative terms are referred to the surroundings conditions. Thus for an airfoil specifically:

$$R_e = \frac{\rho_\infty U_\infty c}{\mu} \qquad (3.14)$$

For a wind-turbine blade U_{REL} is employed instead of U_∞. Thus for such cases:

$$R_e = \frac{\rho_\infty (U_{REL} c)_r}{\mu} \qquad (3.15)$$

where, for horizontal-axis turbines, U_{REL} is a function of radius r and c may also be a function of r. More rigorous derivations of the Reynolds number can be found in most texts on fluid mechanics.

From wind-tunnel tests and other practical experience with airfoils it has been shown, by many workers as reported in the technical literature (Hoerner, 1965; Hoerner and Borst, 1975), that for most airfoils the drag coefficient, C_D, drops significantly, and the lift coefficient, C_L, increases, when the Reynolds number, as presented in equation (3.14), exceeds about 300,000, and from that point onwards the airfoil performance continues to improve slightly, but at a decreasing rate of improvement, as R_e increases. For wind-turbine situations the same comments apply but with U_{REL} substituted for U_∞ as in equation (3.15).

Typically, representative values of R_e can range from about 100,000 for small, high solidity, low-tip-speed-ratio machines to about 4×10^6 for very large, high tip-speed ratio, wind-electric type turbines. The influence of R_e on the value of C_D for a typical airfoil is significant and can involve a ratio of about 5 to 10 between the value of C_D applicable for an R_e value of, say, 100,000 and that for an R_e value of several million. The influence of R_e on C_L is opposite to that on C_D and is weaker. The value of C_L can typically increase by about 20% over the range $100 \times 10^3 \le R_e \le 4 \times 10^6$. An additional factor that can influence, strongly, airfoil drag and, to a lesser extent, lift is the aspect ratio and also the condition of the airfoil surface. It has been found that contamination with small grit particles can have a serious deleterious influence particularly on high performance airfoils.

3.4. Blade Aspect Ratio

The aspect ratio, A_R, of an airfoil, or a wind-turbine blade, is defined as:

$$A_R = \frac{\text{Span}^2}{\text{Area}} = \frac{b^2}{\bar{c}b} = \frac{b}{\bar{c}}$$

where $\bar{c}$ is the average chord.

Whilst the aspect ratio is a commonly used parameter with respect to aircraft wings it is seldom referred to directly in the case of wind-turbine blading. For the propeller-type turbines of wind-electric machines the influence of the relatively high aspect ratio of such blades is taken into

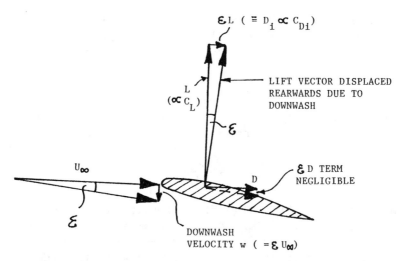

Figure 3.4. The influence of downwash on the performance of finite aspect ratio airfoils.

account implicitly in terms of the axial and tangential induction factors and the tip-loss factor. Nevertheless, many water-pumping turbines often have much lower aspect ratios than those typical of wind-electric machines. Hence it is well worthwhile looking at the influence of the aspect ratio on airfoil performance independently of the more complex issues surrounding the operation of a complete turbine rotor.

Considering a lifting airfoil of finite aspect ratio the influence of the finite span is to permit high-pressure fluid from the pressure surface to "leak" towards the lower-pressure, suction, surface via the airfoil ends or tips, This fluid motion can be shown to create, for the airfoil orientation shown in Fig. 3.4, a small downwash flow velocity, w, in which the airfoil is immersed. For what are termed elliptically loaded airfoils w is uniform over the airfoil span. Hence the flow approaching the airfoil is, therefore, tilted downwards, relative to the free stream of velocity U_∞, by the small angle ε, the downwash angle. Hence the lift vector, which is normal to the oncoming flow, is also deflected by angle ε as indicated in Fig. 3.4. This gives rise, relative to the direction of the horizontal flow, in a component, εL, of the lift acting in a downwind direction thereby augmenting the airfoil drag otherwise experienced without the induced flow. The term εL is the induced drag D_i.

It can be shown (Glauert, 1948) that the minimum value of the drag coefficient, C_{D_i}, corresponding to the induced drag D_i is given by:

$$C_{D_i} = \frac{C_L^2}{\pi A_R} \tag{3.16}$$

and hence from Fig. 3.4 and equation (3.16) the corresponding minimum downwash angle, ε, is given by:

$$\varepsilon = \frac{C_L}{\pi A_R} \tag{3.17}$$

Strictly, equations (3.16) and (3.17) are only applicable to elliptically loaded airfoils but can be applied to other cases with small error; the error, an under-estimate of C_{D_i} and ε, increases as A_R diminishes. The downwash angle ε corresponds to the increase in incidence angle required to achieve a prescribed lift coefficient. In addition to the introduction of an induced drag a finite aspect ratio also results in a loss of pressure differential, concentrated at the tips, due to the "leakage" flow. This effect can, in practice, sometimes be partially offset by a delay of flow separation due to the downwash tending to maintain attached flow on the airfoil suction surface.

By way of example Fig. 3.5 shows, for a standard, symmetric NACA 0012 airfoil section the influence on airfoil performance of finite aspect ratio. These data apply to an airfoil of (NACA) standard roughness for a chord-based Reynolds number of 6×10^6. It can be seen from the left-hand portion of the diagram that the maximum value of C_L for infinite aspect ratio is only about unity. This relatively low value is due to the NACA "standard roughness" which is analogous to a slightly dirty airfoil such as might occur in service. The same airfoil with a smooth, ie., clean, surface has a maximum lift coefficient of 1.6 at the same Reynolds number! The slope, $dC_L/d\alpha$, of the linear portion of the C_L versus α curve is the same for both the clean and standard roughness cases (Abbott and von Doenhoff, 1959).

The reduction of the lift curve slope, $dC_L/d\alpha$, apparent with decreasing aspect ratio is due to the additional angle, ε, added to the value of α otherwise applicable to the infinite aspect ratio case. The infinite aspect ratio experimental results were obtained with the airfoil fully spanning the wind-tunnel (Abbott and von Doenhoff, 1959). The remaining curves were derived analytically, using equations (3.16) and (3.17), from the result for infinite aspect ratio. An empirical tip-loss was assumed corresponding to the effective elimination of lift at each tip for a portion

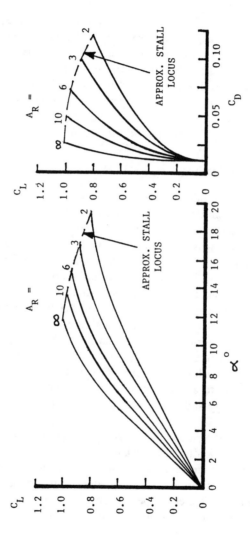

Figure 3.5. The influence of aspect ratio on the performance of an NACA 0012 airfoil of standard roughness; $R_e = 6 \times 10^6$.

of the span corresponding to the effective elimination of lift at each tip
for a portion of the span corresponding to 20% of the airfoil chord. Partial justification for such an assumption has been given by Freris (Freris,
1990). The right-hand portion of Fig. 3.5 is termed a drag-polar diagram
in which C_L is plotted versus C_D.

It can be seen, from Fig. 3.5, that whilst a reduction of aspect ratio
increases the incidence angle range over which the airfoil generates lift,
which can in some cases prove beneficial, there is a considerable penalty
in terms of a drag increase. The drag increase is less penalising for low-
tip-speed rotors, such as those often used in direct-drive water pumpers,
than for turbines operating at high tip-speed ratios. The reason for this
relates to the geometrical proportions of the velocity diagrams applicable
to these cases as shown diagrammatically in Fig. 3.1.

3.5. Separated-Flow Blading

For very-low-aspect-ratio airfoils the flow over the suction surface is separated, extensively, from that surface; that is, it does not follow, closely,
the contour of the suction surface for incidence angles well below those at
which stall occurs. The reason for this phenomenon is due to the flow over
the tips of the airfoil from the pressure to the suction surface forming vor-
tices which trail over, and downwind of, the airfoil covering a significant
portion of the suction surface as shown, diagrammatically, in Fig. 3.6(a).
For such conditions the cross-section selected for the airfoil diminishes in
importance as the aspect ratio diminishes and, presumably, the sensitivity to dirt deposits on the suction surface also diminishes. This, therefore,
suggests the possibility of using simple, low-cost flat plates as low-aspect-
ratio airfoils provided such plates offer sufficient structural stiffness. The
possibilities of adding to a thin plate suitable stiffeners or employing a
corrugated material suggest themselves as potential solutions for structural
problems.

If the planform of a sharp-edged plate is triangular with the apex of
symmetry of the triangle directed upwind, as shown in Fig. 3.6(b), then
the vortex formation is encouraged and strengthened as the flow spills,
progressively, over the swept-back leading edges of the triangle or delta-
wing. This gives rise to interesting performance characteristics in which a
gentle stall occurs, relative to a conventional airfoil, at a very high angle
of incidence or attack. Figure 3.7 presents the experimentally obtained
wind-tunnel performance of a sharp-edged, flat-plate, delta-wing. The
delta-wing, of aspect ratio 2, was of the plain type that is without any flap
surfaces (Kentfield, 1988(b)). The delta-wing results, which were obtained
at a Reynolds number of approximately 10^5, have been compared with

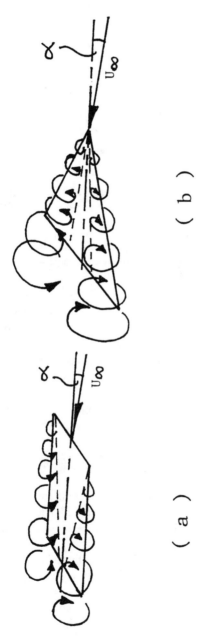

Figure 3.6. Flow around very-low-aspect-ratio airfoils with large areas of separation (diagrammatic): a) rectangular planform; b) delta-wing planform.

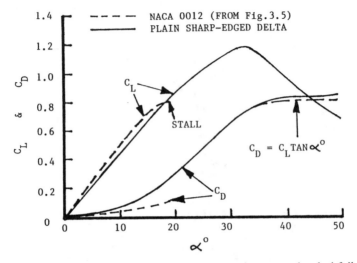

Figure 3.7. Comparison of the performances of a conventional airfoil and a plain, sharp-edged delta-wing. Aspect ratio = 2 in both cases.

C_L and C_D versus incidence angle curves, extracted from Fig. 3.5, for an NACA 0012 airfoil, also of aspect ratio 2, operating at a Reynolds number of 6×10^6. The higher Reynolds number of the NACA 0012 airfoil should assist the performance of that airfoil relative to the delta-wing although the assumption of standard roughness for the NACA 0012 has an opposite influence.

Since the delta-wing is a thin flat plate it could be expected that, when skin friction drag is ignored, the drag coefficient would, by simple force resolution, be given by:

$$C_D = C_L \tan \alpha \qquad (3.18)$$

In fact equation (3.18) is applicable, as a first approximation, up to the stall incidence angle of 33° and between 33° and 50° the departure is very little with the actual measured drag being only slightly greater than that suggested by equation (3.18).

Whilst the high drag coefficient of the delta-wing is, for a wind-turbine blade, a disadvantage, the relatively wide range of incidence angle over which such a blade can operate is a major advantage compared with a conventional airfoil when both are to be employed in simple, fixed-pitch, high starting-torque-coefficient rotors. The drag disadvantage of a delta-wing as a turbine blade tends, as mentioned previously, to be minimised when applied to relatively low-tip-speed ratio rotors.

3.6. Rotor Aerodynamic Performance

So far consideration has been given to the principle of a turbine (§3.1), the concept of induced velocity (§3.2), the significance, with respect to blade performance, of Reynolds number (§3.3), blade aspect ratio (§3.4) and simple, easily fabricated blades utilising separated flows (§3.5). However it remains to provide an explanation of the superior performance, in terms of power coefficient, expected from relatively high-tip-speed-ratio rotors, such as those generally used in wind-electric machines, compared with corresponding performance expectations for low-tip-speed-ratio, high-torque-coefficient units commonly used for such duties as water pumping.

The required explanation is derived from a study of the loss of kinetic energy, in the form of whirl, residing within the flow leaving a wind-turbine. The greater the whirl the greater the loss of kinetic energy. Correspondingly the greater the torque generated by the turbine rotor the greater the proportion of the kinetic energy of the flow passing through the turbine converted into a whirl, or vortex, form. This situation is amenable to quantitative study, at the fundamental level, on the basis of modifying, suitably, the flow model introduced previously in Chapter 2 and illustrated in Fig. 2.1(a).

With reference to the flow model shown in Fig. 2.1(a) and from equation (2.13), which is applicable to situations in which there is residual whirl at station 2, the tangential reactive force, F_T, corresponding to the whirl is given by:

$$F_T = \dot{m} U_1 \left(\frac{U_T}{U_1} \right) \tag{3.19}$$

Also from equation (2.1):

$$\dot{m} = \frac{\rho_\infty S}{2} U_1 \left[1 + \frac{U_2}{U_1} \right] \tag{3.20}$$

hence from substitution for $\dot{m}$ in equation (3.19) from equation (3.20):

$$F_T = \frac{\rho_\infty S}{2} U_1^2 \left[1 + \frac{U_2}{U_1} \right] \frac{U_T}{U_1} \tag{3.21}$$

and hence the reactive torque acting on the turbine rotor corresponding to F_T is, following the form of equation (2.19), with no radial pressure gradient at station 2:

$$\text{Torque} = \frac{\rho_\infty U_1^2}{2} \left[1 + \frac{U_2}{U_1} \right] \frac{U_T}{U_1} \cdot \frac{2\pi}{3} \frac{D^3}{8} \tag{3.22}$$

Invoking equation (2.9) to convert equation (3.22) into an expression for torque coefficient:

$$C_T = \frac{2}{3}\left[1 + \frac{U_2}{U_1}\right]\frac{U_T}{U_1} \qquad (3.23)$$

As was demonstrated in §2.1, the condition for maximum energy conversion is given by $U_2/U_1 = 1/3$. Thus when this condition is applied equation (3.23) yields the result:

$$C_T = \frac{8}{9}\frac{U_T}{U_1} \qquad (3.24)$$

It can be shown, with reference to Fig. 2.3, that when $U_2/U_1 = 1/3$ the maximum value of U_T/U_1 corresponding to a stationary (ie., $\lambda = 0$), loss-free, ideal, turbine rotor is given by:

$$\left(\frac{U_T}{U_1}\right)_{MAX} = \sqrt{\frac{8}{9}} = \frac{\sqrt{8}}{3} = 0.9428 \qquad (3.25)$$

thus from equations (3.24) and (3.25)

$$C_{T(MAX)} = \frac{8\sqrt{8}}{27} = 0.838 \qquad (3.26)$$

Note that this value of $C_{T(MAX)}$ is slightly less than that given by equation (2.20). This is due to U_2/U_1 here being restricted to a ratio of 1/3 corresponding to maximum energy extraction whereas the optimum value of U_2/U_1 corresponding to the maximum possible torque for a stationary rotor was shown to be 1/2. The latter ratio yielded a maximum torque coefficient of $\sqrt{3}/2 = 0.866$, a value just over 3% greater than that given by equation (3.26).

The maximum energy obtainable, ΔE, from an ideal turbine rotor without residual whirl is, from equation (2.2):

$$\Delta E = \frac{\dot{m}}{2} U_1^2 \left[1 - \left(\frac{U_2}{U_1}\right)^2\right] \qquad (3.27)$$

and the kinetic energy remaining in the residual whirl, ΔE_T, when the entry whirl, at station 1, is zero is:

$$\Delta E_T = \frac{\dot{m}}{2} U_1^2 \left(\frac{U_T}{U_1}\right)^2$$

Thus the net ideal useful output with residual whirl is:

$$\Delta E - \Delta E_T = \frac{\dot{m}}{2} U_1^2 \left[1 - \left(\frac{U_2}{U_1}\right)^2 - \left(\frac{U_T}{U_1}\right)^2 \right] \quad (3.28)$$

and from equations (3.27) and (3.28) the ratio $(\Delta E - \Delta E_T)/\Delta E$ is given by:

$$\frac{\Delta E - \Delta E_T}{\Delta E} = \frac{\left[1 - \left(\frac{U_2}{U_1}\right)^2 - \left(\frac{U_T}{U_1}\right)^2 \right]}{\left[1 - \left(\frac{U_2}{U_1}\right)^2 \right]}$$

or when $U_2/U_1 = 1/3$:

$$\frac{\Delta E - \Delta E_T}{\Delta E} = \left[1 - \frac{9}{8} \left(\frac{U_T}{U_1}\right)^2 \right] \quad (3.29)$$

and the corresponding power coefficient, C_P, with residual whirl is:

$$C_P = 0.593 \left[1 - \frac{9}{8} \left(\frac{U_T}{U_1}\right)^2 \right] \quad (3.30)$$

C_T and C_P were evaluated for selected values of U_T/U_1 from equations (3.24) and (3.30), respectively. The corresponding values of λ were subsequently derived following rearrangement of equation (2.12) namely:

$$\lambda = \frac{C_P}{C_T} \qquad \cdot \qquad (3.31)$$

The results obtained from evaluation of equations (3.24), (3.30) and (3.31) are presented graphically in Fig. 3.8. The steepness of the C_P versus λ curve is noteworthy, showing that even direct-drive water pumpers having power coefficients peaking in the range $1 \leq \lambda \leq 2$ should be able to achieve peak power coefficients of from about 0.34 to 0.43 assuming that 80% of the ideal value is attainable in practice. It can also be seen that on this basis a high-tip-speed unit capable of peaking in the range $6 \leq \lambda \leq 7$ should, correspondingly, be capable of achieving a peak power coefficient in the region of 0.47. The ideal C_P versus λ curve shows that from the performance viewpoint alone turbines attaining their peak power coefficient at yet higher-tip-speed ratios do not seem to be warranted. From the practical viewpoint, when blade drags are taken into account, it

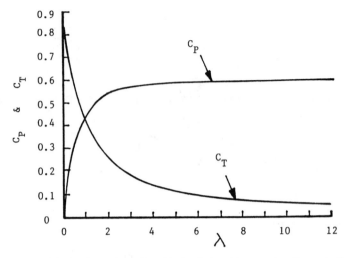

Figure 3.8. Performance of an ideal wind-turbine on the C_P and C_T versus tip-speed ratio, λ, planes.

will be very difficult to achieve a good performance at ultra-high tip-speed ratios. This can be deduced, implicitly, from Fig. 3.1(b).

3.7. Rotor Wakes

Interest in the wakes of wind-turbine rotors relates to the relative position-ing of individual turbines in arrays of machines, as in a typical wind-farm, primarily to maximise the cost-effectiveness of the project. In so far as water-pumping wind-turbines are concerned, arrays of machines are very unusual but are not completely unknown. Arrays of wind-electric units can, of course, be dedicated to water-pumping duties and there is at least one array of small wind-electric machines employed in this manner. Most of the studies carried out so far on array situations have been directed at wind-electric, wind-farm type operations. Array studies, or even stud-ies of the wake of a single turbine, are difficult to carry out in a wind-tunnel because of the small turbine model size, low Reynolds number and the considerable length of tunnel working-section required. Hence most studies to date have been based on either theoretical modelling or wake measurements made downwind of full-scale turbines.

   A review of the findings to date relating to turbine array spacing has been presented in an American Wind Energy Association (AWEA) Standard 8.2 (Bailey, 1993). Summarising the AWEA recommendations it is suggested that a downwind spacing of approximately 10 rotor diameters be used and that a lateral spacing of not less than 3 rotor diameters be provided. Evidence exists to show that a lateral spacing of only 2 rotor diameters is usually too small and leads to lateral wake-overlap, or wake merging, problems. These reduce the rate of mixing of the wakes with more energetic, surrounding fluid thereby penalising, heavily, turbines in rows downwind of the first row. For a single row of turbines, arranged normal to the prevailing wind, turbines are often located as closely as possible, with a gap of say half a rotor diameter or less between adjacent blade tips, to form what is sometimes termed a wind wall.

The principle difference between the wakes of high-tip-speed-ratio, low-torque, wind-electric turbines and low-tip-speed-ratio, high-torque, direct-drive water pumpers is the greater residual whirl occurring in the wakes of the latter. At least one analytical study was made in which account was taken of this factor (Kentfield, 1988(c)). A conclusion was that at a distance of about 10 rotor diameters downwind only a small difference in wake whirl angle prevailed between a typical propeller type turbine and a mechanical water pumper. The wake whirl angle of the mechanical water pumper, 10 rotor diameters downwind, was approximately $0.9°$ whilst that of the wind-electric turbine was less than $0.3°$.

3.8. Drag-Type Rotors

A key elementary type of turbine that does not employ the principle of aerodynamic lift is the drag-type rotor. In this device, which is usually arranged with a vertical axis, the torque is generated as a consequence of the difference in drag forces between blades running from the wind, in the manner of the sails of a square-rigged ship, and blades on the opposite side of the rotor advancing into the wind. The drag of the advancing blades is minimised by the use of upwind fairings, by arranging for the blades to retract or by the provision of a shield or by a combination of these. Most drag-type turbines, without blade retraction, have the advantage of a very simple and robust construction and a very low runaway tip-speed ratio under storm conditions. The penalty is, as will be shown here, an inherently low value of $C_{P(MAX)}$.

A simple, common example of an unloaded drag-type turbine, operating at runaway conditions, is a cup-anemometer. In this device the drag of the advancing cups is minimised because they present a faired shape to the oncoming flow whilst the retreating cups offer a much greater resistance to the flow impinging upon them.

What in effect represents the ideal performance of a turbine of the drag type can be established, quite easily, by simple analysis. With reference to Fig. 3.9 and on the basis of the assumption that the drag of the advancing blades can be ignored and that, effectively, an area A is continuously active:

$$\text{Drag} = \frac{\rho_\infty C_D A}{2} (U_\infty - U_\omega)^2 \qquad (3.32)$$

and the corresponding work done per unit time, WD, is:

$$WD = \text{Drag} \cdot U_\omega \qquad (3.33)$$

Hence from equations (3.32) and (3.33)

$$WD = \frac{\rho_\infty C_D A}{2} \left[U_\infty^2 U_\omega - 2U_\infty U_\omega^2 + U_\omega^3 \right] \qquad (3.34)$$

differentiating equation (3.34) with respect to U_ω and equating to zero gives the result:

$$0 = \frac{\rho_\infty C_D A}{2} (U_\infty - 3U_\omega)(U_\infty - U_\omega)$$

Since neither $\frac{\rho_\infty C_D A}{2}$ nor $(U_\infty - U_\omega) = 0$ (the latter condition corresponds to $WD = 0$) hence: $(U_\infty - 3U_\omega) = 0$ and thus $U_\omega = U_\infty/3$ for maximum WD.

Substitution of $U_\omega = U_\infty/3$ in equation (3.34) and dividing by $\rho_\infty U_\infty^3 S/2$ to express the maximum value of WD in terms of a power coefficient gives:

$$C_{P(MAX)} = \left(\frac{4}{27} \right) \frac{C_D A}{S} \qquad (3.35)$$

A general expression for the power coefficient is obtained by dividing equation (3.34) by $\rho_\infty U_\infty^3 S/2$ giving:

$$C_P = \frac{C_D A}{S} \left[\frac{U_\omega}{U_\infty} - 2 \left(\frac{U_\omega}{U_\infty} \right)^2 + \left(\frac{U_\omega}{U_\infty} \right)^3 \right] \qquad (3.36)$$

and the corresponding expression for torque coefficient is, from equations (3.32) and (2.9):

$$C_T = \frac{C_D A}{S} \left[1 - \frac{U_\omega}{U_\infty} \right]^2 \qquad (3.37)$$

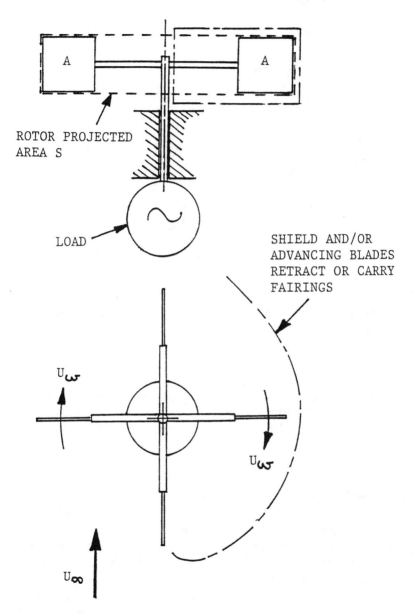

ROTOR PROJECTED
AREA S

LOAD

SHIELD AND/OR
ADVANCING BLADES
RETRACT OR CARRY
FAIRINGS

U_ω

U_ω

U_∞

Figure 3.9. Diagrammatic illustration of a drag-type turbine.

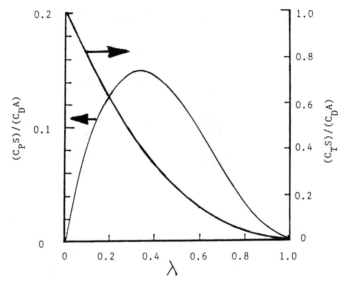

Figure 3.10. Power coefficient and torque coefficient parameters versus tip-speed ratio, λ, for an idealised drag-type wind-turbine.

Clearly, from equation (3.37), C_T is a maximum at zero rotor speed, a condition desired for most water pumping and similar duties. The nominal tip-speed ratio of a drag-type machine can be expressed, most simply, in a form independent of the details of machine geometry as:

$$\lambda = \frac{U_\omega}{U_\infty} \tag{3.38}$$

Figure 3.10 is a presentation, derived from equations (3.36) to (3.38) inclusive, of what can be termed the ideal performance of a drag-type turbine. Details of the rotor geometry and also the blade drag coefficient have not been specified in order to make Fig. 3.10 as general as possible. Consequently the ordinates of Fig. 3.10 are $(C_P S)/(C_D A)$ and $(C_T S)/(C_D A)$ rather than simply C_P and C_T.

Speculatively, the greatest realistic value that can be assigned to C_D is approximately 1.25 and the largest value of A/S that could be incorporated is, perhaps, 0.4. Based on these estimates $C_D A/S = 0.5$. This suggests a maximum ideal power coefficient for a drag-type turbine of only about 0.07, or 7%, and a maximum ideal torque coefficient of about 0.5, a respectable value, at $\lambda = 0$. However modern, practical, real, drag-type turbines do not incorporate retraction, or shielding, of the advancing blades because of the complications involved. This implies that the drag of the upwind-moving blades must be taken into account. This drag has the deleterious effect of reducing significantly C_P and C_T. It also has the effect of reducing substantially the value of λ at runaway conditions which can, in practice, be beneficial since it can eliminate the need for storm protection of the rotor, a further simplification.

It is perhaps worth noting that the historic Chinese type turbine, the origin of which appears to be lost in antiquity, was of the vertical-axis drag-type. It featured retraction of the advancing blades by permitting them to swing freely, thereby presenting themselves edgewise to the flow. The writer is not aware of turbines of this type having been applied to water pumping.

3.9. Savonius Rotors

The Savonius rotor is a much newer concept than the pure drag-type turbine although it retains some of the functional aspects of the latter. The Savonius rotor configuration was introduced, in 1928, by a Finn, S.J. Savonius (Savonius, 1931). The geometry of a Savonius rotor, which is normally arranged with a vertical axis, presents, in planform, an essentially S-shaped rotor with two blades which can be joined on the rotor axis as shown in Fig. 3.11(a); in the form of two separated circular arcs, Fig. 3.11(b), or as two separate blades with circular arc plus tangential surfaces as indicated in Fig. 3.11(c). Many other geometrical variations are of course possible.

At start-up, or when operating at very low tip-speed ratios, a Savonius rotor functions somewhat as a drag-type turbine when the rotor is broadside to the wind as illustrated in the upper diagrams of Fig. 3.11. However, for the configurations shown in Fig. 3.11(b) and (c) fluid is diverted, beneficially out the rear face of the advancing blade. This is not normally a feature of pure drag-type turbines. Also at start-up, or at very low tip-speed ratios, aerodynamic lift can, in principle, be generated when the rotor is edgewise to the flow as implied in the lower set of diagrams of Fig. 3.11. Because it is often found that the rotor torque at start-up can be zero for certain angular positions of the rotor it is usual, to ensure good starting, to stack two rotors one above the other on the same shaft but orientated at 90° relative to each other.

Because of the complexities of the flow through, and around, a Savonius rotor it is not amenable to a simple analytical prediction of ideal performance similar to that in the previous section for drag-type turbines. Numerous experimentally obtained performance measurements are available for many Savonius rotor geometries. A fairly recent paper describes

NOTE MOST ROTORS
PROVIDED WITH END-
PLATES. TYPICAL
ROTOR LENGTH/DIAM. ≃1

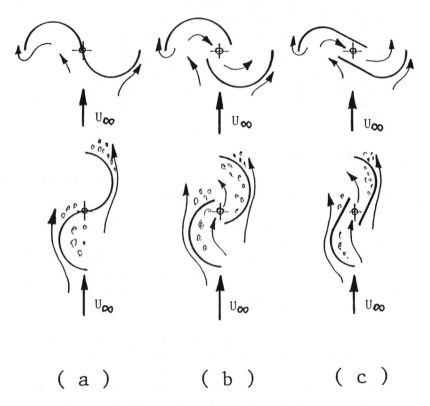

(a)   (b)   (c)

Figure 3.11. Diagrammatic illustration of Savonius rotors: a) joined blades (S-rotor); b) separated circular-arc blades; c) separated circular-arc blades with tangential extensions.

a prototype Savonius rotor-driven irrigation pump and presents some test results (Modi et al., 1985). A later work presents the results of a numerically evaluated analytical study directed at improving the understanding of Savonius rotor flow fields (Fernando and Modi, 1989).

It has been found experimentally that the peak power coefficient of a typical Savonius rotor is in the region of 0.20 to 0.25 and that the runaway tip-speed ratio is generally about 1.5. Whilst the starting torque of a stacked Savonius rotor is usually quite high, making it suitable for water-pumping duties, the maximum rotor torque coefficient is commonly developed at a tip-speed ratio within the range $0.3 \leq \lambda \leq 0.6$. Small, very simple, free-running S-type Savonius rotors are quite commonly used for commercial advertising purposes where they serve as rotary sign-boards.

CHAPTER 4

Wind Characteristics

Whilst, clearly, some knowledge is needed of the wind, at the very least an annual average wind speed, in the area where a wind-driven water pumper is to be installed it is rarely economically justifiable making a detailed wind survey of the site. The reasons for this are that the cost of an average, individual, small, wind-driven water pumper is relatively low and also the siting of the machine is, in most cases, prescribed by the location of the water source. This is particularly true when the machine is of the direct-drive type. Air-lift pumping permits some latitude in locating the wind-turbine unit remotely from the water source. A reasonable distance is, perhaps, about 500 m before the cost of the air-hose required to couple the wind-driven air compressor to the well site, or water source, becomes excessive. A somewhat greater range can be entertained for wind-electric systems although this depends to some extent on the transmission voltage. A high-transmission voltage reduces the wire diameter required and, in a properly designed system, transmission energy losses but may introduce the need for, and cost of, a transformer.

At least an indication of the average wind speed, and direction, for the general area of the wind-turbine site can often be obtained from the local airport or, in some cases, from tabulated data. An example of tabulated wind data, for the United States, has been given by Park (Park, 1981). Another source of information can be national weather service organisations. However, it is important to realise that the information generally available is most likely to be based on airport data. The usual, accepted, height for mounting anemometers is 10 m above ground level but not all anemometers, even some of those at airports, conform to this specification. Data of the kind discussed here can at least give an idea as to whether or not suitable winds are even likely to prevail at the area of the proposed wind-site but such information is not always conclusive since local conditions can have profound influences.

Very important parameters, usually independent of the local airport situation, capable of having a major influence on an individual wind-site, are the local terrain, surface roughness, altitude, wind direction and obstructions, particularly those upwind of the site. An example, relating to the siting of wind-electric machines, where terrain has had a profound influence is the San Gorgonio Pass near Palm Springs, California. Here several thousand turbines are located on a plateau-like area between two mountains. The mountains serve to concentrate the wind and produce a much stronger flow than would otherwise occur. The Altamont Pass, also in California, is another example involving terrain-induced wind-energy concentration.

Clues that can sometimes assist in assessing the suitability of a potential wind-site without resorting to time-consuming wind speed and direction measurements, with the associated data processing, can sometimes be obtained from people already familiar with the area. Another possible source of information are flora the growth of which tends to be deflected, in a downwind direction, by strong prevailing winds. According to available data (Park, 1981) the potential gustiness of a site can be estimated, indirectly, on the basis of the upwind terrain in combination with knowledge of the local average wind speed. The likelihood of gusts of a specific strength, for example, sufficiently strong to double, transiently, the average wind speed prevailing prior to the gust, increases strongly with increasing upwind surface roughness and decreases with increasing average wind speed. In a general sense gustiness is a poor site property since it increases the number of fatigue-loading cycles to be withstood by the wind-turbine, but it can, however, also increase energy output.

If the financial investment in a wind-turbine project is to be large it becomes important to conduct a properly executed wind survey of the proposed site. The cost of such a survey can well offset the potential financial losses involved due to failure to take this precaution. An inherent problem with site surveys is that to gather really reliable information the survey should be conducted over a period of several years. The wind speed distribution usually varies not only from season to season but also, more randomly, from year to year.

Clearly a site wind survey lasting several years is not likely to be acceptable. However data gathered over one year, or at least for a duration corresponding to that of one operational season, is better than no information. It is usually possible to check with the local weather station, probably at a nearby airport, to determine, on the basis of long-term records, whether the year, or the season, during which data were collected at the proposed wind-site corresponded to an above average, below average or a normal year at the weather station. Such a correlation should then allow the site measurements to be adjusted to provide a more meaningful estimate of the site potential.

4.1. Wind Measuring Devices

Two commonly used wind speed and wind direction indicating devices are depicted in Fig. 4.1. Figure 4.1(a) illustrates a cup-type anemometer, a device which is in effect a simple drag-type turbine operating in the runaway mode. The wind speed is directly proportional to the rotational speed of the rotor above an almost negligible "cut-in" wind speed necessary to overcome the very low bearing friction of the device. The output speed is detected, on current cup-anemometers, by the voltage produced by a very small generator. Since the cup-anemometer output is independent of wind direction the latter is indicated by means of a weather-cocking vane. Again an electrical output allows the wind direction to be read, and recorded, remotely in an analogous manner to the wind speed.

Figure 4.1(b) shows an alternative, also widely used, form of anemometer consisting of a runaway horizontal-axis wind-turbine integrally combined with a wind direction indicating vane. It is important that in both types of anemometer the rotor must have a very low polar moment so that it can respond to changes of wind speed as accurately as possible. The term used to define the responsiveness of an anemometer is the time constant of the device (Freris, 1990).

Figure 4.2(a) shows a very elementary wind speed measuring installation in which a simple cup-anemometer, without the provision of a wind direction indicator, is mounted at the hub-height of the proposed turbine. Since most wind-driven water pumpers employ relatively low towers, a length of piping or a wood-pole can often be used as a support mast. A much more sophisticated arrangement is represented, diagrammatically, in Figure 4.2(b). Here four anemometers, each with a direction indicating capability, are mounted at the equivalent of the perimeter of the proposed turbine. This degree of elaboration is usually reserved for monitoring when a large, and expensive, turbine is being considered. In such a case the anemometer tower, instead of being a simple tube, may well be a built-up lattice structure hinged at ground level and cable-guyed as indicated. Usually a sophisticated monitoring system of this type will be hired from a contractor specialising in wind surveying who will also conduct the survey and process the data. More thorough descriptions of wind-monitoring equipment, and the techniques used, can be found elsewhere (Freris, 1990; Rohatgi and Nelson, 1994).

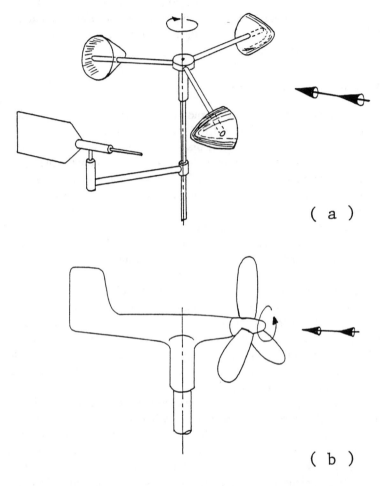

Figure 4.1. Cup and propeller type anemometers (diagrammatic): a) cup-anemometer with wind direction vane; b) propeller anemometer with integral wind direction indicator.

4.2. Influence of Tower Height

The boundary layer due to wind-driven flow over the surface of the earth is generally turbulent and results, within the boundary layer, in the wind speed increasing, at a decreasing rate, with increasing height above the earth surface. A commonly used, simple model of the boundary layer is based on a well-known experimentally derived result, due to Prandtl, to

SIMPLE CUP-ANEMOMETER
(NO WIND DIRECTION INDICATOR)

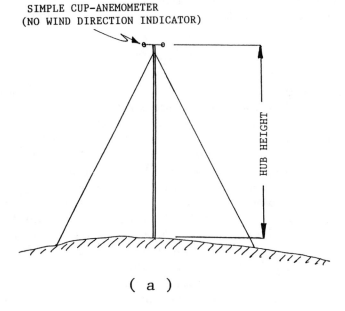

(a)

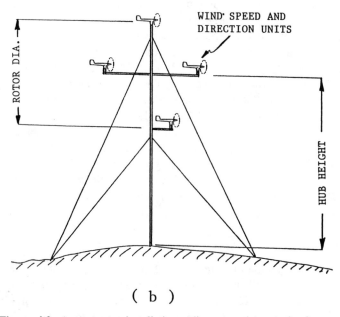

(b)

Figure 4.2. Anemometer installations (diagrammatic): a) simple cup-anemometer without wind direction vane; b) multiple propeller-type anemometer installation.

describe the velocity distribution within a turbulent boundary layer in flow passing over a smooth flat surface. Thus in accordance with Prandtl:

$$\frac{U}{U_{MAX}} = \left(\frac{Y}{Y_{MAX}}\right)^{\gamma} \tag{4.1}$$

where U_{MAX} is the flow velocity at the outer edge of the boundary layer which is of thickness Y_{MAX}. Hence provided both Y_{MAX} and γ are known the boundary layer is defined and, consequently, the velocity U is also defined as a function of Y. It should be noted that the Prandtl power law is not an exact relationship. It can be shown that the most severe departures from reality occur where $Y/Y_{MAX} \to 0$ and for $Y/Y_{MAX} = 1$. For the first condition the gradient $d(Y/Y_{MAX})/d(U/U_{MAX})$ approaches zero, when $\gamma < 1$, which is too small a value, and for the second condition the gradient should be infinity whereas it actually has a value of $1/\gamma$. Nevertheless the Prandtl relationship is quite realistic within the range of Y/Y_{MAX} values of interest in the wind-turbine field.

Prandtl found, from laboratory experiments on smooth plates, that $\gamma \simeq 1/7$ (= 0.143). Field measurements in the boundary layer of the earth reveal that both γ and Y_{MAX} are functions of the roughness of the surface over which the flow passes. The sensitivity of the boundary-layer velocity profile to variation of γ is presented, graphically, in Fig. 4.3. However it had been found experimentally that both γ and Y_{MAX} increase with increasing surface roughness. The approximate relationship between γ and Y_{MAX} is presented in Fig. 4.4. The information for Fig. 4.4 was extracted, via interpolation by the writer, from material available in the literature for the simple power-law boundary-layer model (Park, 1981; Freris, 1990; Rohatgi and Nelson, 1994).

Since the nominal height above ground level of weather-station anemometers is 10 m it is useful to compare the variation of wind speed, and the energy available, which is proportional to the cube of the local wind velocity as shown in Chapter 2, as ratios of the values applicable at $Y = 10$ m. Thus from equation (4.1) when U is replaced by the wind velocity U_{∞}:

$$\frac{U_{\infty}}{U_{\infty(Y=10m)}} = \left(\frac{Y}{10m}\right)^{\gamma} \tag{4.2}$$

Evaluation of equation (4.2) for $\gamma = 0.2$, a value representative of typical open countryside, leads to the results presented in Fig. 4.5 which, in view of their basis in a simple power law, should be regarded as approximate only. As can be seen from Fig. 4.5 employing a tower of just over 30 m in height can double the potential output of a wind-turbine whereas a tower of 60 m height will increase the potential output by a factor of 3 compared

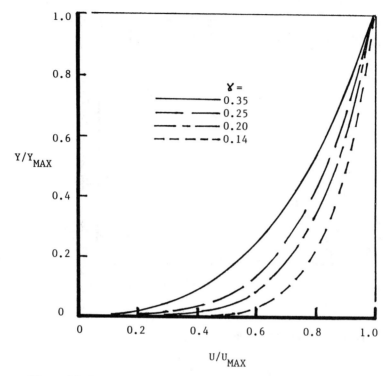

Figure 4.3. Power-law boundary-layer velocity profiles for several exponents.

with that when the rotor is mounted at the usual anemometer height of 10 m. Clearly cost considerations mitigate against the employment of very tall towers since a law of diminishing returns is apparent from inspection of Fig. 4.5.

The model presented here for consideration of the influence of tower height is of very simple form but takes into account the major factors involved. Superior, but much more complex, models are available which include such things as atmospheric stability, roughness-height as a parameter for categorising surface roughness and variation with Y of both pressure and temperature (Freris, 1990; Rohatgi and Nelson, 1994).

Whilst the variation with Y of pressure and temperature over the range of practical wind-turbine tower heights is small the variation of pressure, in particular, with terrain elevation can be significant. For example at an altitude of 1000 m above sea level the (absolute) ambient pressure is typically 12.5% lower than that at sea level. Hence account

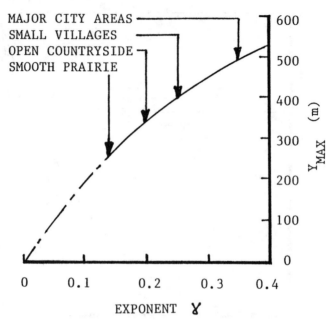

Figure 4.4. Approximate thickness, Y_{MAX}, of the boundary layer of the earth versus exponent γ.

should be taken of wind-turbine site absolute pressure and temperature values when calculating the local density ρ_∞. Thus since in general from ideal gas laws:

$$\rho = P/RT$$

therefore:

$$\rho_\infty = P_\infty/RT_\infty \tag{4.3}$$

where R is the characteristic gas constant for air which, in the S.I. unit system, has a value of 287 Nm/kg·deg K. When P_∞ is expressed in N/m^2 and T_∞ in degrees Kelvin the density, ρ_∞, is in units of kg/m^3.

4.3. Influence of Obstructions

Obstructions in the vicinity of a wind-turbine can have influences on machine output which are either bad or good. In some cases the role of an obstruction can change as a function of wind direction. Water-pumping turbines seem to be particularly vulnerable to performance reduction due to obstructions because such machines are usually small on fairly short

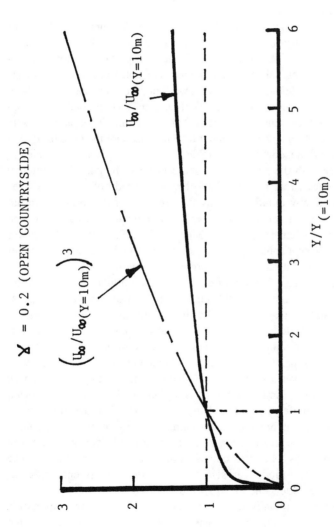

Figure 4.5. Increase of velocity, and energy available, with increasing turbine hub-height.

towers and hence are easily screened by, for example, nearby trees or houses even when these are of modest size. Another factor is that where the water table is close to the ground surface tree growth is likely and, because of the small depth of the water table, it is also likely to be the preferred area from which to pump water. This situation tends to pose more problems for direct-drive water pumpers than for systems employing remote air-lift or electric pumps.

By rule of thumb, supported by practical experience, a building, or tree, shielded wind-turbine should be a minimum of ten building, or tree, heights downwind of the obstruction. If trees in particular cannot be removed another empirical rule, regarded as applicable to large wind-electric turbines, suggests that an increase of tower height corresponding to 3/4 of the tree height will result in a turbine output equal to that obtainable when the trees are not present. It seems that this rule should be applied with considerable caution since it does not take into account the possibility that a very small turbine, completely shielded by trees, may remain completely shielded even with the suggested increase in tower height. Experimental evidence suggests that the wind speed at an altitude of four times tree height is essentially uninfluenced by the presence of the trees. A partial justification of these empirical rules and a more detailed discussion of the tree-shielded problem is available (Nierenberg, 1993). It should always be kept in mind that subsequent tree growth can render inadequate earlier provisions to take into account the presence of trees.

A turbine mounted on top of an escarpment normal to the prevailing wind may, or may not, benefit from such a location. A very steep escarpment is shown, diagrammatically, in Fig. 4.6(a) with flow separation occurring, as indicated, resulting in poor flow in the vicinity of the turbine. An otherwise similar escarpment with a well-rounded crest serving to prevent flow separation can, on the other hand, be shown to be very beneficial. Flow over a shape such as that depicted in Fig. 4.6(b) can be analysed quite easily, in two dimensions, by potential flow techniques (ie., a source plus a uniform stream). This shows that, when the influence of the boundary layer is ignored, a substantial velocity increase is obtained in the vicinity of the crest of the escarpment, a result known to conform to practical findings where, of course, a boundary layer must exist. The rounded escarpment model can also be considered to represent a ridge as indicated by the dotted line in Fig. 4.6(b).

A study of artificially contouring land to increase the output of a wind-turbine shows that, on the basis of potential flow analyses, turbine output increases of more than 100% are possible by this means (Fuhs et al., 1978). The Fuhs et al. work shows also, by implication, how, on a

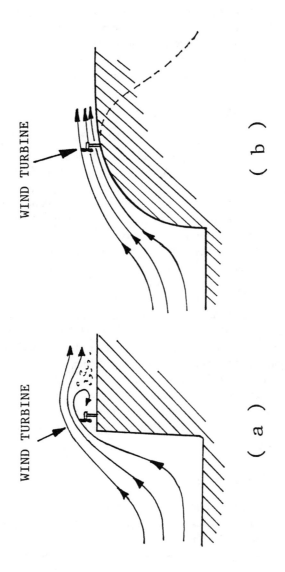

Figure 4.6. Flow over escarpments and ridges (diagrammatic): a) abrupt escarpment; b) rounded escarpment or ridge.

much bigger scale with many turbines involved the natural contouring of the San Gorgonio Pass serves to augment turbine performance.

An inherent problem with utilising obstructions, natural or otherwise, to augment turbine performance is that associated with variable wind direction. An otherwise helpful obstruction, serving as an augmenter, may become exactly the opposite due to a change of wind direction. The results of detailed studies of flows over, and around, various obstructions and terrain features are available (Rohatgi and Nelson, 1994).

4.4. Temporal Wind-Velocity Distributions

Even when the average wind at a site is known it is, in order to evaluate the potential time-averaged output of a turbine or other wind-energy conversion device, also necessary to know how the wind speed varies with time. Normally, at most sites, the wind speed varies cyclically with the season and also, in some cases, on a daily basis and, additionally, in a random manner minute-by-minute or even more rapidly. Daily, or diurnal, cycles in wind speed usually occur in mountainous regions or in a mountain pass through which air flows to compensate for air convected upwards from a solar-heated plain downwind of the pass. An example of this type is the Altamont Pass in California within which are located thousands of wind-electric turbines.

Clearly the true situation prevailing at a site can only be established from wind speed and direction measurements. However, it seems that many sites conform to relatively simple mathematical models of time-dependent wind speed variation. This cannot, of course, be known beyond doubt at a specific site without a wind survey being conducted. If such a survey has been carried out at a nearby location, with a similar topography, it may be construed as reasonable to apply the data to the non-surveyed site although, of course, a full set of applicable experimental data for the site are preferred.

4.4.1. Typical Experimental Results

Results obtained experimentally from wind speed surveys carried out at two sites in the British Isles are presented in Fig. 4.7. The surveys, reported by Golding (Golding, 1956), represent one site at which the average annual wind speed was 4.47 m/s (10 mile/h) and another site with a rather high average annual wind speed of 6.7 m/s (15 mile/h). The diagram shows the hours per year for which the wind speed exceeds the corresponding ordinate value. For example, from the curve for 6.7 m/s average annual wind speed, the wind speed exceeds 9 m/s for just over

2000 h. The maximum value on the abscissa, 8760 h, represents 365 days of 24 h each. The dotted curves are corresponding results predicted theoretically based on what is known as a Rayleigh wind speed distribution model. This model will be described later following a discussion of a very adaptable model known as a Weibull distribution. The Rayleigh distribution is, it will be shown, a special case of a Weibull distribution.

4.4.2. Weibull Distribution

A fairly general, flexible model for evaluating what is termed the probability density function (PDF) of statistical data is the Weibull distribution. This has been used widely to describe, in terms of two experimentally determined parameters C and K, the PDF applicable to the wind speed at a particular location. With respect to the time-dependent wind speed, U_∞, the Weibull distribution based PDF, $f(U_\infty)$, is given by:

$$f(U_\infty) = \left(\frac{K}{C}\right) \left(\frac{U_\infty}{C}\right)^{(K-1)} \exp\left[-\left(\frac{U_\infty}{C}\right)^K\right] \qquad (4.4)$$

Adjustment of the values of C and K allow the form and magnitude of the PDF to vary over a wide range. The constant C has the dimensions of velocity and K is dimensionless. A PDF is evaluated, for prescribed values of C and K, by assuming that U_∞ can vary from zero to infinity. In fact for situations typical of wind speed distributions the PDF becomes vanishingly small for values of U_∞ several times that of the site average wind speed $\overline{U}_\infty$.

As has been demonstrated previously (Pennell and Miller, 1982) the parameter K controls the spread of the PDF. A relatively large value of K, for example $K = 4$, results in a wind speed distribution tightly packed around the site average wind speed whereas a relatively low value of K results in a much more diffuse distribution. This point is illustrated, diagrammatically, in Fig. 4.8 which shows for hypothetical sites, each with an annual average wind speed, U_∞, of 7 m/s, the influence of K on wind speed distribution. The constant C is normally found to be in the region of 1.13 times the average annual wind speed $\overline{U}_\infty$. Constant C is identified as the scale parameter and K as the shape (of the PDF distribution curve) parameter.

As can be seen from equation (4.4), bearing in mind that K is dimensionless and that C has the dimensions of velocity, the PDF, $f(U_\infty)$, has units which are the inverse of the dimensions of velocity. Hence integrating the area under a PDF versus U_∞ curve, for example, any of the three curves of Fig. 4.8, yields a dimensionless result. Further, it is also

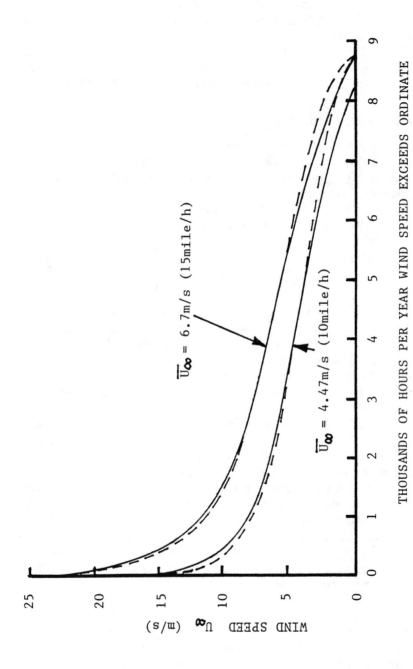

Figure 4.7. Experimentally obtained velocity distributions (Golding, 1956); corresponding, predicted, Rayleigh-type distributions shown dotted.

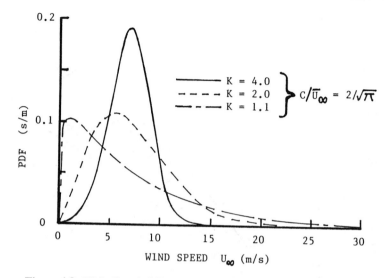

Figure 4.8. Weibull probability-distribution-functions versus wind speed for three values of the shape parameter K. Site average wind speed 7 m/s for each case.

found that the resultant numerical value is, in each case and as a fundamental rule, unity. Thus when the PDF ordinate is multiplied by the hours per year, 8760 h, and the integration is repeated in steps between specific values of U_∞, the annual hours of operation are obtained, for each step, between the limits of U_∞ of the integration.

Justus (Justus, 1978) analysed wind data from a number of sites in the continental United States. On the basis of the assumption of a Weibull distribution in each case Justus established, from these experimental data, K and C as functions of the site average wind speed. The findings of Justus are presented for K and C in Figs. 4.9 and 4.10, respectively. Points of particular interest are that, from Fig. 4.10, $C/\overline{U}_\infty$ is close to being constant for all values of $\overline{U}_\infty$ and, from Fig. 4.9, the value of K is within the range $1.5 \leq K \leq 2.5$ for the average wind speed range 3.5 m/s $\leq \overline{U}_\infty \leq 6$ m/s. This wind speed range covers most of the probable sites where water-pumping wind-turbines are likely to be installed. A simplification suggests, therefore, that a value of $K = 2$ should be fairly representative of many sites. It can be shown that for the specific case

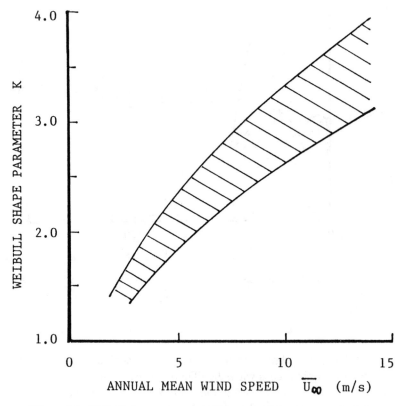

Figure 4.9. Weibull shape parameter, K, versus site mean annual wind speed (Justus, 1978).

where $K = 2$ the Weibull distribution model can be simplified into what is known as a Rayleigh distribution.

4.4.3. Rayleigh Distribution

A Rayleigh distribution, which is a special case, where $K = 2$, of the more general Weibull distribution, is given by the PDF:

$$f(U_\infty) = \frac{\pi}{2} \frac{U_\infty}{\overline{U}_\infty^2} \exp\left[-\frac{\pi}{4} \left(\frac{U_\infty}{\overline{U}_\infty} \right)^2 \right] \qquad (4.5)$$

Once a Rayleigh distribution has been assumed the need to conduct a wind survey is eliminated provided the site annual, or seasonal, average

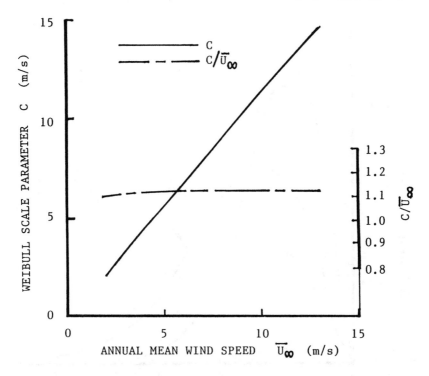

Figure 4.10. Weibull scale parameter C, and $C/\overline{U}_\infty$, versus site mean annual wind speed $\overline{U}_\infty$ (Justus, 1978).

wind speed, $\overline{U}_\infty$, is known. From putting $K = 2$ in equation (4.4) and comparing with equation (4.5) it can be shown that the value of $C/\overline{U}_\infty$ corresponding to a Rayleigh distribution is $2\sqrt{\pi} = 1.128$. This value is essentially the same as that of Fig. 4.10 over the full range of U_∞ for which data are available. The curve of Fig. 4.8 for $K = 2$ is a Rayleigh distribution. It can be seen that the $K = 2$ curve lies between the other two, hypothetical, more extreme cases for large and small K.

The practical importance of the Rayleigh distribution hinges not only upon realism but also because of the use made of it by wind-turbine manufacturers who usually specify expected machine performances in terms of Rayleigh distributions since, for prescribed $\overline{U}_\infty$, these are unambiguous. Comparisons of Rayleigh distribution predictions with examples of actual site data are presented in Fig. 4.7. The predicted results, shown dotted, model quite well the experimental data except at very low wind speeds. The dotted curves were obtained from the corresponding Rayleigh PDF

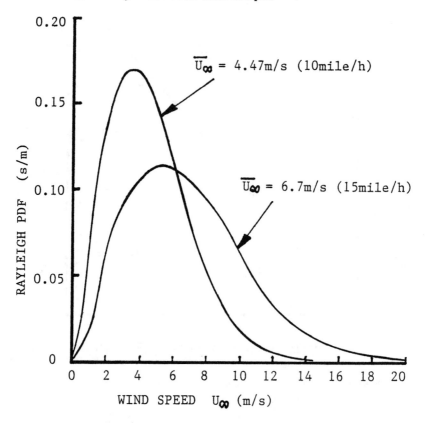

Figure 4.11. Rayleigh probability-distribution-functions versus wind speed for $\overline{U}_\infty = 4.47$ m/s (10 mile/h) and $\overline{U}_\infty = 6.7$ m/s (15 mile/h).

versus U_∞ curves of Fig. 4.11 by means of the integration procedure described in the previous subsection. It can be seen from Fig. 4.11 that as $\overline{U}_\infty$ is increased the trend is for the PDF curves to become less steep and spread over a widening range of U_∞.

It seems, from the foregoing, that for situations in which the cost of, and the time required for, comprehensive wind surveys cannot be justified the best course of action, in the absence of specific knowledge of nearby sites, is to assume that a Rayleigh velocity distribution applies. This then allows more sophisticated performance predictions to be made than can be carried out based only on the site average wind speed at, or adjusted to correspond to, the hub height of the proposed turbine. Knowledge, or a good estimate, of the site average wind speed is, of course, an essential ingredient for this performance prediction process. For some water-pumping wind-turbines, for example those tested at the Alberta Renewable Energy Test Site (ARETS) in Alberta, Canada, the pumping performance is available, directly in terms of the water lift and flow rate as a function of site average wind speed, $\overline{U}_\infty$, assuming a Rayleigh velocity distribution (Atkins and Proctor, 1993).

4.5. Influence of Gusting

The gustiness of the wind has essentially two impacts on wind-turbines. One influence, touched upon previously in this chapter, concerns machine fatigue-loading cycles. Gustiness also affects performance either favourably or unfavourably. Typical gusts can involve rapid transient local velocity excursions as large as $\pm 50\%$, or more, of U_∞, the average prevailing wind speed, with associated transient changes of local flow direction.

Gusting is relatively frequent at sites with low average wind speeds as indicated by the experimental evaluation of the Weibull shape factor K by Justus (Justus, 1978) the results of which are reproduced here, in Fig. 4.9, showing that K decreases as $\overline{U}_\infty$ decreases. As demonstrated graphically in Fig. 4.8 a small value of K implies a large variation, or scatter, of velocity about the site time-averaged velocity $\overline{U}_\infty$. Park (Park, 1981) not only implies that sites with low values of $\overline{U}_\infty$ tend to be more gusty than sites with high values of $\overline{U}_\infty$, but he also presents evidence showing that winds that have passed, previously, over rough surfaces, as indicated by a relatively large Prandtl boundary-layer exponent γ, tend to have greater gustiness than flows for which γ is small.

An implication of gustiness, from the structural viewpoint, is that a relatively high fatigue count will usually occur at weak wind-sites downwind of obstructions, etc., but, due to the low average wind speed, the associated stress levels, and cumulative damage if any, will be correspondingly low. For good sites with high average wind speeds the frequency of the fatigue-inducing loadings can be expected to be relatively low but the occasional strong gusts are more likely to cause critical cumulative damage or even, in very extreme situations, to exceed the permitted survival loads of the structure. The chances of the latter situation occurring are, it appears, relatively remote for well-designed machines with survival wind speeds in the region of 55 m/s. A preliminary study of the likely frequency of very strong destructive gusts has been reported by Milborrow (Milborrow, 1994).

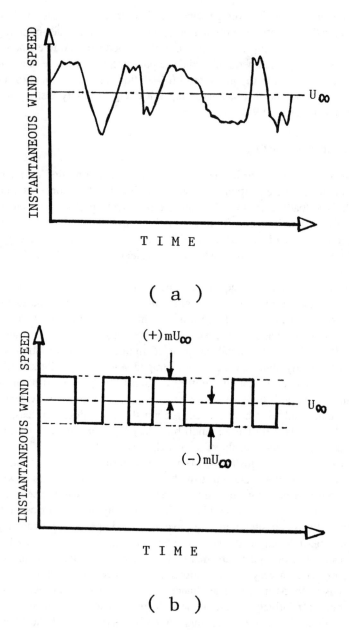

Figure 4.12. Wind gustiness characteristics: a) typically observed form; b) simplified square-law model.

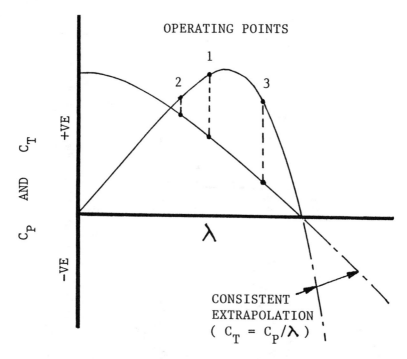

Figure 4.13. Diagrammatic illustration of wind-turbine performance characteristics showing operating points with and without gusting.

At least one study has been made of the influence of gusting on the performance of various types of wind-turbine rotor (Kentfield, 1986(a)). This study was based on the simplifying assumption that random gustiness about a nominal, steady, wind speed U_∞, as illustrated diagrammatically in Fig. 4.12(a), can be represented as a square wave oscillation, of random frequency, as illustrated in Fig. 4.12(b), where m is the gust-strength parameter. It can be shown, from such a model, that over a time interval of sufficient duration to ensure independence from the influence of the randomness of the gusts depicted in Fig. 4.12(b) and with reference to Fig. 4.13 showing operating points 1, 2 and 3:

$$\overline{C}_P = \frac{1}{2}\left\{C_{P2}(1+m)^3 + C_{P3}(1-m)^3\right\} \qquad (4.6)$$

where $U_1 = U_\infty$, $U_2 = (1+m)U_1$, $U_3 = (1-m)U_1$, and where $\overline{C}_P$ is the time-averaged power coefficient based on the prevailing average wind

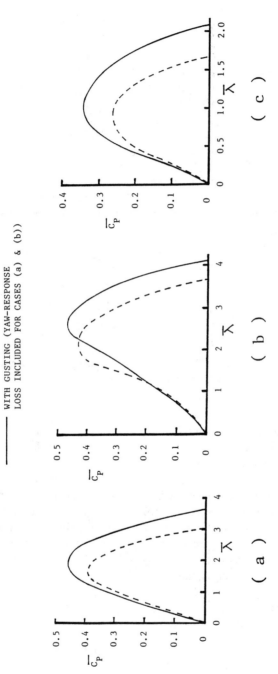

Figure 4.14. Experimentally obtained water-pumping-turbine performance characteristics modified analytically to include the influence of gusting (*m* = 0.4): a) delta-wing bladed rotor; b) Dutch CWD (WEU-I-2) rotor; c) Savonius rotor.

velocity, U_∞, at operating point 1. The variation of λ between operating points 2 and 3 is due to the assumption that the turbine rotor speed remains invariant whilst the wind speed at operating point 2 is $(1 + m)U_\infty$ and that at operating point 3 is $(1 - m)U_\infty$. The assumption of a constant rotor speed is clearly justified for fixed-speed grid-connected wind-electric machines and will approach the truth for water pumpers when the typical frequency of the random step-wave of Fig. 4.12(b) is sufficiently high to prevent significant sympathetic variations of rotor speed. For the water pumper case the nominal steady running speed will increase due to gusting because of the characteristics of the load unless the pump size and/or lift are increased to compensate.

Results obtained from application of equation (4.6) to the analysis, for $m = 0.4$, of three types of water-pumping wind-turbine are presented in Fig. 4.14 and, for comparative purposes, a horizontal-axis fixed-pitch propeller type turbine in Fig. 4.15(a) and a variable pitch, horizontal-axis, propeller turbine in Fig. 4.15(b). The types of water-pumping turbine studied were, in Fig. 4.14(a), a horizontal-axis rotor with delta-wing type blades; in Fig. 4.14(b) a Dutch CWD (WEU-I-2) horizontal-axis rotor, and in Fig. 4.14(c), a Savonius vertical-axis rotor. These turbine types are discussed in more detail in subsequent chapters. In each case the results for the horizontal-axis machines were corrected to include a performance loss, under gusting conditions, due to an expected inability to align, continuously, with the oncoming flow. The yaw error was assumed to correspond to an angle of Tan^{-1} (m/2). It can be seen that the predicted gust responses of the delta-wing bladed rotor and the Savonius rotor are such that these turbines benefitted, throughout their operating ranges, from gusting whilst the remaining horizontal-axis machines suffered performance degradations at low tip-speed ratios with gains apparent only at higher tip-speed ratios.

4.5.1. Gustiness and Turbulence

The term "gustiness" has been used here extensively to describe transient changes of wind speed and direction. In terms of the large-dimensional scale of the boundary layer of the earth these velocity changes can usually be described as a consequence of the turbulence in the boundary layer. However viewed from a dimensional scale representative of a small wind-turbine the term "gustiness" seems appropriate since one perturbation may completely engulf a small wind-turbine or a significant portion of a very large turbine. In fluid-mechanics terminology "turbulent flow over a surface" usually refers to random, disordered, time-dependent flow over a

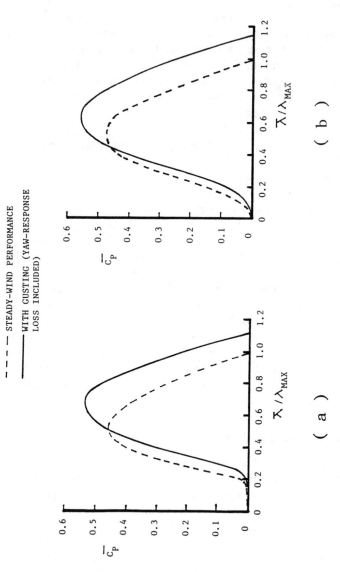

Figure 4.15. Typical wind-electric propeller-type turbine performance characteristics modified analytically to include the influence of gusting ($m = 0.4$): a) fixed-pitch rotor; b) variable-pitch rotor.

surface the chordwise length of which far exceeds a dimension representative of a typical perturbation in the flow.

Hence whether the term gustiness or turbulence is used depends upon the perspective of the observer. What is turbulence in the boundary layer of the earth appears to be gustiness from the viewpoint of another observer focussing on a wind-turbine immersed in such a flow. An analogous situation often occurs in aviation where atmospheric turbulence can lead to transient three-dimensional changes in flow direction and velocity relative to an aircraft. This circumstance is often perceived by the occupants of an aircraft as gustiness but to atmospheric scientists as turbulence in the atmosphere. With wind-turbines velocity components normal to the surface of the earth tend to be suppressed due to the proximity of the turbines to the ground.

CHAPTER 5

Types and Performances of Horizontal-Axis Turbine Rotors

Numerous forms of turbine rotor have been applied to water-pumping applications. It is the objective, in this chapter, to describe not only the basic geometry of each of the main categories dealt with but also to present, where possible, the corresponding rotor aerodynamic performance data as deduced from wind-tunnel, or other, tests. An underlying, very desirable characteristic of the rotors of water-pumping wind-turbines directly coupled to either reciprocating or rotary, positive-displacement pumps is a high torque coefficient at zero rotor speed. This enables the wind-turbine to start the pump, under load, most effectively. A similar comment applies to simple air-lift systems in which a positive-displacement air-compressor is directly coupled to the turbine rotor.

In some cases the need for the torque coefficient to be a maximum at zero rotor speed has been ameliorated by such devices as pump bleed-orifices, or pump, or air-compressor, transient short-circuit arrangements. In other cases centrifugal clutches have been used to unload the turbine rotor completely until it has reached a speed high enough to generate a torque coefficient sufficient to carry the pump load. Modern developments, in The Netherlands, involving pumps with small bleed, or leakage, holes and the alternative, and more efficient, use of floating valves have been reported (Cleijne et al., 1986). This work was undertaken in order to match light-weight, relatively low-solidity, low-cost rotors to water-pumping applications. Partly because of their low solidity these rotors do not produce their maximum torque coefficients at zero tip-speed ratio but at $\lambda \simeq 1.5$.

In the past at least one commercial water-pumping wind-turbine employed a propeller-like rotor, similar to those normally used on wind-driven electric-power generators, direct coupled to a reciprocating water pump. Because of the poor starting torque coefficient produced by this rotor a centrifugally actuated clutch was employed to completely disconnect the turbine rotor from the pump during start-up. A more detailed description of this unusual American machine has been given by Baker (Baker, 1985). More conventional rotors of direct-drive water-pumping wind-turbines are of relatively high solidity and generate their maximum torque coefficients at, or close to, the zero tip-speed ratio condition. Horizontal-axis rotors of this kind currently dominate the wind-driven water-pumping scene.

5.1. Cretian Rotors

The origin of the design of Cretian wind-turbines appears to be lost in antiquity. The name associates this configuration with the Mediterranean area in general and with the island of Crete in particular. So far as the writer is aware the classical application of Cretian turbines has been to drive grain-milling equipment; their use in water-pumping seems to be comparatively recent. The turbines used for grain milling are usually supported on short, relatively large diameter masonry towers which also house the grain mills. Those used for water-pumping are often mounted on narrow lattice towers of wood or metal and are controlled in yaw by means of a conventional downwind vertical-tail surface. Typically Cretian turbines have either 8, 10 or 12 blades or sails. A representative configuration, actually a drawing of a model 8-sail rotor built specially for performance testing in a wind-tunnel, is shown in Fig. 5.1.

The upper portion of Fig. 5.1 illustrates the rotor-frame assembly. The only rigid members are the spokes, the steel welding rod in the 508 mm diameter model rotor, and the "bowsprit-like" extension of the main shaft. The perimeter members joining the tips of the spokes and the members connecting the upwind tip of the "bowsprit" to the outer ends of the spokes were of thin nylon chord, in the model, representative of rope in full-scale units. The lower portion of Fig. 5.1 depicts, diagrammatically, a compliant cloth sail, in a typical operating position, added to the rotor frame. The locations A and B mark the outer corners of the triangular sail and stations B and C identify each end of the rope attaching the top of the sail to the next spoke.

Because there did not appear to be any definitive rules defining an optimum geometry for Cretian rotors the wind-tunnel tests were carried

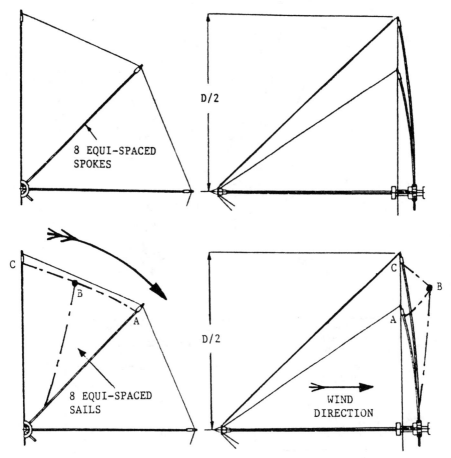

Figure 5.1. Frame of wind-tunnel model Cretian rotor.

out in a parametric manner in an attempt to establish, from the water-pumping application viewpoint, an optimal configuration. Accordingly the tests covered four sail sizes and four values of a sail-setting parameter identified as ϕ. Flat, or taut, generations of the four sets of sail surface tests are illustrated in Fig. 5.2. The sail-setting parameter, ϕ, is defined as the path length from A to C following the curvature formed by the top edge of the sail plus rope length BC (see Fig. 5.1) divided by the straight-line length XY between the spokes.

Hence for the settings illustrated in Fig. 5.2, where the rope length BC is shortened such that point B lies on the straight line XY, $\phi = 1$. Values of ϕ greater than unity imply a blade pitch angle, β, greater at

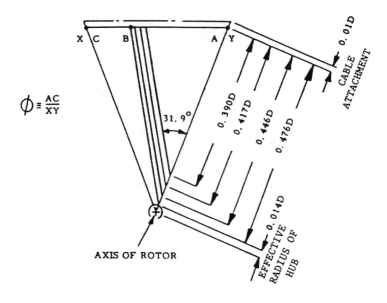

$$\phi \equiv \frac{AC}{XY}$$

MAXIMUM DIMENSION OF SAIL	ROTOR SOLIDITY σ' $\equiv \dfrac{\Sigma \text{SAIL AREA}}{\text{ROTOR PROJECTED AREA}}$
0.476D	0.57
0.446D	0.50
0.417D	0.44
0.390D	0.38

Figure 5.2. Flat generations of model Cretian rotor sails, subjected to wind-tunnel testing, and corresponding solidity table.

the outer edge of the sail than zero or, correspondingly, a blade stagger angle of less than 90°. The rotor solidities achieved with each of the four sets of blades are tabulated in Fig. 5.2. Because the sail curvature is not known, and hence the blade chord is not known apriori, the solidity has been expressed in terms of the full surface area of one side of each set of sails divided by the rotor disc area and is identified as σ'. It is difficult to achieve a significantly greater σ' value than 0.57 without seriously obstructing the flow path through the rotor and also generating an excessive, counter-productive, back-curvature of each sail.

Tests of the dynamometer-equipped model rotor were carried out in an open-jet wind-tunnel at the University of Calgary. The jet width and height were 1.37 m and 0.76 m, respectively. A summary of the results obtained is presented in Figs. 5.3 to 5.6 inclusive. The performance shown in Fig. 5.3 on the C_P and C_T versus λ planes was judged to be the best achieved from the tests when account was taken of the performance requirements of turbines driving positive-displacement water pumps. The dotted curves represent model test data corrected to take into account the higher Reynolds number of typical full-scale turbines of 3 m to 4 m diameter, operating in a 7 m/s wind, and also correct for the loss of rotor area of the model due to the cable-anchor fixtures which would be relatively smaller in a full-scale machine. Such corrections were not applied to Figs. 5.4, 5.5 and 5.6 which were derived from cross-plotting from Fig. 5.3 and many similar diagrams. It can be seen from Figs. 5.4 and 5.5 that the best results were obtained with the highest solidity, σ', tested. It can also be seen that ϕ values corresponding to $C_{P(MAX)}$ and maximum C_T at $\lambda = 0$ are not identical but the value of $\phi = 1.06$, applicable to Fig. 5.3, is close to the optimum for both conditions. It can also be seen that, from Fig. 5.6, the runaway tip-speed ratio, λ_{MAX}, increases with both increasing solidity and decreasing ϕ. Further details of the test procedure and results are available elsewhere (Kentfield, 1983).

An advantage of Cretian rotors is their very simple construction in conjunction with a performance which, whilst not outstanding compared with other types of turbine, is acceptable for many applications, particularly in developing nations. A problem is that the rotor uses cloth for the blade surfaces which, in some developing nations is a scarce and relatively costly material, and, in any case, is one that tends to deteriorate fairly rapidly with exposure to the atmosphere. Further, the Cretian rotor design does not lend itself well to the application of automatic control to furl the machine in stormy conditions. Whilst automatic control strategies, for example, an automatic increase in rope length BC due to overspeeding and/or an aerodynamic load increase on the sails, can be envisaged, control is normally by stopping the unit, by braking or yawing, and reducing the exposed sail area, manually, by wrapping each sail around the spoke to which it is attached. It appears that the low tower height usually associated with Cretian rotors is to provide access to the sails from ground level. Clearly a taller tower supporting a raised platform just below the sails is also a possibility.

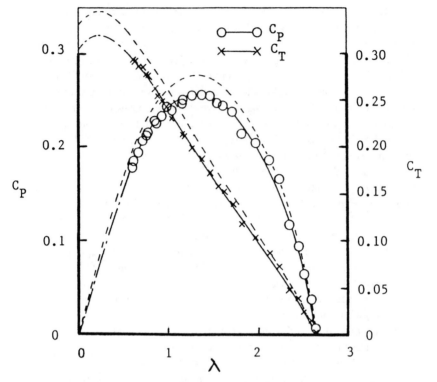

Figure 5.3. Best performance of model Cretian rotor. Solidity $\sigma' = 0.57$, $\phi = 1.06$. Projected full-scale performance shown dotted.

5.2. Slatted Rotors

Multibladed rotors, constructed of wood, featuring thin, flat-plate, slat-like blades constituted the most common form of rotor for water-pumping wind-turbines in North America during the latter half of the nineteenth century. Towards the end of the nineteenth century and during the early part of the twentieth century wood-slatted rotors were gradually displaced by the now classical multibladed form featuring cambered sheet-metal blades. The essential aerodynamic differences between the two types were primarily the introduction of blade camber and secondarily a reduction of flow blockage due to the thinner cross-section of the metal support structure compared with the timber structure of the wood, flat-plate, slatted rotors. Some of the wood-slatted rotors were of the so-called sectional type an example of which is illustrated, diagrammatically, in Fig. 1.2. Others were, however, of a rigid nature. Relatively recently interest in

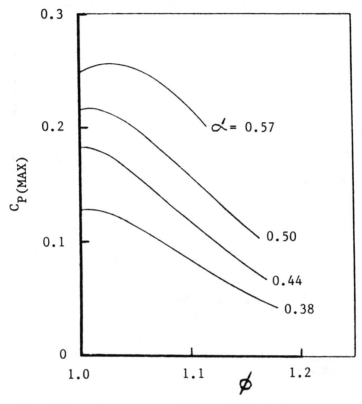

Figure 5.4. Maximum power coefficient of model Cretian rotor versus sail-setting parameter ϕ.

the rigid form of slatted rotor has been revived for water-pumping duties in developing countries in which timber, for indigenous construction, is readily available.

A fairly comprehensive series of tests of wood-slatted rotors was undertaken in 1882, and the following year, by T.O. Perry on behalf of the United States Wind Engine and Pump Company of Batavia, Illinois. Due, it seems, to the proprietary nature of Perry's study, which also included work on rotors with metal, cambered, sheet-metal blades, the results were not published until 1899 (Perry, 1899). At that time there was little interest in Perry's data since attention had, by then, already been diverted from wood-slatted rotors to those of the now classical metal form with cambered blades. Whilst Perry's tests were quite comprehensive in nature his results were obtained by what must, by the practices of today, be regarded as

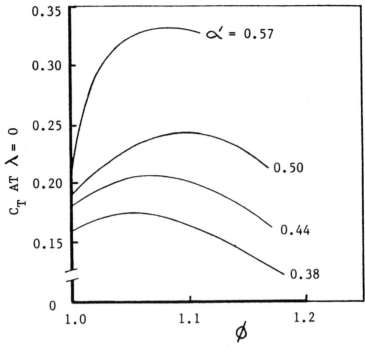

Figure 5.5. Torque coefficient at $\lambda = 0$ of model Cretian rotor versus sail-setting parameter ϕ.

most unconventional means. Perry mounted 1.525 m (5 ft) diameter, dynamometer-equipped, model rotors at the end of a power driven radial arm rotating about a vertical axis. The turbine axis was both horizontal and normal to the centre-line of the radial arm. Concerns with this procedure, which had previously been employed in England by Smeaton more than a hundred years earlier (Smeaton, 1759), arose due to the difference in the apparent stream velocity across the turbine face, which would tend to lead to a performance over-estimate, and the tendency of the system to cause the air in the test laboratory to be pushed into an orbital motion about a vertical axis. The latter influence could be expected to lead to an under-estimate of the performance of the test wind-turbine rotor. Accordingly a 508 mm (20 in) diameter model was built of Perry's best rotor for which full performance data were available, his no. 6 unit illustrated in Fig. 5.7, for testing in the University of Calgary 1.37 m × 0.76 m open-jet wind-tunnel referred to previously in §5.1.

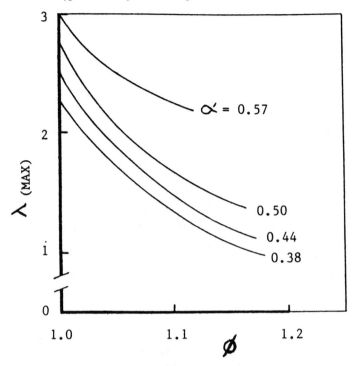

Figure 5.6. Runaway tip-speed ratio of model Cretian rotor versus sail-setting parameter ϕ.

The results obtained from the University of Calgary facility are presented in Fig. 5.8. It should be noted, however, that only the test data points are presented. The solid curves were extracted, without the application of any corrections, directly from Perry's results of approximately a century earlier. There was a very slight discrepancy between the Calgary data, obtained by the writer, and Perry's results adjacent to the $\lambda = 0$ condition. Actually the very closeness of the two sets of results does indicate, since Perry's tests took place at a Reynolds number about three times greater than that of the later wind-tunnel tests, that Perry's technique leads to a very slight under-estimate of performance. Hence it would appear to be reasonable to regard all of Perry's results as what would have been obtained from the University of Calgary wind-tunnel had Perry's tests been repeated using that facility. The dotted curves shown in Fig. 5.8 present the expected performance of 3 m to 4 m diameter full-scale Perry no. 6 rotors operating in a 7 m/s wind. The Reynolds number correction employed was based on half of the Reynolds number correction advocated by

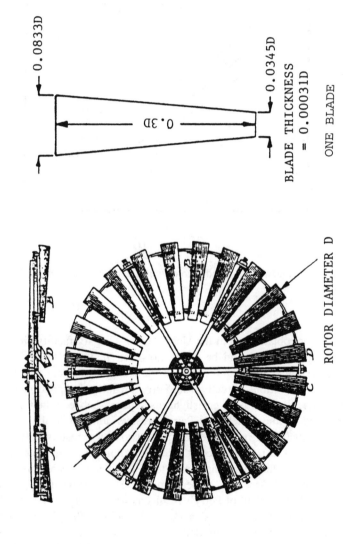

0.0833D

0.0345D

BLADE THICKNESS = 0.00031D

ONE BLADE

0.3D

ROTOR DIAMETER D

Figure 5.7. Typical slatted rotor as tested by Perry (Perry's rotor no. 6 (Perry, 1899)).

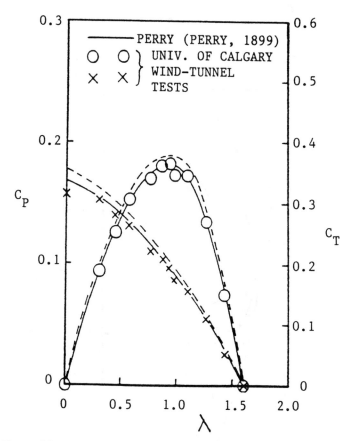

Figure 5.8. Comparison of performance of Perry's rotor no. 6 ($\sigma' =$ 0.544, 24 blades, $\beta = 30°$) with that of University of Calgary replica. Projected full-scale performance shown dotted.

Hawthorne as applicable to a full reaction turbine stage consisting of both nozzle and rotor blading (Hawthorne, 1964). The same form of correction was employed to take into account the Reynolds number portion of the two corrections applied to the Cretian rotor data of Fig. 5.3.

Figures 5.9, 5.10 and 5.11 were compiled directly from Perry's results, without corrections being applied, and are presented here as data that could have been expected from the University of Calgary open-jet wind-tunnel without any correction to convert the results from model to full-scale Reynolds numbers. It is noteworthy, from Fig. 5.9, that for a solidity σ ($= \sigma'$ for flat blades) of 0.666 a slightly better performance was

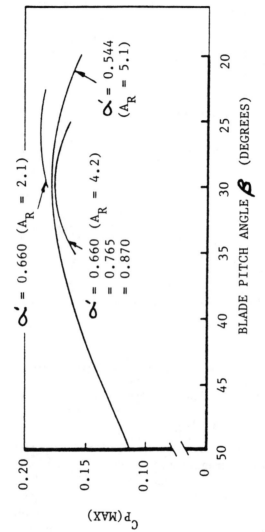

Figure 5.9. Maximum power coefficient versus blade pitch angle, β, for Perry's slatted rotors.

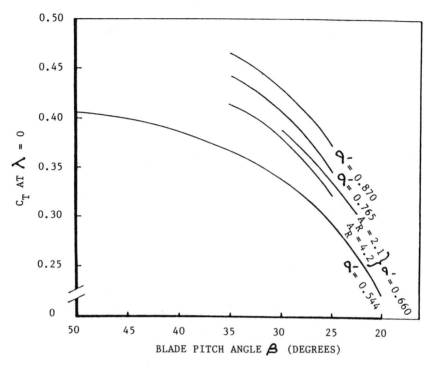

Figure 5.10. Torque coefficient at $\lambda = 0$ versus blade pitch angle, β, for Perry's slatted rotors.

obtained with blades of aspect ratio 2.1 than for blades of twice the aspect ratio. Since the aspect ratio reduction was obtained using only 12 blades of the same thickness as the 24 blades of the $A_R = 4.2$ rotor it seems that the reduction of blockage overwhelmed the apparent advantage of the higher aspect ratio case. It can be seen from Fig. 5.10 that, as might be expected, increasing solidity corresponds, over the range investigated by Perry, to an increasing starting-torque coefficient. Figure 5.11 shows that, again as might be expected, decreasing the blade pitch angle increases the runaway tip-speed ratio, but at a decreasing rate, with a maximum occurring, it would appear, at a pitch angle, β, of about 20°.

It is clear from Fig. 5.7 that the 6 timber spokes of Perry's rotor no. 6 constitute a fairly substantial blockage in 6 of the 24 flow passages between adjacent blades. Whilst for an all-timber rotor Perry's construction appears, in general terms, to be essential it seems that a performance improvement could be expected using much thinner metal spokes. A

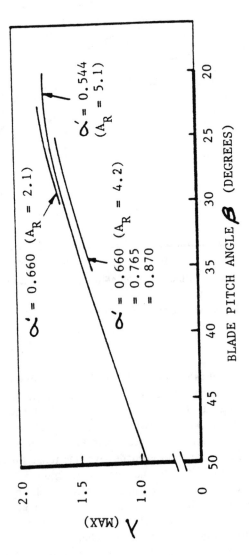

Figure 5.11. Runaway velocity ratio versus blade pitch angle, β, for Perry's slatted rotors.

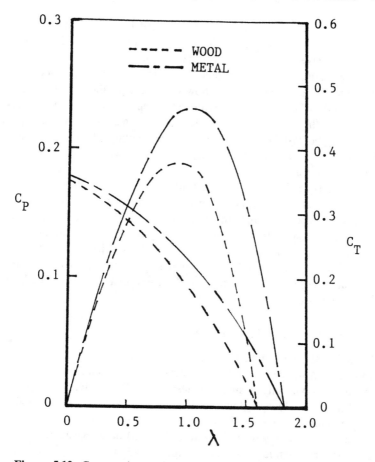

Figure 5.12. Comparative projected full-scale performances of wood and metal versions of Perry's no. 6 rotor. Derived from University of Calgary wind-tunnel test data.

wind-tunnel test of a modified version of Perry's no. 6 rotor confirmed this expectation. The results of this experiment, with a Reynolds number correction applied, are compared with the dotted curves of Fig. 5.8 in Fig. 5.12. However the use of a metal rotor frame in conjunction with wood blading tends to defeat the perceived advantages of a wholly timber construction. More details of Perry's results and the corresponding tests in the University of Calgary wind-tunnel are available (Kentfield, 1983).

It can be seen, in summary, that Perry's rotor of solidity $\sigma = 0.870$ is probably the most suitable for water pumping since it has the highest torque coefficient at zero tip-speed ratio and is only slightly inferior, in terms of maximum power coefficient, to his other rotors. However full, comprehensive, data are not available for the $\sigma = 0.870$ rotor. It seems that the main aerodynamic problem with the slatted rotor concept lies in the lack of ability to deflect the flow within the parallel-walled blade passages. Most of the flow deflection must, it appears, occur in the vicinity of the slat leading-edges for simple, flat slats. A small performance improvement may be possible by radiusing the slat leading edges and chamfering the suction surfaces at the trailing edges. This would, however, weaken already thin slats.

A considerable advantage of slatted rotors is their generally low tip-speed ratio at runaway conditions. This implies that, in many cases, positive-displacement reciprocating pumps can be driven directly from the turbine shaft without resorting to very small pump strokes to avoid excessive pump-rod accelerations. This topic will be dealt with in more detail, later, in Chapter 8. The rigid slatted rotor also lends itself to automatic furling by overspeed control systems that yaw the rotor edgewise to the wind direction.

5.3. Classical Multibladed Rotors

Multibladed rotors with cambered sheet-metal blades, also commonly known as American multibladed rotors, have become, over the past 80 to 90 years virtually a standard design for direct-drive water-pumping wind-turbines. However few aerodynamic performance data are available. Hence apart from the results of an early test of a multibladed rotor presented comparatively recently (Eldridge, 1975) little appears to be known of rotor aerodynamic performance expectations. Or at least little has been presented in the open literature.

Accordingly it was decided, by the writer, to attempt to establish a sound basis from which to assess the influence on performance of various geometric features of the designs available commercially. Four rotor designs were composed based on the rotors of several well-known, fairly similar, production turbines. Dynamometer-equipped models of 508 mm diameter were made of these rotors which were subsequently tested in the 1.37 m × 0.76 m open-jet wind-tunnel at the University of Calgary referred to previously in §§5.1 and 5.2. Since the full-scale rotor diameters of greatest interest were in the 3 m to 4 m range it was decided, following a study of corresponding commercial units, that the models should each have 18 blades supported on a wheel-like structure comprising six double spokes carrying two blade-support rings. This configuration, which was common for all the tests, is illustrated in Fig. 5.13; it represented,

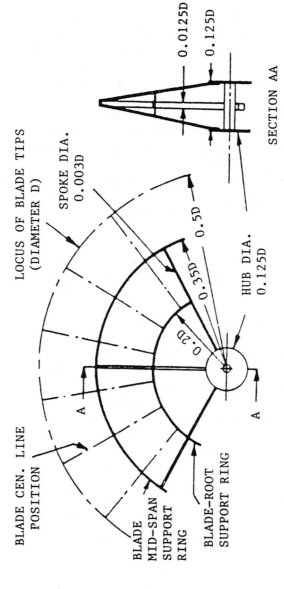

Figure 5.13. Rotor-blade support frame for wind-tunnel model American multibladed rotors (18 blades).

in model form, both past and current typical practice in blade-support structure construction.

Four blade configurations were tested. In each case the radial dimension, or span, of the blades was 0.3 D. Flat generations of each blade shape tested are shown in the upper portion of Fig. 5.14. Concurrent examination of the upper and lower portions of Fig. 5.14 shows that Configurations 1 and 2 reveal no differences in blade entry and exit angles but only a variation in local solidity between the inner and outer ends of the blades. The local solidity, σ'_L, of the inner blade ends for all four configurations was unity whereas the local solidity, σ'_L, based on the outer dimensions of the blade blanks was unity for Configurations 2, 3 and 4 but was only 0.69 for Configuration 1. The area based solidity, σ', based on the area of the flat blade blanks was 0.66 for this configuration. The geometry of the flat blade blanks for Configurations 2, 3 and 4 was identical and the corresponding value of σ' was 0.84 in all three cases. These configurations differed from each other in blade curvature with leading-edge angles of 50°, 40° and 30°, respectively, as can be seen from the lower portion of Fig. 5.14.

The results obtained from the tests are presented in Figs. 5.15 to 5.18 inclusive for Configurations 1 to 4, inclusive, respectively. The dotted curves added to each diagram represent the expected performances of full-scale rotors of 3 m to 4 m diameter operating in winds of approximately 7 m/s. The Reynolds number correction employed to convert the model test results to projected full-scale performances was of the form described previously in §5.2. Generally it can be seen that the poorest performance, both in terms of the torque coefficient at zero tip-speed ratio and maximum power coefficient, was that of Configuration 1. Increasing the rotor solidity by adding blade area in the outboard region, as represented by Configuration 2, increased the torque coefficient at start-up by about 6% and also increased, slightly, the maximum power coefficient. The most impressive improvements, in terms of increasing the torque coefficient at $\lambda = 0$, decreasing the runaway tip-speed ratio and increasing, slightly, $C_{P(MAX)}$ were obtained by progressively increasing the blade camber such that the blade leading-edge angle was reduced from the 50° value shown in Fig. 5.14, corresponding to Configuration 2, to 40°, corresponding to Configuration 3, and then to 30° corresponding to Configuration 4. A comparison is made in Fig. 5.19 of the expected full-scale performance of Configuration 4, shown in Fig. 5.18, with the results presented by Eldridge (Eldridge, 1975). It can be seen that the two performances are fairly similar.

The main aerodynamic difference between classical multibladed rotors and slatted rotors, discussed in §5.2, is the flow turning that occurs,

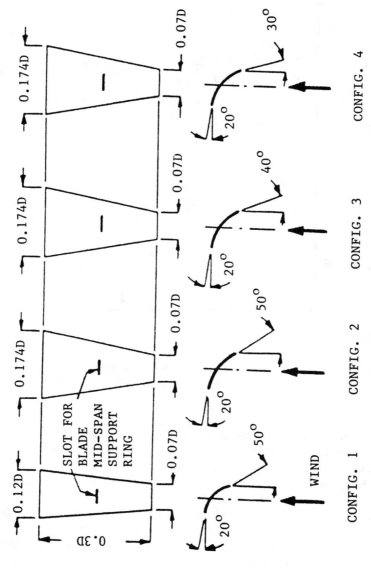

Figure 5.14. Blade configurations of 18-bladed model American multibladed rotors subjected to wind-tunnel testing.

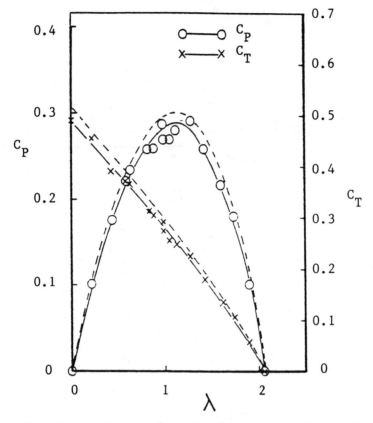

Figure 5.15. Performance of model multibladed rotor Configuration 1, solidity $\sigma' = 0.66$. Projected full-scale performance shown dotted.

inherently, in the rotor due to the use of blade camber in the former case. The cambered blades also serve as nozzles since the passage cross-sectional area at exit is less than that at inlet. A comparison can be made of the slatted rotor performances for $\sigma (= \sigma') = 0.666$ of Fig. 5.12, with that of a classical multibladed rotor for which $\sigma' = 0.66$ (note: σ is slightly smaller than σ' for cambered blades) presented in Fig. 5.15. This reveals that the classical multibladed rotor has a much better performance, both in terms of the torque coefficient for $\lambda = 0$ and $C_{P(MAX)}$, than the slatted rotors even when the latter employs a low-blockage, metal, rotor-support structure. Furthermore, it can also be seen, from comparison of the data presented in this and the previous section of Chapter 5, that a slatted rotor for which $\sigma = 0.87$ has an inferior performance, except in terms of the

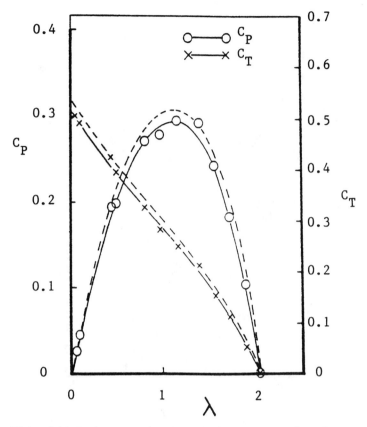

Figure 5.16. Performance of model multibladed rotor Configuration 2, solidity $\sigma' = 0.84$. Projected full-scale performance shown dotted.

runaway tip-speed ratio, compared with all the classical multibladed rotors tested. More details relating to the tests of the model classical multibladed rotors have been presented elsewhere (Kentfield, 1982).

In common with the slatted rotor case, classical multibladed rotors lend themselves to automatic overspeed control by means of turning the rotor edgewise to the wind direction. It may, perhaps, be possible to obtain further performance improvements if airfoil-like cross-section blades are substituted for the thin, sheet-metal, cambered blades of traditional, classical, multibladed rotors. The use of airfoil-like blades is already normal practice in most turbo machines. The new blade form would possess the benefit of radiused leading edges thereby rendering the blading performance less sensitive to changes of flow incidence angle. Rotor blading

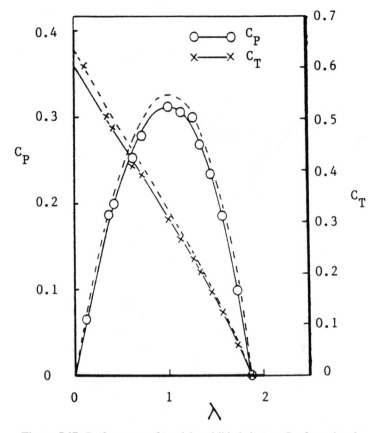

Figure 5.17. Performance of model multibladed rotor Configuration 3, solidity $\sigma' = 0.84$. Projected full-scale performance shown dotted.

made in this manner would have an appearance similar to that shown, in cross-section, in Fig. 3.1(a). Unfortunately the use of airfoil cross-section, cambered blading, whilst easily fabricateable in, say, fiberglass, tends to negate the inherent simplicity of the thin sheet-metal blades of the traditional version. It is, perhaps, noteworthy that, for small machines, the slightly higher tip-speed ratios of classical multibladed rotors compared with typical slatted rotors often requires, for reciprocating pumps, that reduction gearing be introduced between the turbine and the pump drive in order to prevent excessive pump-rod accelerations. The alternative are pumps with rather short strokes driven directly from the turbine shaft.

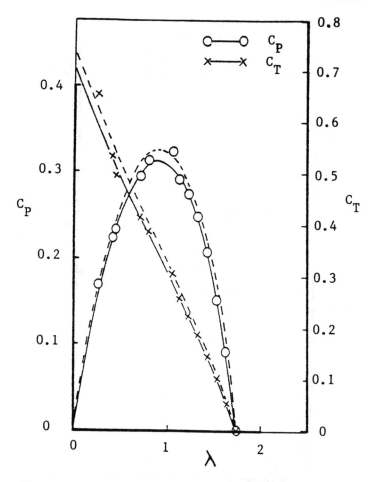

Figure 5.18. Performance of model multibladed rotor Configuration 4, solidity $\sigma' = 0.84$. Projected full-scale performance shown dotted.

5.4. CWD Rotors

CWD (Consulting Services, Wind Energy, Developing Countries) known initially, until 1984, as SWD (Steering Committee, Wind Energy, Developing Countries) was, until dissolution in 1990, a group, based in The Netherlands, devoted to developing wind-energy systems primarily for application in developing nations. CWD was a joint activity of the Eindhoven and Twente Universities of Technology and DHV Consulting Engineers of Amersfoort. CWD was financed by the Netherlands Programme

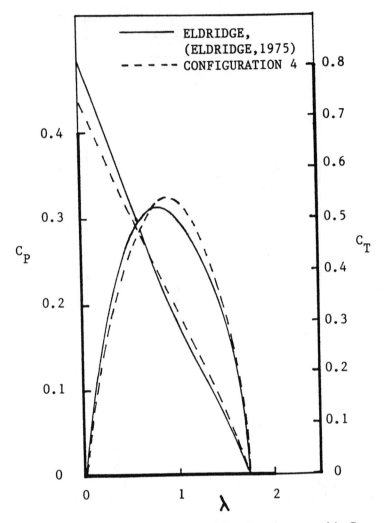

Figure 5.19. Comparison of projected full-scale performance of the Configuration 4 model rotor with the results presented by Eldridge (Eldridge, 1975).

for Development Cooperation. CWD commenced operations, as SWD, in 1975. The main activity of CWD was designing, fabricating, component testing under laboratory conditions and subsequently field-testing, simple, light-weight, low-cost, direct drive water-pumping wind-turbines for use, and in large part manufacture, in developing nations.

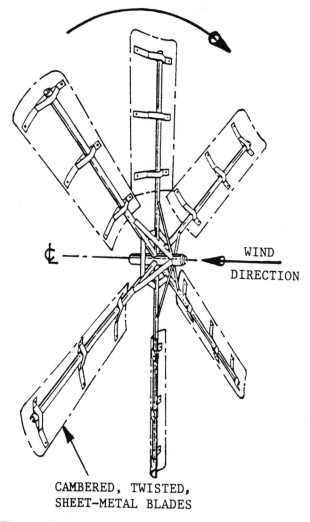

CAMBERED, TWISTED,
SHEET-METAL BLADES

Figure 5.20. Typical construction of a CWD rotor (diagrammatic).

The design philosophy, focussed as it was on lightness, low-cost and structural simplicity, led to the development of light-weight turbine rotors which, relative to conventional multibladed water-pumping turbines, were of low solidity and ran at high tip-speed ratios. The requirement of simplicity plus Reynolds number considerations resulted in the selection of a relatively small number of blades per rotor. The number of blades

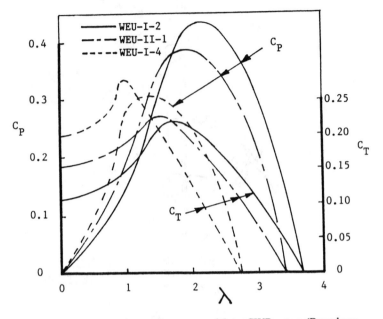

Figure 5.21. Comparative performances of three CWD rotors (Beurskens et al., 1980; Kragten, 1985).

used ranged from 4 to about 16 for prototype rotors with the most usual number of blades being either 6 or 8 for the majority of units. The most commonly used blades were cambered metal plates supported, on their concave surfaces, by tubular spokes radiating from the rotor hub. Ribs, attached to the radial spokes and to which the blade surfaces were in turn attached, served to assist in maintaining the correct camber and pitch angle. Generally rotor blades were twisted in an attempt to improve performance by optimising the local blade setting.

A typical CWD turbine is depicted, diagrammatically, in Fig. 5.20. This shows the main design features of a six-bladed rotor. The blade spokes and reinforcing ribs are located on the concave, or pressure, surface only leading to a smooth convex, or suction, surface. The performances of three CWD rotors, deduced from wind-tunnel tests carried out by CWD using an open-jet wind-tunnel at the Delft University of Technology in The Netherlands, are presented in Fig. 5.21. These results were selected to show the general character of the data obtained by CWD and are for rotors identified as WEU-I-2, for which $\sigma' = 0.30$, WEU-II-1 ($\sigma' = 0.40$) and WEU-I-4 ($\sigma' = 0.43$). No Reynolds number correction was needed

Table 5.1

Leading Parameters of Five CWD Rotors

CWD notation	Number of blades	Solidity σ'	$C_{P(MAX)}$	$C_{T(\lambda=0)}$
THE-I-1	4	0.23	0.36	0.07
THE-I-2	6	0.34	0.39	0.11
WEU-I-2	8	0.30	0.43	0.11
WEU-I-4	8	0.43	0.30	0.21
WEU-II-1	12	0.40	0.38	0.15

since the test took place at Reynolds numbers typical of full-scale rotors. It is noteworthy that in general terms $C_{P(MAX)}$ decreased as $C_{T(\lambda=0)}$ was increased. It is also noteworthy that very high peak power coefficients were achieved for rotors of water pumpers and also for rotors of such simple construction. However a low value of $C_{T(\lambda=0)}$ had to be accepted as the price for a high $C_{P(MAX)}$ although, as was demonstrated by CWD, partial amelioration of the low $C_{T(\lambda=0)}$ problem can be achieved by rounding the blade leading edges.

The performances shown in Fig. 5.21 should be taken as representative only since adjustment of blade pitch angles, and twist, resulted in small performance variations. The main parameters of five CWD rotors are listed in Table 5.1. Again the performances quoted are indicative rather than exact. The rotor diameters of machines built by CWD, or under their guidance, ranged from 2 m to 8 m. During the short life span of SWD, and latterly CWD, a large number of complete water-pumping wind-turbines were built and put into operation.

Since low production cost was a major concern of CWD the use of reduction gearing between the turbine and pump drive was avoided. Hence, in order to prevent excessive pump-rod accelerations, it became necessary to employ very short-stroke pumps driven directly from the turbine rotor. Also because of the generally low values of rotor torque coefficients for the $\lambda = 0$ condition it became necessary to unload a pump in order to permit the turbine to start up in low winds with the pump still connected to the turbine rotor shaft. This was accomplished by CWD in two alternative ways. One method was to employ a small leak effectively short-circuiting the pump at low turbine speeds. The other technique was to utilise a floating pump-delivery valve to do, in effect, a similar job more efficiently. Both pump leaks and floating valves have been described in detail previously (Cleijne et al., 1986) and have also been referred to, briefly, in the first portion of this chapter. The method of furling adopted by CWD was the same as that applied to solid-slatted and classical multibladed turbines, that is, by positioning the rotor edge-on to the wind.

The work of CWD has been well documented in terms of reports and technical papers. A paper is available describing some of the turbine rotor test work (Beurskens et al., 1980). A report describing, briefly, the rotor design techniques employed by CWD is due to Jansen and Smulders (Jansen and Smulders, 1977). Another paper reporting some of the rotor test work is by Smulders and Schermerhorn (Smulders and Schermerhorn, 1984). Also work directed at maximising starting-torque coefficient whilst maintaining a relatively low solidity, resulting in the WEU-I-4 rotor referred to previously, is the subject of a separate report (Kragten, 1985).

5.5. Delta-Wing-Bladed Rotors

Another fairly recent development in the wind-pump turbine-rotor field is the introduction of rotors featuring delta-wing-like blades. What is believed to be the first paper describing, and presenting the performance of, rotors of this type, a concept originated by the writer and Dr. D.H. Norrie, a colleague at the University of Calgary, was published in 1978 (Kentfield and Norrie, 1978). The concept of wind-turbines employing delta-wing-like blades, usually abbreviated to delta-turbines, was introduced in an attempt to create a rotor which, because of the high angle of incidence typically associated with the stalling of sharp-edged delta-wings (see Figs. 3.6(b) and 3.7), could be arranged to generate maximum torque coefficient at $\lambda = 0$ and yet run sufficiently fast to have a fairly high value of $C_{P(MAX)}$. Furthermore the use of sharp-edged delta-type blades implied that the sharp leading edge associated with simple sheet-metal blades could be turned from a disadvantage to an advantage in so far as rotor performance was concerned. There was also a hope that such rotors may have a lower solidity, and hence be somewhat lighter, than the rotors of traditional multibladed turbines of equal diameter. Figure 5.22 shows, diagrammatically, the arrangement of a typical 8-bladed delta-turbine employing flap-equipped blades.

Because of a lack of funding for research work on the delta-turbine project the investigation of the potential of the concept took place intermittently, when opportunities arose, over a period of approximately 14 years. The model testing work was undertaken, exclusively, in the University of

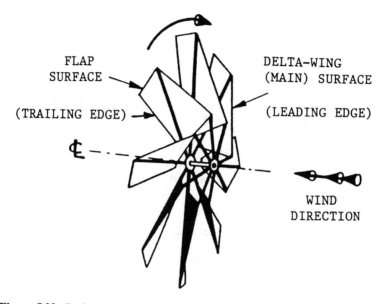

FLAP
SURFACE

DELTA–WING
(MAIN) SURFACE

(TRAILING EDGE)

(LEADING EDGE)

WIND
DIRECTION

Figure 5.22. Basic arrangement of an eight-bladed delta-turbine (diagrammatic).

Calgary 1.37 m × 0.76 m open-jet wind-tunnel referred to previously, on several occasions, in this chapter.

Early during the first phase of development an attempt was made to match experimentally obtained data on the $C_P \sim \lambda$ and $C_T \sim \lambda$ planes with predicted performances based on the experimentally obtained C_L versus α characteristics of an isolated, model delta-wing with and without a flap. This procedure, whilst somewhat crude, did include, empirically, the influence of flow-induction causing the flow approaching the rotor to slow down upwind of the turbine face (see Chapter 3, §3.2). The results of this comparison between experiment and theory are presented in Fig. 5.23 for simple delta-turbine rotors with, and without, trailing edge flaps.

For both the flap-equipped and non-flap-equipped rotors it is clear, from Fig. 5.23, that the biggest discrepancies between experiment and theory occurred at small values of λ. The experimental results produced notably better performances than were predicted theoretically. This was, it appeared, due to blade-on-blade interactions occurring in the experiment which were omitted from the theoretical treatment. It is also noteworthy that at higher values of λ there did not appear to be any detrimental blade-on-blade interactions which would be expected for rotors of similarly high solidity employing conventional airfoils (see Fig. 3.2). A more detailed

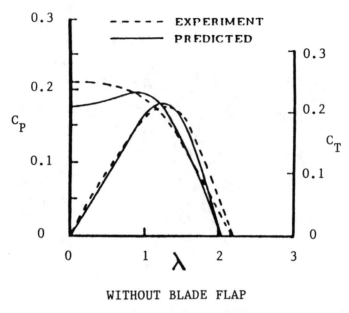

WITHOUT BLADE FLAP

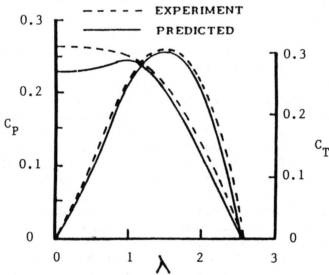

WITH BLADE FLAP

Figure 5.23. Comparison of predicted and experimentally obtained performances of two elementary, model delta-turbines.

description of the analytical procedure employed has been given elsewhere (Kentfield, 1980(a)).

Largely because the study of the delta-turbine concept took place intermittently three designs arose each of which was regarded as an optimum at the end of the phase of the activity associated with it. The Mark 1 delta-turbine marked the end of the first phase of intensive effort. The geometry of the Mark 1 rotor, dating from 1978, is shown in Fig. 5.24. The opportunity also arose to build a 3.3 m diameter full-scale prototype and to subsequently test this in the National Research Council of Canada 9.2 m × 9.2 m (30 ft × 30 ft) working section, closed-type wind-tunnel. The results obtained from wind-tunnel tests of the prony-brake-equipped 3.3 m diameter rotor, after correcting the results for wake blockage, are presented in Fig. 5.25. The dotted curves were obtained from tests of the corresponding model rotor in the University of Calgary open-jet wind-tunnel. The major differences in performance between the model and the full-scale rotors were attributed to the influence of Reynolds number which was about one order of magnitude greater for the full-scale turbine than for the model (Kentfield, 1979).

The next stage of development was hastened by some preliminary interest, in Canada, in the delta-turbine concept. This resulted in further experimentally conducted development work directed at refining the geometry of the Mark 1 version to improve the performance and also to arrive at a configuration suitable for fabrication in large diameters. The result of this process was identified as the Mark 2 rotor. The geometrical details of the Mark 2 rotor are presented in Fig. 5.26. The prime function of the circumferential blade-support members apparent in Fig. 5.26(b) was to reduce, essentially to zero, the large blade-root bending moments that could otherwise occur when the rotor was in a furled position edge-on to the wind. The blade-support rings of the solid-slatted and classical multibladed rotors also serve this purpose.

A model of a large-scale Mark 2 rotor complete with the rotor-blade-reinforcing ribs, necessary for large-scale units, was built and subsequently tested in the University of Calgary wind-tunnel. In parallel with this a complete full-scale machine, having a rotor of 16 m diameter, was fabricated industrially based, in large part, on a design prepared by the writer. This machine was subsequently field tested. A comparison of the model and full-scale test results is presented in Fig. 5.27.

The full-scale results presented in Fig. 5.27 indicate the achievement of a peak power coefficient of approximately 0.41. The scope of the full-scale tests was restricted as only the performance in the vicinity of the peak power coefficient was of interest. This was because the full-scale machine was provided with a variable-stroke water pump that

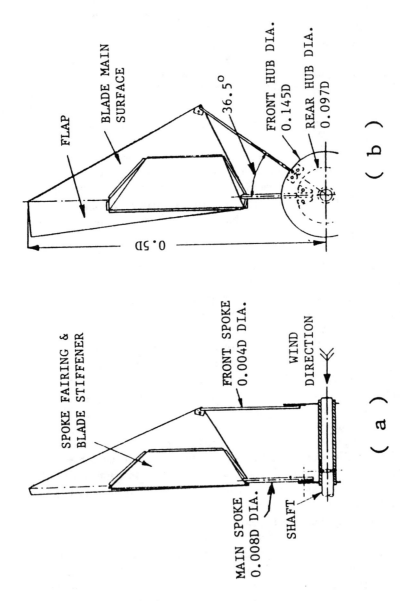

Figure 5.24a,b. Geometry of an 8-bladed Mark 1 delta-turbine: a) side view; b) view downwind.

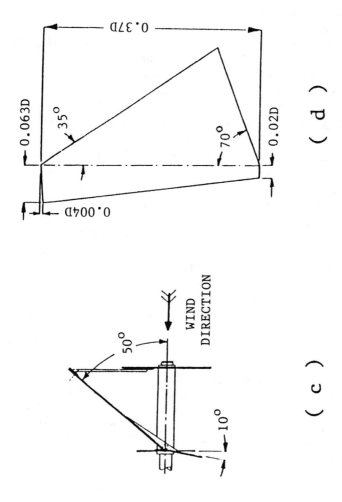

Figure 5.24c,d. Geometry of an 8-bladed Mark 1 delta-turbine: c) radial view along spoke (one blade); d) flat generation of a blade surface.

would, ideally, ensure that the turbine always operated in a mode close to the maximum power coefficient over a wide wind-speed range. Further information relating to this project, including the procedures used for the full-scale testing, is available (Baker, 1986; Alberta Energy Scientific and Engineering Services, 1987).

The final phase, to date, in the development of the delta-turbine concept has resulted in what has been termed the Mark 3 configuration. This consists of a basic Mark 2 model rotor, without blade-reinforcing ribs, equipped with vortex-flaps on the inboard leading edges of both the delta-wing surfaces and main flaps and on the radially outboard leading edges of the main flaps only. In addition snags were attached to the outer portions of the delta-surface leading edges. Details of the logic behind these modifications, which represented the outcome of an intensive fundamental, experimental study, have been given elsewhere (Kentfield, 1988(b)). Figure 5.28 illustrates the basic Mark 3 configuration. The corresponding Mark 2 configuration was identical to the Mark 3 version but with the vortex flap and snag surfaces removed. The differences in diameter between the upwind and downwind hub discs was not found to be a significant aspect of rotor geometry.

A performance comparison between the corresponding Mark 2 and Mark 3 configurations is presented in Fig. 5.29. The dotted curves of Fig. 5.29 show the projected performance of a 2.44 m diameter Mark 3 rotor. The Reynolds number-based correction to convert from model to full-scale results was derived from the known response of delta-wing performances to changes of Reynolds number (Kentfield, 1987). Several full-scale 2.44 m diameter Mark 3 rotors have been built for a special water-pumping application but, unfortunately, no attempt has yet been made to deduce turbine rotor performance separated from the measured overall performance of a complete machine.

The tip-speed ratio range of delta-turbines implies the need, if driving conventional reciprocating water pumps by means of small diameter rotors, for reduction gearing unless ultra-short strokes are employed as was the case for the CWD wind pumps. Typically, for a 3.5 m diameter turbine driving a pump with a 150 mm stroke a 4:1 reduction gear ratio is required to ensure safe operation, thereby avoiding excessive pump-rod accelerations, when the turbine is free-running in a 13.4 m/s wind. The experimental 16 m diameter delta-turbine referred to earlier did not employ any reduction gearing. The large-diameter rotor was a major help in avoiding the need for a speed reducer.

The delta-turbine, as developed to date, is capable of generating not only maximum torque at $\lambda = 0$ but also a peak power coefficient in the region of 0.4. The rotor solidity, σ', based on a flat generation of the

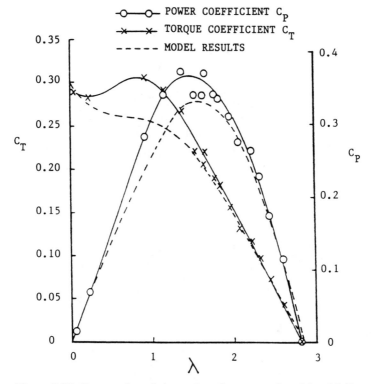

Figure 5.25. Comparative wind-tunnel performances of model and full-scale (3.3 m diameter) Mark 1 delta-turbines.

rotor blading is approximately 0.62 and 0.68 for the Mark 2 and 3 rotors, respectively. The greater value of σ' for the Mark 3 rotor is due to the additional surface area of the vortex flaps and leading edge snags. Hence it can be expected that for a prescribed rotor diameter a well-designed delta-turbine rotor will be heavier than a typical CWD rotor but, possibly, lighter than a typical classical multibladed turbine.

5.6. Perimeter-Bladed Rotors

The concept of what has been termed the perimeter-bladed rotor followed, at the University of Calgary, as an extension of the delta-bladed turbine development described in the previous subsection. The prime incentive was to eliminate the need for a reduction gear box, in an attempt to reduce capital costs and complexity, when a delta-turbine is direct coupled to a

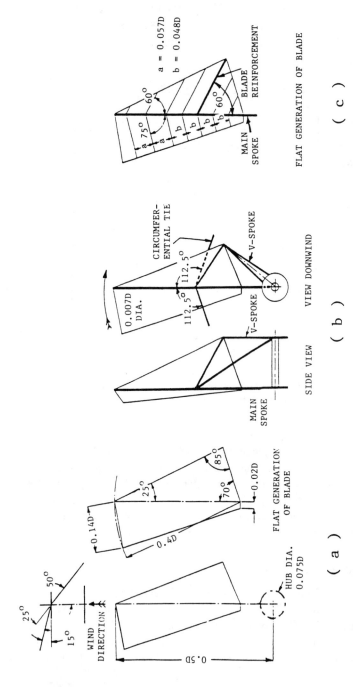

Figure 5.26. Geometric arrangement of a Mark 2, 8-bladed delta-turbine: a) blade geometry; b) structural support system of rotor; c) blade reinforcement for large units.

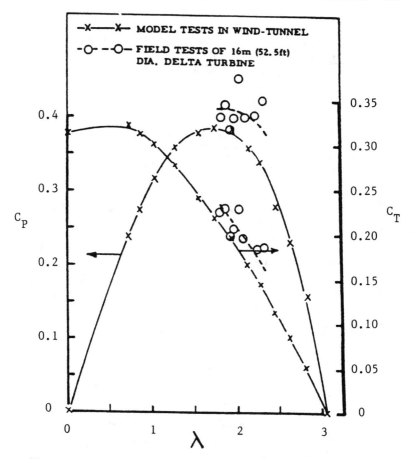

Figure 5.27. Comparative performances of model and full-scale (16 m diameter) Mark 2 delta-turbines.

conventional reciprocating water pump. The method adopted to accomplish this was, in effect, to move the delta-wing-like blades outwards to a larger radius, on a rotor of increased diameter, without increasing the total blade area relative to a corresponding delta-turbine of the type described in the previous subsection. The aim, in so far as the performance of the perimeter-bladed rotor was concerned, was to simultaneously reduce the rotor speed and correspondingly increase the torque generated relative to a corresponding conventional delta-turbine.

The main structural consequences of adopting the perimeter-bladed design was, in addition to eliminating the cost, and complication, of a

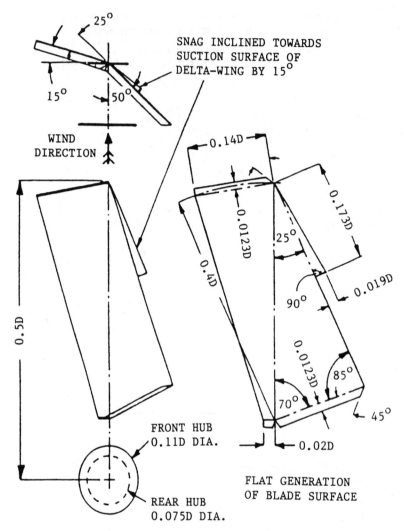

Figure 5.28. Geometry of a blade of a Mark 3, 8-bladed delta-turbine.

speed-reducing gearbox, to add some additional material costs due in
large part, but not completely, to the longer rotor spokes required. An
incidental benefit derived from the perimeter-bladed concept was to provide a relatively good flow path, through the open centre of the rotor, over
the yaw-control tailvane. Figure 5.30 shows, diagrammatically, a sector
of two eight-sector perimeter-bladed, or annular, rotors one carrying 24

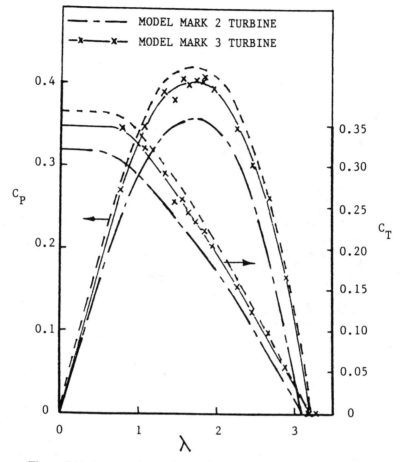

Figure 5.29. Comparative performances of models of small Mark 2 and Mark 3 delta-turbines without the blade-reinforcing ribs shown in Fig. 5.26. Projected performance of a 2.44 m diameter full-scale turbine shown dotted.

blades, without the provision of vortex flaps, the other a 32-bladed rotor with vortex flaps. The configurations shown in Fig. 5.30 depict straight blade-support tubes, chosen for simplicity, with the blades mounted in a "shish-kebab" manner to limit the maximum torsional loadings on the blade-support tubes.

It is, perhaps, worth noting that at least one annular wind-turbine rotor, employing 120 slat-type blades, was used previously to drive a corn mill in England (Major and Watts, 1992). The writer is not aware of the

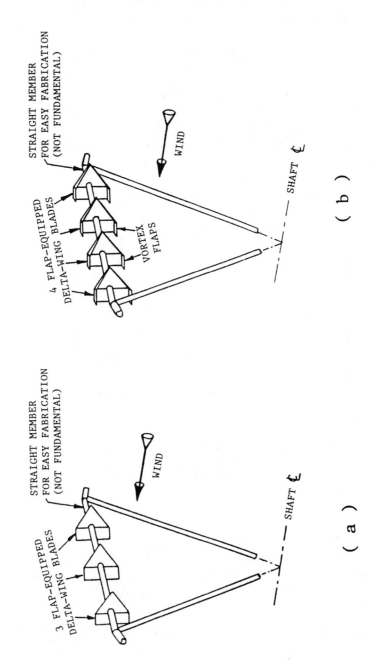

Figure 5.30. Arrangement of an 8-sector perimeter-bladed rotor (diagrammatic): a) 24-bladed turbine without vortex flaps; b) 32-bladed turbine with vortex flaps.

logical reasons for the adoption of this design. The annular rotor was roughly equal in diameter to a conventional traditional Dutch-type rotor that it might otherwise have been expected would be used. It is unlikely that the intention could have been to increase rotor torque and decrease rotor speed since the grinding stones of a corn mill are normally driven by the turbine rotor via speed-increasing gearing (Reynolds, 1970). Hence the use of a high torque ~ low speed turbine would have required an even greater speed-increase ratio assuming the use of conventional, windmill-type grinding equipment.

It is quite easy to correlate the expected performance characteristics of a perimeter-bladed rotor (subscript p) with those of a corresponding conventionally proportioned rotor (subscript c) having geometrically similar blading. It is not necessary to assume the use of delta-wing-like blades specifically. For the conventional rotor the effective radius, $r_{c(eff)}$ at which the blades can be considered to be concentrated can be expressed as a fraction, H, of the rotor maximum radius $r_{c(MAX)}$ thus:

$$r_{c(eff)} = H r_{c(MAX)} \tag{5.1}$$

Provided the radius, or diameter, ratio, M, of the perimeter-bladed rotor to that of the conventional turbine is sufficiently large, say 2 or greater, then:

$$r_{p(eff)} \simeq r_{p(MAX)} \tag{5.2}$$

Thus from equations (5.1) and (5.2):

$$\frac{r_{p(eff)}}{r_{c(eff)}} = \frac{M}{H} \tag{5.3}$$

It then follows that for equal blade velocities at the effective radii of the conventional and perimeter-bladed rotors:

$$\frac{\omega_p}{\omega_c} = \frac{H}{M} \tag{5.4}$$

and since in general $\lambda = (\omega r_{(MAX)})/U_\infty$ then for prescribed U_∞:

$$\frac{\lambda_p}{\lambda_c} = H$$

Also from the definition of C_P (equation (2.8)) and assuming equally effective use of the equal blade areas of the conventional and perimeter-bladed rotors their power outputs will be equal, for invariant U_∞ and ρ_∞, thus:

$$C_{Pp} D_p^2 = C_{Pc} D_c^2 \tag{5.5}$$

hence it follows for the equal power condition:

$$C_{Pp} = C_{Pc}/M^2 \qquad (5.6)$$

and also since, in general, from equation (2.12) $C_T = C_P/\lambda$:

$$C_{Tp} = C_{Pp}/\lambda_p \text{ and } C_{Tc} = C_{Pc}/\lambda_c$$

thus:

$$C_{Tp} = C_{Tc}/(M^2 H) \qquad (5.7)$$

Further, where C'_{Tc} represents the output torque coefficient of the conventional rotor referred to an output shaft driven by the conventional rotor but geared down to run at the same rotational speed as the turbine shaft of the perimeter-bladed rotor then:

$$\frac{C'_{Tc}}{C_{Tc}} = \frac{M}{H} \qquad (5.8)$$

and from the definition of C_T (equation (2.9)):

$$C_T D^3 \propto \text{Torque}$$

Hence:

$$C_{Tp}D_p^3 \propto \text{Torque}_p \text{ and } C_{Tc}D_c^3 \propto \text{Torque}_c$$

therefore:

$$\frac{\text{Torque}_p}{\text{Torque}_c} = \frac{C_{Tp}}{C_{Tc}} M^3 \qquad (5.9)$$

substituting from equation (5.7) in equation (5.9) for C_{Tp}:

$$\frac{\text{Torque}_p}{\text{Torque}_c} = \frac{M}{H} \qquad (5.10)$$

Comparison of equations (5.8) and (5.10) shows that the output torque of a geared-down shaft driven by the conventional turbine to run at the same rotational speed as the turbine shaft of the perimeter-bladed rotor will generate the same torque as that available directly, without reduction gearing, from the perimeter-bladed rotor. The required ratio of the reduction gearing applied to the conventional rotor is, from equation (5.4), M/H.

The analysis will be illustrated by means of a simple example based on the transformation of a classical multibladed rotor, for which $H \simeq 2/3$, into a perimeter-bladed version for which $M = 2$. For this example the effective speed reduction ratio is, from equation (5.4), 3:1. The corresponding power coefficient expected from the perimeter-bladed rotor is, from equation (5.6), $C_{Pc}/4$ with a torque coefficient, established from equation (5.7), of $(3/8)C_{Tc}$. In reality a problem arises if a perimeter-bladed rotor is derived, for large M, from a classical multibladed rotor. The difficulty is due to the very large number of blades required for the perimeter-bladed version. If the blade area of the conventional rotor is redistributed around the perimeter of a rotor M times larger in diameter than the conventional rotor, it can be shown that for geometrically similar blades, with an equal pitch $\sim$ chord ratio, the number of blades, n_p, equals $n_c M^2$, where n_c is the number of blades of the corresponding conventional rotor.

Thus it is apparent that for, say, a 20-bladed conventional classical multibladed rotor the corresponding perimeter-bladed rotor will require, for $M = 2$, 80 geometrically similar, but smaller, blades the span and chord of which will be $1/M$, or half, of the span and chord of the blades of the conventional version of the rotor. Figure 5.31 shows, diagrammatically, a comparison of corresponding conventional and perimeter-bladed rotors.

If, alternatively, the conventional rotor is a delta-turbine, as described in the previous subsection, an 8-bladed delta-turbine transforms into a 32-bladed rotor, also with delta-wing-like blades, as depicted in Fig. 5.30(b). Due to the disposition of the blades of a perimeter-bladed rotor, with the possibility of flow passing relatively symmetrically both inboard and outboard of the blade tips, the form of delta-wing-type blades required is essentially symmetric. Symmetric blades are implied in Fig. 5.30. Hence the blades of a perimeter-bladed version of a delta-turbine are not truly geometrically similar to those of the delta-turbines described in the previous section. Furthermore M values occurring in practice are likely to be within the range $1 < M < 2$. This implies that an additional departure can be expected from the simple theoretical treatment valid for relatively large M values and geometric similarity between the blading of the perimeter and corresponding conventional turbines.

Wind-tunnel testing of model perimeter-bladed rotors has been carried out at the University of Calgary in the open-jet wind-tunnel described elsewhere in this chapter. The earliest reported work, which includes in addition to early wind-tunnel test results comparative performance predictions, dates from 1988 (Kentfield, 1988(d)). More recently obtained wind-tunnel test data are presented in Fig. 5.32 for a 32-bladed model turbine, the geometry of which is depicted in Fig. 5.33, of solidity $\sigma' = 0.34$ based on flat generations of the rotor blades. The relatively large, Reynolds

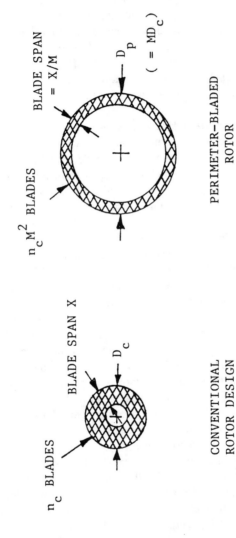

Figure 5.31. Transformation of a conventional rotor into a corresponding perimeter-bladed unit.

number-based correction to convert the wind-tunnel results into the expected full-scale performance was due, essentially, to the low Reynolds number of the model-sized blades. It is clear from Fig. 5.32 that, in general accordance with the trends revealed by the analytical treatment presented earlier, the maximum power coefficient is low, although this is also partially due to tuning the configuration of the model to produce the greatest possible torque coefficient for the $\lambda = 0$ condition. This also helped to minimise the value of λ at runaway. A full-scale water pumper, in large part designed by the writer, incorporating a rotor the performance of which is presented in Fig. 5.32, subsequently attained production status in Canada (Kentfield and Cruson, 1989; Kentfield, 1989(a)).

The geometry of one blade of a 24-blade perimeter-bladed turbine, also tested in model form, is shown in Fig. 5.34. The corresponding test results, including the projected full-scale performance, are presented in Fig. 5.35. The solidity, σ', of this rotor was 0.51 resulting, relative to the rotor described previously, in significantly greater values of $C_{T(\lambda=0)}$ and $C_{P(MAX)}$ with a comparatively small penalty in terms of an increase in λ at the runaway condition. However for a prescribed overall diameter this rotor will be heavier, and generate greater tower loadings, etc., than the lower solidity, 32-bladed, version for which $\sigma' = 0.34$. More details of the developmental path leading from the configuration of Fig. 5.33 to that of Fig. 5.34 are available elsewhere (Kentfield and Panek, 1993).

Perimeter-bladed rotors lend themselves to two alternative methods of furling. One method involves mounting each group of blades, each group constituting one sector of the rotor, on a tube such that the rotor can furl in a manner similar to that of the so-called sectional rotor of Fig. 1.2. However this introduced complications because of the number of moving parts involved. The other method, preferred by the writer, is to build the rotor in rigid form and arrange for it to be turned edgewise to the wind in the manner described previously in this chapter.

Limited testing was also carried out on a version of the model rotor of Fig. 5.34, the performance of which is presented in Fig. 5.35, with a non-rotating dome-like component, located immediately upwind of the turbine, effectively filling the open centre of the rotor. The dome was expected to act as a mild augmenter by virtue of accelerating the flow passing over the dome and through the rotor blading. The device increased $C_{T(\lambda=0)}$ of the model by approximately 25%, to a value of 0.55, and increased $C_{P(MAX)}$ to over 0.3, about a 76% increase. The runaway tip-speed ratio also increased by 11% to 1.78. Whilst these results are of some interest doubts remain about the cost effectiveness of the dome which by virtue of blocking the flow over a single, centrally positioned, tailvane can in any case, only be used, conveniently, with a downwind rotor location.

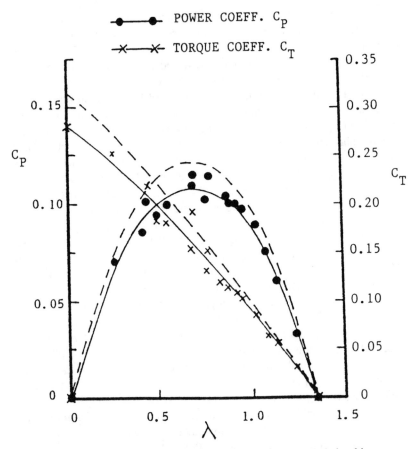

Figure 5.32. Performance of a model 32-blade perimeter-bladed turbine, solidity $\sigma' = 0.34$. Projected full-scale performance shown dotted.

5.7. Rotors for Wind-Electric Power

Whilst wind-electric turbines are not a specific topic of this monograph they do impact the field of wind-driven water-pumping when what are usually standard wind-electric machines are coupled, directly or otherwise, to electric pumps. The systems employed vary widely in nature. For example, a wind-turbine-driven DC generator, or AC alternator, can be arranged to charge batteries, the latter via a converter. The batteries discharge to either a DC motor driving the pump or, alternatively, via an inverter, to an AC pump-drive motor. In some cases a wind-turbine-driven alternator is directly connected to an AC pump-motor in such a manner

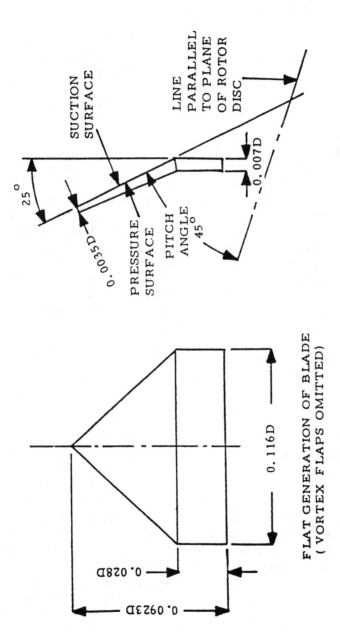

Figure 5.33. Blade geometry of the rotor the performance of which was presented in Fig. 5.32.

that the alternator ~ pump-motor combination operates in a variable frequency mode at a frequency dictated by the speed of the wind-turbine. Systems of this type avoid the need for costly battery energy storage.

The pumps of wind-electric systems can be either surface mounted, if the lift is sufficiently low to permit this, or, more likely, a submersible pump will be used. Most systems employ centrifugal, rotor-dynamic pumps although positive-displacement rotary pumps are an option. In other cases a surface-mounted electric-motor-driven pump jack can be used connected, mechanically, to a conventional reciprocating positive-displacement pump.

It appears that in all cases classical, low-solidity, 2- or 3-bladed wind-electric, propeller-type turbines are employed. In the past various turbines with more than three blades, and relatively high solidities, have been used in small wind-electric units but these do not appear to have prevailed. Important requirements of stand-alone (ie., non-grid connected) wind-electric turbines without on-site energy storage are that the turbine must be capable of self-starting and the safety system must be self-acting without the need for external power. Largely because of the latter consideration the usual method of furling in small systems is of the type where the rotor is turned edge-on to the wind. The movement necessary to achieve furling is based on either a yawing-type motion of the rotor about a vertical axis or, in some cases, a tilt-up motion about a horizontal axis.

Figure 5.36 shows two sets of performance curves for propeller-type turbines. The curves for a large, relatively high-performance turbine were derived analytically and are shown as solid lines. The curves drawn with dotted lines are for the other extreme and apply to a very small, simple, propeller-type unit. They were established experimentally in the University of Calgary open-jet wind-tunnel. The differences in performance are in large part due to the difference in the applicable, typical, blade-chord-based Reynolds numbers which were 2×10^6 and 6×10^4 for the solid and dotted curves, respectively. In both cases the performances are for fixed-pitch turbines, the type most likely to be found in water-pumping applications. The two sets of curves can be thought of as bounding the range of operation of the turbines likely to be used for wind-electric pumping. The performances of relatively large, sophisticated turbines will tend to approach the solid curves whilst those of very small, simply constructed turbines will tend to approach the dotted curves.

The main functional advantage of a wind-electric system relative to a directly connected mechanical unit is the ability to install the wind-turbine remotely from the well site at a preferred location, possibly on a nearby hill, not constrained by the environment in the immediate vicinity of the well head. Another advantage is that, when rotary pumps are employed,

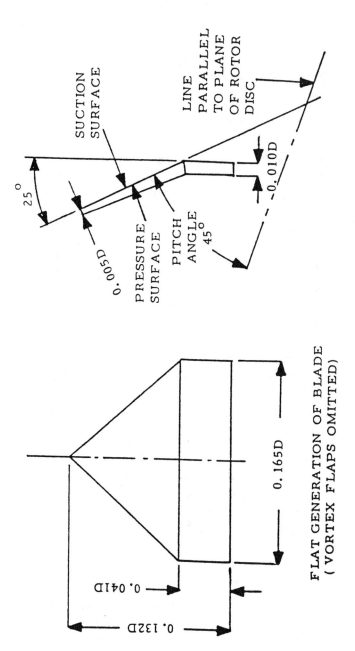

Figure 5.34. Blade geometry of a 24-blade perimeter-bladed rotor ($\sigma' = 0.51$).

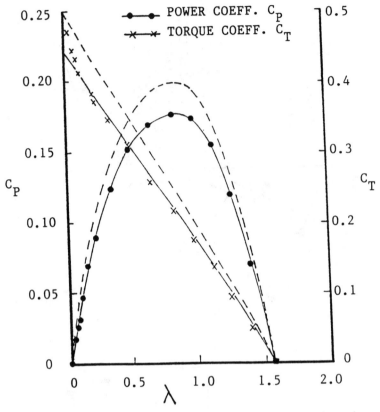

Figure 5.35. Performance of a model rotor of the geometry shown in Fig. 5.34. Projected full-scale performance shown dotted.

better use can be made of strong winds, which however usually occur relatively irregularly at most sites, than is the case for direct coupled systems with reciprocating pumps. Limitations due to the maximum permissible acceleration of pump rods tends to inhibit the performance of the latter in strong winds.

5.8. Turbine Performance Comparison

Comparisons of the performances of the turbines dealt with in this chapter can be carried out on several bases depending upon the focus of interest. Since one of the main considerations is the suitability of the rotors

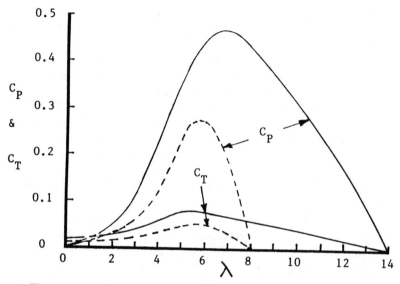

Figure 5.36. Performance range encompassed by propeller-type, fixed-pitch turbines (diagrammatic). Dotted lines very small, simple machines: solid lines large, sophisticated machines.

described in all but the previous subsection for driving simple positive-displacement pumps, turbines of the propeller type will be omitted from the comparison. A commonality between the remaining turbines is that, in each case, the blades are fabricated from a single layer of sheet material. In the case of the Cretian rotor the material is compliant cloth, in all the other cases it is a rigid substance.

The most commonly used comparison is based on rotor performances presented on the C_P and C_T versus λ planes. This mode of comparison is meaningful, for prescribed ρ_∞ and U_∞, when the diameter of the rotor is considered to be invariant. A problem arises with this method on the C_T versus λ plane since different types of rotor generally operate at different tip-speed ratios. The turbine torque characteristics of most interest are those applicable at the output shaft of the transmission gearbox, if any. In order to allow such a comparison to be carried out on a common basis the rotor torque coefficient has here, in each case, been unified by multiplying by the rotor tip-speed ratio, Λ, corresponding to $C_{P(MAX)}$ for that rotor. Hence, in this way, the torque coefficient is, for each case, referred to a common output shaft speed: that of a hypothetical turbine for which $C_{P(MAX)}$ occurs at $\lambda = 1.0$. It is, perhaps, worth noting that if the runaway tip-speed ratio had been used instead of Λ essentially the same ranking of the rotors would be obtained since, for most turbines, the runaway tip-speed ratio $\simeq 2\Lambda$.

A performance comparison on the C_P versus λ plane is shown in Fig. 5.37 with the corresponding unified coefficient of torque, ΛC_T, versus λ presented in Fig. 5.38. It can be seen from Fig. 5.37 that the CWD WEU-I-2 rotor and the Mark 2 and Mark 3 delta-turbines exhibit the highest maximum energy-conversion efficiencies and the low-solidity perimeter-bladed rotor the least value. Figure 5.38 shows that the highest unified torque coefficients at $\lambda = 0$ are produced by the classical multibladed rotor and the Mark 2 and Mark 3 delta-turbines. Again the lowest value is that of the low-solidity perimeter-bladed rotor. However, it is clear from both diagrams that this rotor has the lowest runaway tip-speed ratio.

Bearing in mind that with equal rotor diameters the total blade area provided is inversely proportional to the solidity, σ', a measure of the effectiveness of the utilisation of the blade area provided can be obtained by dividing the ordinates of Figs. 5.37 and 5.38 by σ'. This process results in Figs. 5.39 and 5.40, respectively. It is apparent from Fig. 5.39 that the maximum performances of the multibladed and the perimeter-bladed rotors are closely clustered showing that the perimeter-bladed rotors are about as effective, in terms of blade area utilisation, as the multibladed form. From Fig. 5.40 it can be seen that the Mark 2 and Mark 3 delta-turbines utilise their blade areas most effectively in producing torque at the $\lambda = 0$ condition. With respect to torque production per unit blade area at $\lambda = 0$ the Cretian, CWD and the multibladed rotors together with the high-solidity perimeter-bladed rotor are all fairly comparable.

For low tip-speed ratio, high-solidity rotors capable of generating a high torque coefficient at zero tip-speed ratio, the maximum wind loads acting on the head and tower of such a wind-turbine can be shown, to a first approximation, to be proportional, for prescribed ρ_∞ and U_∞, to the rotor blade area. This is in contrast to conventional low-solidity, high tip-speed ratio, wind electric, propeller-type turbines where a corresponding approximation is to base estimates of maximum tower loads not on blade areas but on the areas of the rotor discs. Hence for the majority of high-solidity water-pumping turbines it is meaningful to compare rotor performances, for prescribed tower loadings, on the basis of equal blade areas rather than equal rotor-disc areas. For equal blade areas and a rotor diameter D:

$$\sigma' D^2 = D^{*2}$$

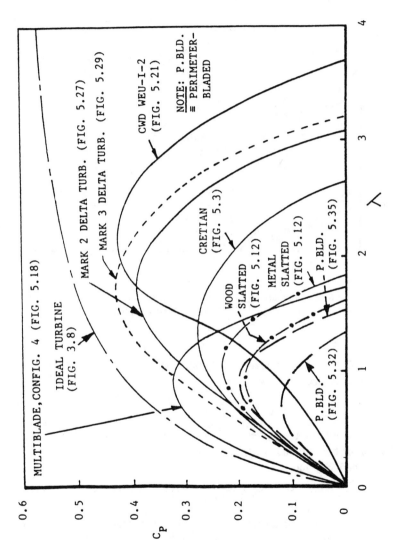

Figure 5.37. Comparison of water-pumping turbine rotor performances on the C_P versus λ plane.

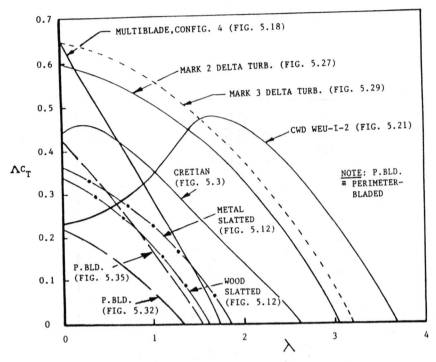

Figure 5.38. Comparison of water-pumping turbine rotor performances on the unified torque coefficient (ΛC_T) versus λ plane.

where D^* is the diameter of a hypothetical reference rotor for which $\sigma' = 1.0$. Hence:

$$\left(\frac{D}{D^*}\right)^2 = \frac{1}{\sigma'} \tag{5.11}$$

Thus multiplying the power coefficient, C_P, by the rotor area normalised by that of the reference rotor gives, after invoking equation (5.11) and for prescribed P_∞ and U_∞:

$$\text{Power output} \propto C_P/\sigma' \tag{5.12}$$

which is the same parameter as that for power output per unit blade area. Further, when comparing rotors of equal blade areas but differing diameters the torque produced is, from equation (2.9), proportional to the product $C_T D^3$. Thus normalising D with respect to D^* and invoking equation (5.11):

$$\text{Rotor torque} \propto C_T/(\sigma')^{3/2} \tag{5.13}$$

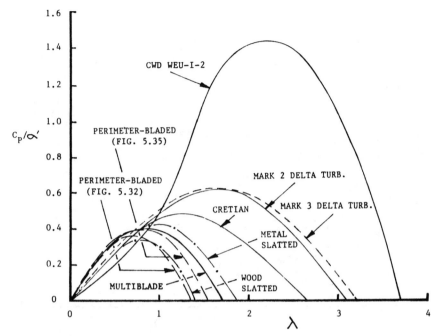

Figure 5.39. Comparison of water-pumping turbine rotor performances on the specific power coefficient (C_P/σ') versus λ plane.

When contemplating the operation of low-speed, deep-well, reciprocating pumps specifically an alternative parameter to λ is the rotor angular velocity, ω, since this will reveal the need, or otherwise, for a reduction gear-box. In fact the maximum accelerations, and decelerations, of a pump-rod moving sinusoidally are directly proportional to the product of the square of the angular velocity of the crank, or eccentric, shaft generating the motion and the corresponding pump stroke. Hence a yet more useful parameter than ω is ω^2. Thus since $\lambda = (\omega D)/(2U_\infty)$ then for prescribed U_∞:

$$\omega \propto \lambda/D \tag{5.14}$$

Thus normalising D with D^* and substituting in (5.14) from equation (5.11):

$$\omega^2 \propto \lambda^2 \sigma' \tag{5.15}$$

Figure 5.39 can now be replotted, if desired, with the abscissa, λ, replaced by the variable $\lambda^2 \sigma'$ which, from (5.15), is proportional to the square of the rotor angular velocity ω. The ordinate, which remains the

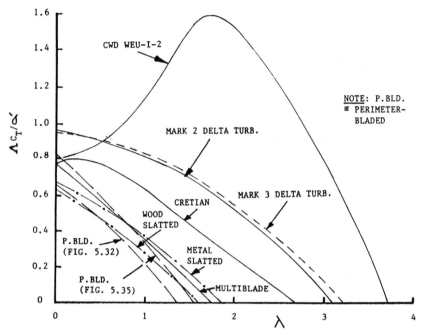

Figure 5.40. Comparison of water-pumping turbine rotor performances on the specific unified torque coefficient ($(\Lambda C_T)/\sigma'$) versus λ plane.

same as in Fig. 5.39, can then be interpreted as a variable proportional to power output for a variety of turbines all of which are of equal total blade area. A more useful presentation is to plot the variable $C_T/(\sigma')^{3/2}$ versus $\lambda^2\sigma'$. This has been done and the results are presented in Fig. 5.41.

Figure 5.41 shows that the low-solidity perimeter-bladed rotor produces, for a prescribed rotor blade area, the highest starting torque of any of the rotors coupled with the smallest value of ω^2 at runaway. The value of the square of the maximum angular velocity of the perimeter-bladed rotor is less than 10% of that of the Mark 3 delta-turbine implying that, at least for small rotors and moderate pump strokes, a reduction gear will be necessary for the latter. Alternatively the Mark 3 rotor must be furled at a relatively low wind speed or a combination of early furling and a speed-reduction gear-ratio is likely to be required. Because Fig. 5.41 refers to rotors of equal blade area there are considerable differences in their diameters. Table 5.2 lists the diameter ratio D/D^*, derived from equation (5.11), and the corresponding solidity, σ', of each turbine type.

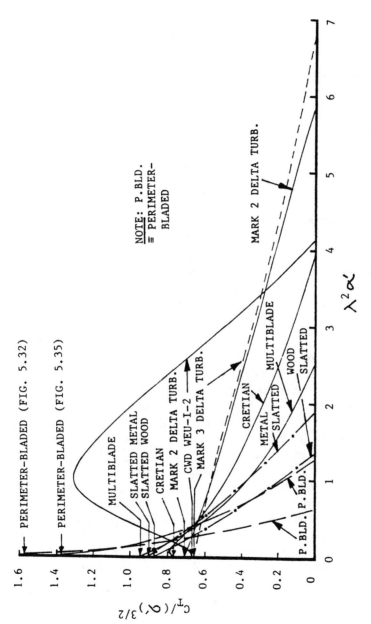

Figure 5.41. Comparison of water-pumping turbine rotor performances for rotors of equal blade area on the $C_T/(\sigma')^{3/2}$ versus $\lambda^2 \sigma'$ plane.

Table 5.2

Relative Diameters of Turbine Rotors of Equal Blade Area

Identity of rotor		Diameter ratio
Description	Solidity σ'	$D/D*$
Reference rotor (hypothetical)	1.00	1.000
Cretian rotor	0.57	1.325
CWD (WEU-I-2)	0.30	1.826
Delta-turbine Mark 2	0.62	1.270
Delta-turbine Mark 3	0.68	1.213
Multiblade	0.84	1.091
Perimeter-bladed	0.34	1.715
Perimeter-bladed	0.51	1.400
Slatted-blade (metal)	0.54	1.361
Slatted-blade (wood)	0.54	1.361

It can be concluded, from Figs. 5.39 and 5.41, that for equal blade areas the energy conversion capability of the low-solidity perimeter-bladed rotor approaches that of the smaller diameter multibladed turbine. However the starting torque of the former is much greater and the runaway angular velocity much less. This implies that the perimeter-bladed rotor is inherently more suitable for driving reciprocating pumps directly, without an intervening speed reducer, than a typical multibladed rotor. Figures 5.37 and 5.38 show that, provided a relatively high turbine-shaft speed is acceptable, then for rotors of prescribed diameter, the Mark 2 and Mark 3 delta-turbines combine a high unified torque coefficient, ΛC_T, at $\lambda = 0$, comparable with that of a classical multibladed rotor, with a high energy conversion capability.

It would appear that the CWD-type rotor is less justifiably included in the comparisons presented in Fig. 5.41, and hence by implication also in Figs. 5.39 and 5.40, than any of the other turbine types due to the low torque coefficient at $\lambda = 0$. It has, in fact been included only for the sake of completeness.

CHAPTER 6

Major Factors Influencing the Design of Horizontal-Axis Machines

The finalised design of a horizontal-axis wind-turbine-driven water pump depends upon the interaction of many factors. The type of turbine rotor selected depends, for example, on the choice of pump and whether or not reduction gearing is to be employed and even, in some cases, on the size, or scale, of the unit. Also the design is strongly influenced by the furling arrangements provided to protect the machine from damage due to overspeeding under strong wind conditions. Additionally it is necessary to provide some means for stopping the machine, manually, when pumping is no longer required or when maintenance work is to be undertaken. Damage due to overspeeding can take at least two forms. One obvious influence of overspeeding is the resultant risk of bursting the turbine due to excessive centrifugally induced loads. Another is the result of imposing high accelerations on the pump-rod, sometimes termed the sucker rod, of conventional reciprocating pumps.

High pump-rod accelerations can lead to very high loads in the mechanism during the pumping (up) stroke and, on the downstroke, pushing the pump-rod down the well-bore with an acceleration greater than that achievable due to gravity acting on the pump-rod and piston. The latter situation can result in disastrous buckling of the pump-rod and also, possibly, jamming of the pump mechanism. Normally, for a direct-drive water pumper with a high-solidity rotor it is not sufficient, under strong wind conditions, to prevent overspeeding by simply stopping the rotor by means of, say, a brake. In order to prevent excessive wind-induced loads on the rotor, also transmitted to the tower, it becomes necessary to either open up the flow area through the rotor or to turn the rotor edgewise to the wind. Either action will serve to both prevent overspeeding and minimise wind-induced structural loads.

The tower structure employed to support the wind-turbine rotor, head and the furling mechanism is itself subjected to several external influences. At the most fundamental level the possibilities are tubular towers or towers of the lattice, or space-frame, type. In general terms tubular towers usually involve less field-assembly work than lattice towers but, if erected over the well, tend to make pump withdrawal for servicing more difficult unless there is provision to, say, lower the tower clear of the well. On the other hand a lattice tower in the dismantled state is usually more easily transported than a tubular tower and, when assembled at the site, can, if suitably designed, be used very easily as a derrick to assist in pump removal for servicing and subsequent reinstallation. Also lattice towers can be designed with wide bases to straddle manually dug wells.

Both lattice and tubular tower designs can be adapted to various self-erection schemes whereby small machines can be site-assembled without the need for a crane. This can be accomplished by, for example, hinging the tower at ground level and subsequently raising it into the upright position, by means of a gin-pole, with the tower top assembly in place. Alternatively a slide-up system can be used. These and other aspects of tower design are discussed in more detail in Chapter 11. Tubular and lattice towers can be either free-standing or cable-guyed structures. Normally, for water pumpers, lattice towers are free standing whilst tubular towers are usually based on relatively small-diameter commercial piping and, consequently, are cable guyed. Free-standing, light-weight, rolled sheet-metal tubular towers are commonly used for large wind-electric machines.

It can be seen, therefore, that machine design, configuration and appearance are, in general, strongly influenced by the design priorities. Of course in each case it is imperative that the machine design selected should be as cost-effective, and inherently reliable, as possible. Of the factors considered in more detail here one of the most fundamental is the location of the turbine rotor, which can be positioned either upwind or downwind of the tower. Other areas warranting further consideration relate to the use, or otherwise, of reduction gearing, the scaling of successful designs to other sizes and designs suitable for unusual pumping modes.

6.1. Upwind Rotor

An upwind rotor location is the most common arrangement found in practice. It has the inherent advantage of positioning the rotor in relatively undisturbed flow, assuming no significant upwind obstructions, thereby serving to maximise the turbine output. It does, however, imply the need for a tailvane, or some alternative device, to maintain the rotor in an upwind orientation under all operating conditions. It is noteworthy that an upwind rotor running at a high tip-speed ratio, higher than is customary with high-solidity rotors such as those used on most water pumpers, can be shown to be inherently stable in yaw provided the wind direction does not deviate suddenly, by a substantial angle, from alignment with the turbine axis of rotation (de Vries, 1981).

The tailvane and support boom, located downwind of the yaw axis of an upwind rotor, can also serve as effective counter-weights to balance the tower bending moment induced by the weight of the rotor. An alternative to a tailvane is the use of paddle-like, autonomous, wind servo rotors, illustrated diagrammatically in Fig. 6.1. These spin only when the turbine axis is malaligned with the wind direction and serve to realign the turbine by means of a pinion, or worm, on the servo-shaft which meshes with a ring-gear fixed to the tower top (de Vries, 1981). Arrangements of this kind, employing a single servo-rotor known as a fan-tail, have been used in the past on British corn-grinding windmills (Reynolds, 1970; Major and Watts, 1992). However the servo-rotor yaw control system is relatively complex and does not lend itself to permitting the automatic furling of the turbine unless additional provisions are made for this.

In the case of a vane-steered upwind rotor the turbine and the rotor-supporting head are most commonly arranged to fold, under storm conditions, about a vertical axis such that the axis of the turbine rotor shaft lies approximately at right angles to the tail boom. This then orientates the rotor edgewise to the wind direction, and essentially parallel to the tail-vane, thereby stopping the machine. A less common system, frequently used in the past, employs a so-called sectional rotor, of the type depicted in Fig. 1.2, which opens up under storm conditions to limit the rotor maximum speed. More recently a rotor design of the multiblade type has been proposed in which the pitch angle of each individual blade increases, automatically, under storm conditions by hinging about a radially directed axis to spill flow through the rotor thereby, in that way, controlling speed much in the manner of a sectional rotor.

6.2. Downwind Rotor

At the price of the loss of some rotor power, due to a portion of the rotor lying in the wake of the tower, the tailvane of an upwind rotor can be eliminated. The action of the tailvane of an upwind rotor is replaced, in essential terms, by the drag force acting on the downwind rotor tending to align the rotor face normal to the wind direction. It is usually necessary,

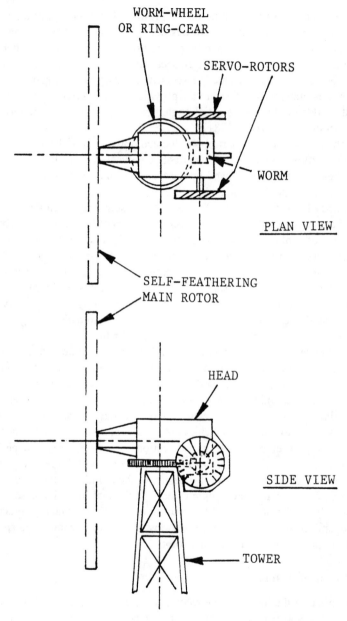

Figure 6.1. Wind-operated servo system for yaw control.

with a downwind system, to introduce a counter-weight upwind of the yaw axis to cancel the tower bending moment due to the weight of the rotor.

It is, with downwind mounted rotors, usually necessary to employ either a sectional rotor, as was commonly the case in the past for water pumpers with downwind-rotor configurations, or a rotor with automatically variable pitch blades. There is at least one, current, commercially available water-pumping wind-turbine featuring a downwind rotor with automatically controlled variable-pitch blades. A downwind rotor usually implies, therefore, a need for a relatively complex rotor instead of the more simple rigid-rotor construction used with traditional, upwind, tailvane-equipped configurations.

An exception to the form of variable geometry rotor normally required for downwind systems employs a fixed-pitch, rigid rotor which is forced to turn edgewise to the flow by operation of an upwind foreplane. However in terms of mechanical complexity such an arrangement is comparable with that of a conventional upwind rigid-rotor system and appears, in general terms, to offer no particular advantages. In one rather exceptional case a rigid-rotor downwind arrangement has been justified on the basis of an unavoidable, very substantial rotor offset downwind from the rotor axis. The offset was due to the use of a flexible-shaft drive directly connecting the downwind turbine rotor to a positive-displacement rotary pump.

A requirement for a long life of the flexible drive was a very gentle bend in the drive cable. This led, directly, to the substantial offset of the turbine rotor from the yaw axis. A water pumper of this type, several prototype units of which have been built, is illustrated in Fig. 6.2. An upwind configuration with such a large rotor offset would have presented considerable yaw-control problems. The large rotor offset of the machine shown in Fig. 6.2 coupled with the relatively narrow, free standing, tubular tower should serve to minimise the loss of performance associated with the rotor operating within the tower wake.

6.3. Directly Driven Pumps

It may not, at first consideration, seem to be a particularly important aspect of machine design to differentiate between systems employing directly driven pumps with, or without, intermediate gear transmissions. However it is possible, by eliminating the need for a geared transmission, to employ an altogether more simple construction than is the case when reduction gearing is used. The use of reduction gearing does, of course, provide a much greater flexibility when matching the performance of a turbine rotor of choice with the requirements of a conventional reciprocating pump.

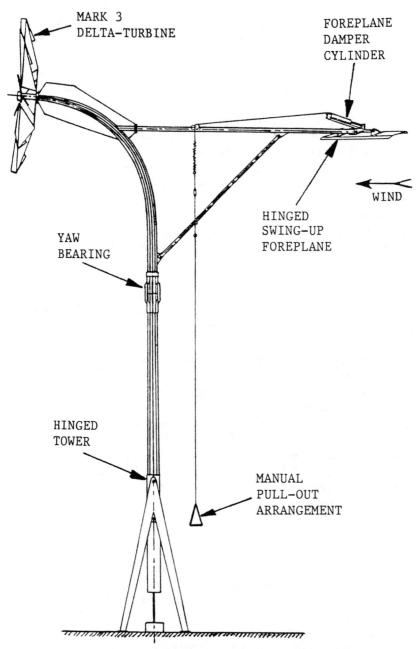

MARK 3
DELTA-TURBINE

FOREPLANE
DAMPER
CYLINDER

WIND

HINGED
SWING-UP
FOREPLANE

YAW
BEARING

HINGED
TOWER

MANUAL
PULL-OUT
ARRANGEMENT

Figure 6.2. Side view of a small (2.44 m rotor diameter) downwind type water pumper with a flexible-shaft transmission.

6.3.1. With Reduction Gearing

Bearing in mind the dynamic limitations of reciprocating pumps, identified by severe restrictions on the maximum pump-rod accelerations acceptable, the use of a reduction gear permits, even in small size units, a relatively fast-running and high-efficiency turbine rotor to be matched, quite effectively, with a reciprocating pump. The essential problem with this is that the reduction gearbox will almost certainly be a dedicated item since it not only carries, on the input shaft, the turbine rotor but also contains, in addition to an oil reservoir, the crank mechanism to convert rotary motion into the reciprocating motion of the pump-rod. This, therefore, implies the need for a machined casting with carefully aligned bearings and the employment of machined gears. Sectioned diagrams of typical reduction gear boxes are included in the literature of various wind-pump manufacturers; a diagram of this type can also be found in "Windpumps, A Guide for Development Workers" (Fraenkel et al., 1993).

It is the cost of special equipment of this type which offers an inducement to the designer to eliminate, if reasonably possible, the need for a reduction gear box. It is also desirable to eliminate the speed-reduction gear box if it is proposed to fabricate the turbine in small plants, with limited machining facilities, such as might be found in developing countries. It is, in some cases, also possible to dispense with a gear box by using a relatively high-speed turbine directly coupled to a rotary positive-displacement type pump. An example is the unit illustrated in Fig. 6.2; this employs a Mark 3 delta-turbine directly coupled to a rotary, progressive cavity, positive-displacement pump. Alternatively it may also be possible, in some circumstances, to use a directly driven rotor-dynamic pump.

6.3.2. Without Reduction Gearing

The elimination of the need for reduction gearing simplifies, very considerably, machine construction because standard, stock, mass-produced, self-aligning, individual, grease-lubricated, sealed, flange-mounted or pillow-block ball or roller bearings can be employed throughout the head assembly. This eliminates much, or all, of the need for machining, and also the requirement for castings, and permits a welded head assembly to be used to which the flange or pillow-block bearings are bolted. The price of this fabricational simplification is that the matching of the turbine rotor performance to the pump requirements is more restrictive than when a reduction gear is employed. The matching problem is generally more acute for very small machines.

A degree of freedom can be obtained, as suggested previously, by employing specially configured turbines, for example, perimeter-bladed rotors described in the previous chapter, so that a direct drive system can be employed without resorting to ultra-short pump strokes. Rotors of the perimeter-bladed type generally require longer spokes than those of otherwise comparable conventional turbines. However the additional cost and weight of these is normally small compared with the cost saving due to the elimination of the speed-reduction gear box. It is also much easier to incorporate a counter-weight to balance a portion of the pumping load, to assist in start-up, in direct-drive systems than in geared units.

6.3.3. Design Scaling

Another factor influencing design can be the scale of the unit. This applies, particularly, to systems employing conventional reciprocating pumps. Scaling down such a system that works satisfactorily can result in unsatisfactory operation of the scaled-down version. It can be shown that for a specific operating condition the tip-speed ratio of the original and scaled-down machines will, to a first approximation, be equal. If it is assumed that the speed-reduction ratio, if any, also remains the same, then with the pump stroke (and bore) of the scaled-down machine reduced by the scale-reduction factor it follows, from reference to the proportionality (5.14), that the pump-rod acceleration will *increase*. This increase will be in direct proportion to the inverse of the scale-reduction factor. Hence the pump-rod acceleration of the scaled-down machine may, therefore, be too great.

This circumstance will, therefore, require an increase in the gear reduction ratio provided or possibly the introduction of a reduction gear if the original unit did not have one. This will, in turn, lead to an adjustment of the pump dimensions such that the pump flow rate will, nominally, be equal to that of the original unit multiplied by the square of the scale-reduction factor. A somewhat undesirable alternative to modifying the speed-reduction ratio is to employ a pump-stroke equal to that of the original unit multiplied by the square of the scale-reduction factor. The corresponding pump-piston area required is equal to that of the original unit multiplied by the scale-reduction factor.

The foregoing considerations show that the direct scaling of systems incorporating conventional reciprocating pumps has to be approached with caution. It can be shown that scaling up a satisfactory system incorporating a reciprocating pump allows the pump-stroke to be increased to equal the original stroke multiplied by the square of the scale-up factor. This results in an invariant pump-rod acceleration. The corresponding pump-piston area should be that of the pump of the original sized unit multiplied by the scale-up factor. It should, however, be realised that, for the suggested scale-up treatment, the pump-plunger velocity is greater, by a ratio equal to that of the scale-up factor, than that of the original unit. This may, or may not, prove to be acceptable from the pump efficiency viewpoint.

6.4. Air-Lift Pumping

The most fundamental decisions here relate to the choice of the type of compressor employed and to the compressor location. The principle of air-lift pumping, which uses a flow of compressed air to achieve a pumping action, is discussed in Chapter 8. If a production air compressor is selected for an air-lift pumping system it will be possible, provided the compressor is suitably sized, to drive it by connecting the compressor shaft directly to the turbine shaft without any intermediate gearing. In the recent past a small air-lift wind-pump was produced commercially in which the turbine rotor was mounted directly on the crankshaft of a standard, production, single-cylinder compressor. The writer does not favour such an arrangement unless the compressor crankshaft is known to be of sufficient strength to support the rotor and withstand, also, the gyroscopic moment generated during yaw.

A multi-cylinder compressor appears to be a superior choice to a single-cylinder unit because the torque loading on the turbine will be more uniform which is beneficial at start-up. Since turbine rotational speeds are generally low compared with those of typical, available compressors it may present a more economical solution to use a smaller compressor than for the direct-drive case in conjunction with a speed-increasing transmission. The latter could, of course, be of the gear type but a toothed-belt transmission appears to be admirably suitably arranged between the turbine shaft and the compressor input shaft.

In each of the foregoing arrangements the compressor is mounted on the head of the machine with the delivery hose passed through the hollow centre of the yaw-bearing assembly. A suitable swivel connection in the delivery hose ensures that the yaw and furling motions of the head are not impeded. A high-speed head-mounted compressor encourages the use of a relatively efficient, high-tip-speed ratio turbine. It is important that the turbine delivers a high torque coefficient at zero tip-speed ratio if the compressor is to be started, easily, under load without the use of a clutch or other compressor-unloading device.

An alternative to a head-mounted compressor is a specially constructed, single-cylinder, pull-rod-operated compressor at the base of the tower at ground level. An arrangement of this type is more convenient, from the viewpoint of accessibility for compressor maintenance, than a head-mounted compressor. Such a compressor can also be arranged more easily for dry lubrication thereby inhibiting the risk of oil contamination of the pumped water. A counter-balance mass can be provided, in the head structure, to minimise torque peaks at start-up much in the manner suggested in §6.3.2. The fixed, ground-level mounted compressor also eliminates the need for a swivel connection in the air delivery hose.

A disadvantage of a ground-level mounted compressor is that the pull-rod, running the height of the tower, will tend to impose operational speed restrictions similar to those discussed previously with respect to reciprocating water pump drives. It may, however, be possible to employ either a ground-level mounted air-cylinder type pull-rod tensioner or, alternatively, a tubular pull-rod that is relatively stiff in compression or a combination of these measures. An easier alternative, to minimise drive-train potential dynamic problems, is to relocate the compressor higher in the tower.

6.5. Other Directly Driven Pumps

Other types of pump employed in wind-driven systems include rotary positive-displacement pumps, usually known generically as progressive cavity pumps or, more specifically, as Mono or Moyno pumps. Other pump types, normally restricted to very low pumping heads, include Archimedian screw pumps, scoop wheels, centrifugal (rotor dynamic) pumps and various forms of pump based on what can be described as the concept of the conveyor belt. In the latter cases an inclined flat-belt, rope or chain, running over two pullies, carries surfaces, normal to the direction of motion, that are arranged to lift water from the lower to the upper end of an inclined channel or pipe. Pumps of these types, including progressive cavity pumps, are described in Chapter 8. In terms of their interaction with horizontal-axis wind-turbines a common requirement of all these pumps is the provision of a transmission to connect them to the turbine-rotor shaft.

In view of the yaw and furling requirements of a horizontal-axis turbine the most convenient form of transmission to convert the rotary motion of the turbine shaft to rotary motion at ground level appears to be one incorporating a vertical rotary shaft. For the progressive cavity and centrifugal pump cases a vertical shaft is particularly convenient since it can be extended below the ground surface and connected directly to the pump shaft. The remaining pump types require a rotary input from a horizontal shaft typically at ground level.

The most obvious way of providing a vertical shaft-drive is to locate such a shaft coaxially with the turbine yaw axis and couple it to the turbine shaft by, say, bevel gears. Alternatively, for small machines, the bevel gears can be replaced by a belt drive. A belt pulley, in a horizontal plane, at the top of the vertical shaft can be connected, via a drive belt, to another pulley, in a vertical plane, on the horizontal shaft of the turbine. A system of this type requires the introduction of two idler pullies to carry the belt through the necessary 90° changes of direction. A ground-level horizontal shaft can be driven from the vertical shaft by similar gear or belt arrangements.

An alternative to using gears or belts to transmit the drive from the turbine rotor to a vertical axis is employed in the machine illustrated in Fig. 6.2. This unit uses a stranded, twisted, steel cable as a flexible drive. The greased cable rotates within a thick-walled plastic tube liner pushed into the tubular steel mast. For the machine shown in Fig. 6.2 the tubular mast was, in fact, adapted from a production "swan neck" type street-lamp standard. Although such a drive appears to be very non-conventional there are many years of successful operational experience with this system in small wind-pumps. The application of the steel-cable flexible drive system to wind-turbines appears to have been pioneered by a Canadian, Mr. B. Massey. It is important to ensure that the drive torque acts to tighten the spiral of the cable twist and not the opposite.

The system shown in Fig. 6.2 drives a vertical-axis progressive cavity pump. Had a horizontal-axis output been required the fixed lower portion of the tower could have been replaced by an appropriately supported, gradual, right-angle bend, similar to that constituting the upper tower section in Fig. 6.2. It is important to note that, with all the systems involving a vertical drive shaft, including a flexible-cable drive, there is a torque reaction tending to yaw the turbine rotor out of the wind. The designer should always take this into account.

The American (Arlington, Virginia) based organisation Volunteers in Technical Assistance (VITA) has designed an ultra-simple wind-pump for irrigation pumping in developing nations. This employs a belt drive connecting, directly, the horizontal shaft of the turbine with a horizontal shaft at ground level for driving a "conveyor belt" type pump. This system is not completely automatic because yaw is accommodated by twisting the flat drive belt. Therefore only a limited range of yaw movement is acceptable.

6.6. Wind Electric Systems

There is a large variety of wind-electric turbines available commercially from which to select a unit for an autonomous wind-electric pumper. Thus the scope of the design decisions that need to be made in relation to such a system is restricted if the system is to be based on an existing wind-electric unit. Essentially the decisions relate to the type of pump chosen and the electrical system selected.

For example, the electrical transmission can be of the AC, DC or mixed type and may, or may not, incorporate energy storage in the form of deep-discharge batteries. If battery storage is selected a DC generator can charge the battery which, in turn, powers a DC pump-motor via a regulator. An AC generator can charge the battery system via a rectifier. An AC pump-motor can be supplied from the battery via an inverter. Yet another possibility is to dispense with the battery energy storage and connect an AC induction type generator directly to an induction type pump-motor. In this case the pump speed will be directly proportional to that of the wind-turbine-driven alternator.

The latter scheme saves the costs involved with the provision of battery energy storage. On the other hand, because of the variable speed of the pump-motor, greater demands are made on the operational flexibility of the pump than when batteries are provided. For deep-well pumping the use of an electric-motor-driven pump-jack can relieve pump difficulties associated with a variable-speed pump-motor. A conventional reciprocating pump operated by the pump-jack will have an efficiency virtually independent of speed up to the maximum permissible speed. However a typical (usually) multi-stage centrifugal pump driven by a submerged motor can be used provided it will generate sufficient pressure to deliver water at some minimum pump-motor speed corresponding to the cut-in wind speed of the system. Such pumps are attractive for wind-electric pumpers since they are modular and mass-produced. Hence the number, and throughput, of the stages used can be selected to correspond to particular, applicable, well conditions.

The overall efficiency of a wind-electric unit is generally fairly low mainly because of a relatively low average pump efficiency, say 60%, for a directly connected AC system employing a multi-stage centrifugal pump. For systems employing energy storage batteries the pump efficiency can be higher, say 70%, because the pump can be arranged to operate closer to the optimum efficiency condition, however battery losses have to be accounted for. Other losses are those in the alternator, connecting wiring and in the pump-motor and in any additional items, for example an inverter or a rectifier.

In general terms the performance characteristic of wind-electric pumping systems differ from those of classical mechanical-type pumpers equipped with conventional reciprocating pumps. Figure 6.3 represents, diagrammatically, a pumping performance comparison between classical mechanical and wind-electric systems of equal rotor diameter. The two sets of

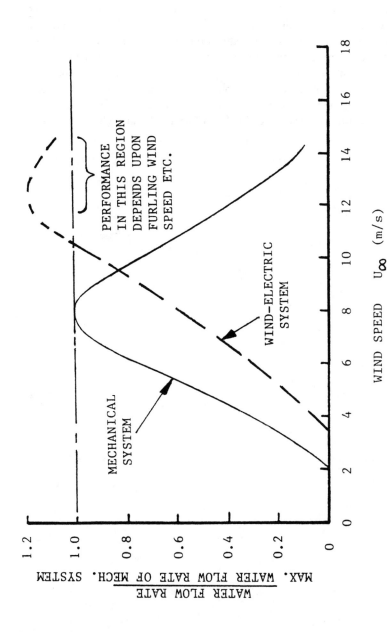

Figure 6.3. Comparative performances, for equal lifts, of equal rotor diameter mechanical and wind-electric water pumpers (diagrammatic).

results, whilst not representing the performances of specific units, are each composites based on test data, for pump lifts of 5.5 m, some of which were obtained at the Alberta Renewable Energy Test Site in Canada. It would appear that the best applications for wind-electric pumping are not only those where displacing the wind-turbine from the immediate vicinity of the well site results in a significantly superior wind regime but also when use can be made of any surplus electrical power generated. Additionally wind-electric pumpers appear to compare most favourably with the classical mechanical types for low-lift, rather than high-lift, pumping applications.

CHAPTER 7

Furling Systems for
Horizontal-Axis Machines

One of the important factors influencing the design of horizontal-axis machines considered, briefly, in the previous chapter is the provision of an automatic system to protect the wind-turbine when strong winds develop and also some form of manually operated device, or pull-out system, for disabling the machine when pumping is no longer required. The latter commonly takes the form of a hand-operated override of the automatic furling system that can usually be activated from ground level.

It has already been pointed out, previously, that wind-turbines directly coupled to reciprocating pumps must not be permitted to overspeed because of the risk of pump-rod damage. It should, however, be realised that even when employing other types of pump less sensitive to overspeeding it is, with very few exceptions, impractical, from the viewpoint of cost-effectiveness, to expect to be able to design a turbine strong enough to withstand "head on" a major storm without, at the very least, suffering severe storm damage if not total destruction. Because machines of the upwind kind are the most common the methods of furling applied to upwind machines deserve to be considered in more detail than in the previous chapter.

7.1. Upwind Machines

Since low tip-speed-ratio upwind turbines are, from the practical viewpoint, essentially unstable in yaw they are almost completely dependent upon some form of yaw-control system. Usually a tailvane, mounted at the extremity of a (nominally) downwind directed boom, is employed to maintain the rotor axis parallel to the wind direction. This arrangement has, because of simplicity, been adopted virtually universally. Factors complicating this otherwise ultra-simple concept relate to the provision of an automatic furling capability coupled with the need for a hand-operated pull-out system to stop the machine when it is not needed or when it is to be serviced.

General questions that can be asked in relation to boom-mounted tailvanes are:

i) Is there a preferred tailvane shape or planform? It is note-worthy that a wide variety of planforms are employed; tailvanes often appear to serve, in part, as trademarks, or logos, of the manufacturers.

ii) Is it preferable, in order to achieve a prescribed yaw-control moment, to employ a tailvane of relatively large area mounted on a relatively short boom or the opposite?

The undesirability of making short, quick, jerky, yaw movements, with overshoots and subsequent corrections, each resulting in the generation of an unwanted gyroscopically induced moment in the turbine shaft and commensurate loads in the rotor, suggests that the designer should strive to achieve gentle, but positive yaw movements with minimal over-shooting. This consideration implies the selection of a low-aspect-ratio tailvane surface which, in the interests of minimising costs, should be of the flat-plate type. Because the gradient, $dC_L/d\alpha$, of the lift curve slope of low-aspect-ratio, flat-plate, delta-wing planforms is particularly small, also delta-wings combine the capability of achieving a fairly high maximum lift coefficient at large values of incidence angle α, the writer has a strong preference for tailvanes with delta-wing planforms. For confirmation of the characteristics of delta-wings see Fig. 3.7 and compare, for $A_R = 2$, with Fig. 3.5.

In the interests of minimising the angular velocity, ω_P, of the yaw, or precessional, motion of the machine the writer's preference is for a relatively small tail surface mounted on a relatively long boom rather than the opposite possibility. Figure 7.1(a) and (b) present, diagrammatically, comparisons of a relatively large tail surface on a short boom with a relatively small tail surface on a long boom. The effective length of the tail boom is identified as $\overline{L}$. For equal yaw directional restoring moments the tail velocities, $\omega_P \overline{L}$, are equal for both cases. Thus with reference to portions (a) and (b) of Fig. 7.1:

$$(\omega_P \overline{L})_{(a)} = (\omega_P \overline{L})_{(b)}$$

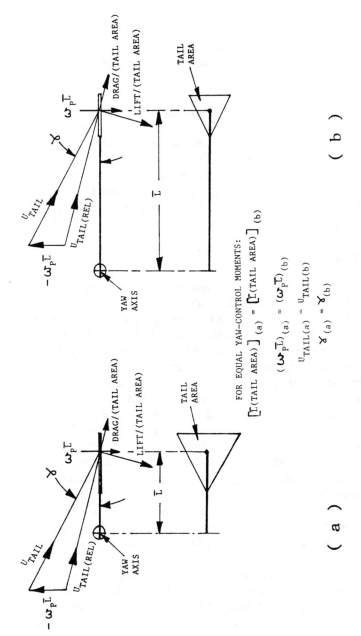

Figure 7.1. Yaw control comparison with tailvane movement ongoing (diagrammatic): a) large tailvane on short boom; b) small tailvane on long boom.

thus:

$$\frac{\omega_{P(b)}}{\omega_{P(a)}} = \frac{\overline{L}_{(a)}}{\overline{L}_{(b)}}$$

Hence the gyroscopic moment, $I\omega\omega_P$, acting on the turbine shaft is inversely proportional to the tail boom length; thus, for prescribed values of I and rotor angular velocity ω:

$$(I\omega\omega_P)_{(b)} \big/ (I\omega\omega_P)_{(a)} = \overline{L}_{(a)} \big/ \overline{L}_{(b)}$$

An additional advantage of a long tail boom is that the tailvane should experience less interference from the rotor wake than a larger surface on a shorter boom. A number of techniques are, or have been, used to adapt the boom-mounted tailvane concept to the requirements of both automatic and manual furling. These will now be considered under appropriate subheadings.

7.1.1. Folding Rotors

Some of the earliest upwind horizontal-axis machines employed a rigidly mounted tailvane in conjunction with a sectional rotor of the type illustrated in Fig. 1.2. The most satisfactory aspects of this type of configuration are the rigid tail boom and the elimination of gyroscopically generated moments associated with the furling of rigid rotors. A sectional rotor can also be expected to respond more promptly to sudden gusts than an edgewise-furling system comprising relatively massive moving parts.

A sectional rotor typically has eight to about twelve moveable sectors; the example shown in Fig. 1.2 is an eight-sector rotor. In addition to the complexity associated with the moveable sectors provision must also be made to coordinate the movement of the sectors which further complicates the rotor. Yet an additional complication is due to the provision of a manually operated arrangement, in some cases dependent upon the provision of a hollow turbine shaft, that can be used to apply a force to the sector-coordinating linkage in order to place all the rotor-sectors in their furled positions to stop the machine.

All this implies, collectively, the inclusion, within the rotor, of a considerable complexity in terms of the number of moving parts. Furthermore the rotor-sector pivots, and those of the coordinating mechanism, are not easily lubricated nor are they readily accessible. Lubrication problems may, perhaps, be avoidable if a modern version of such a rotor were to be built. However wear and tear due to load reversals, at low rotor speeds, and, possibly, grit and rain-water penetration of bearings would be remaining difficulties.

7.1.2. Edgewise-Furling Rotors

When a rigid rotor is used it is normal for furling to take place by arranging for the rotor to be turned edge-on to the wind direction which has the dual effect of reducing, dramatically, the projected area of the rotor normal to the flow and also effectively stopping the rotor. The sideways turning is usually accomplished by employing the drag force acting on the rotor of a configuration in which the rotor axis is offset, laterally, from the yaw axis or, if the rotor axis intersects the yaw axis, by providing an offset drag vane to implement the turning process. In some cases a combination of the two methods is used. In each case the rotor turns bodily, about the yaw axis, together with the head of the machine which also supports the turbine shaft and the pump-drive transmission.

In order to permit the rotor to re-orientate edgewise to the wind direction the tailvane support boom is hinged to the head assembly. A restoring torque, to prevent the head turning relative to the tailvane and support boom prematurely in weak winds, is normally provided by means of either a spring or by gravity acting on the tail. Figure 7.2 shows, diagrammatically, an offset rotor and also a non-offset rotor: the latter machine is, therefore, provided with an offset drag vane. In both the cases illustrated in Fig. 7.2 the restoring torque, or restraint preventing premature furling, is provided by means of a tension spring. It is apparent from Fig. 7.2 that the tailvane is slightly offset from the true downwind direction. This is to balance the tendency of the offset rotor, or the offset drag vane, to deflect the system such that the rotor axis would not align with the wind direction. The tailvane offset angle is typically between about 5° to 10°.

Figure 7.3 shows two configurations, each incorporating a laterally offset rotor axis, in which the action of the restoring spring is replaced by gravity acting on the tail assembly. The tail assembly rises as furling occurs in a manner analogous to the way in which a door on rising hinges is elevated when it is opened. The act of opening the door results, therefore, in the generation of a restoring torque tending to reclose it. An advantage of the rising tail assembly concept is that the need for a restoring spring is eliminated and hence so also is the risk of a breakage of the spring. Such breakage would simply cause the machine to furl. It is normally possible to adjust the furling wind speed by, for example, altering the spring tension of the systems shown in Fig. 7.2 or by modifying the geometry of the arrangements depicted in Fig. 7.3. The configuration of Fig. 7.3(a) lends

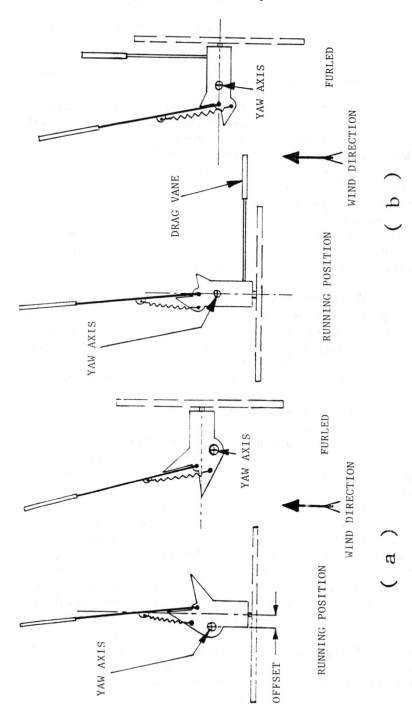

Figure 7.2. Offset rotor axis compared with drag vane system. Restoring torque due to tension spring (diagrammatic): a) offset rotor axis system; b) drag vane system.

itself particularly well to such an adjustment by selecting an alternative attachment location for the tension cable.

In order to prevent, during strong gusting winds, repeated furling and unfurling, with resultant large gyroscopic moments, it is usual practice to adjust the geometry of edgewise furling systems in such a manner that unfurling requires a substantial reduction in wind speed below that required to precipitate full furling. Often the unfurling wind speed is arranged to be in the vicinity of 50% of that required for full furling. Since gust wind speeds are typically $\pm 30\%$ of the average wind speed this implies, therefore, that once the machine has become fully furled on the basis of a peak gust velocity it is unlikely to attempt to unfurl due to a typical transient drop in wind speed.

An unfortunate consequence of many very simple edgewise-furling systems is a tendency for impacts to occur between the tail boom and the stops, depicted in Figs. 7.2 and 7.3, that limit the movements of the head of the machine relative to the tail assembly. An impact can occur during furling since once the angular position has been passed of the head relative to the tail boom at which the resistance to furling is greatest the head assembly tends to accelerate and impact the tail boom at the conclusion of the furling operation.

An impact can also occur when the system realigns into the operating position at the completion of unfurling. This type of impact can be a frequent event since it can follow a partial furling movement due to, say, a wind gust or even a relatively sudden yaw movement of the tail boom towards the furling direction. The writer is, therefore, strongly in favour of an energy-absorbing device, for example, a double-acting damper inter-connected between the head and tail assemblies, which offers negligible resistance to slow furling or unfurling motions but offers substantial resistance to such movements occurring rapidly.

The damper can be an automotive component or it can be fabricated from a dry-lubricated, double-acting air cylinder with a short circuit, containing a flow restriction and, desirably, also a snifting valve inter-connecting the two ends of the cylinder. It is important to ensure that the inherent mechanical resistance of the damper is not sufficient to inhibit proper furling, or unfurling, action. Both types of damper are relatively low-cost items and can, in conjunction with "soft" stops inhibit damage due to furling and unfurling. The writer tends to favour a nominally atmospheric pressure air-cylinder damper since this cannot suffer a gradual loss of working fluid due to slow leakage. It should also, if of a suitable type, have a lower resistance to slow movements than an automotive damper.

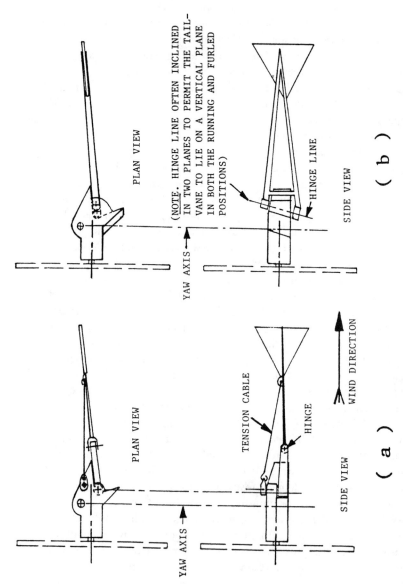

Figure 7.3. Furling systems with gravity generated restoring torque (diagrammatic): a) vertical hinge with offset tension member; b) inclined hinge.

Due to the analytical difficulties involved, particularly if an offset rotor is employed, it is recommended that edgewise furling system designs be based on, or at least checked by, wind-tunnel tests. A question that can be asked in relation to edgewise furling systems is what happens, with respect to furling action, if the pump seizes, or jams, thereby stopping the turbine rotor? Wind-tunnel tests of models in which this circumstance has been simulated by locking the turbine rotor show that for the very-high-solidity rotors typical of water pumpers furling occurs at about the same, or at a slightly lower, wind speed to that for normal full-speed operation. This observation is consistent with the comment made in Chapter 5, §5.8, relating to the drag of non-rotating, high-solidity rotors. Normal full-speed operation approaches, at typical furling wind speeds and when employing a simple pump, the turbine rotor being totally free-running since the power absorbed by a typical simple pump is very small relative to the potential maximum output of the turbine at the furling wind speed.

7.1.3. Hinged Tailvane Systems

A system for governing the rotor speed of upwind rigid-rotor wind-turbines involves a tail boom, rigidly attached to the head of the machine, below the outer end of which hangs a tailvane hinged, along the upper edge, to the horizontal boom. At least two variants of this arrangement are in use. One version, attributed to Kragten (Kragten, 1982), and used on the CWD 2000 water pumper features a rigidly attached boom projecting, in the horizontal plane, at a substantial angle to the turbine rotor axis. This system, which incorporates a rotor offset from the yaw axis on the opposite side to the offset of the suspended tail surface, is illustrated in Fig. 7.4(a). Test results obtained from this kind of system are available (Smulders et al., 1984). These show that, essentially, the hinged tail surface serves as a speed controller by maintaining, when set up correctly, a virtually constant rotor speed at wind speeds greater than a specific threshold value.

This system is, therefore, quite different in concept to the full-furling arrangements described in §7.1.2. The hinged tailvane system has the advantage of only gradually skewing the rotor face to the oncoming wind and hence major gyroscopic moments are not generated. It also has the disadvantage that sustained operation can take place with the rotor heavily mal-aligned with the flow, an operational mode that may contribute, substantially, to fatigue of the rotor structure.

The other version of the hinged tailvane concept is illustrated in Fig. 7.4(b). In the only known application of this arrangement the rotor axis is only slightly offset from the yaw axis and, consequently, an offset drag

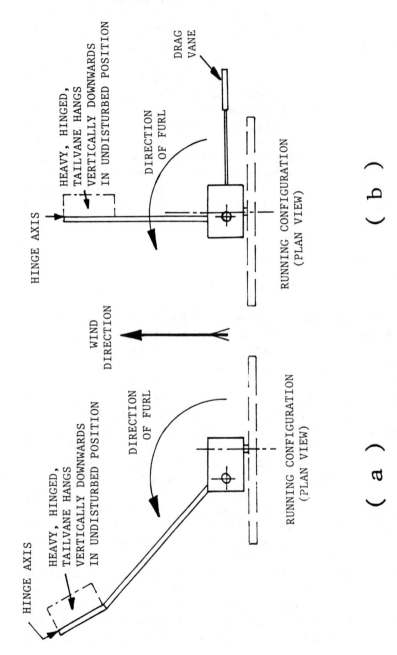

Figure 7.4. Hinged, pendulum type tailvanes: a) Kragten's system; b) Parish's system.

vane is also provided. In this case the tailvane support boom projects substantially downwind. It appears that the mode of operation is essentially similar to that of the system shown in Fig. 7.4(a) and, although detailed information is not available to confirm this opinion, the system could be expected to function more as a rotor-speed governor rather than as an automatic full-furling system. However it has the advantage that a manual pull-out is provided. Operation of this, which simply raises the hinged tailvane into a horizontal plane, should completely furl the rotor with the offset drag vane then substituting as a tailvane, but a tailvane in the plane of the rotor disc.

Provided speed-regulated operation, skewed to the flow in strong winds, is acceptable rather than full-furling the system depicted in Fig. 7.4(b) appears to have considerable merit. It was, it seems, originated by Mr. G. Parish, a Texan, (Baker, 1985). The scheme depicted in Fig. 7.4(b) has not only the advantage of mechanical simplicity, as does Kragten's system (Fig. 7.4(a)), but it is also provided with an ultra-simple hand-operated pull-out mechanism. Apparently the hinged tailvane is also intended to deflect, when impinged upon by a yaw-inducing gust. This, therefore, reduces the severity of the yaw motions which would otherwise occur when the machine is in the normal operating mode.

7.1.4. Retracting Tailvane

A rather unusual furling system has found application on a particular design of small, low-head, drainage water pumper equipped with a centrifugal pump. This machine, made in The Netherlands, is provided with what are, in effect, two alternatively usable tailvanes. One tailvane is mounted conventionally downwind of the four-bladed rotor, the other at right angles to this such that, when it is active, the aerodynamic surface lies parallel to the plane of the rotor disc. The two tailvanes are inter-connected by means of two shafts geared together at the head of the machine. One shaft passes through each tubular vane support. Each tailvane is mounted on the end of one of the shafts. The gearing of the shafts is so arranged that when one tailvane lies in a vertical plane the other is positioned horizontally and can, therefore, be regarded as retracted.

For normal operation the downwind surface lies in a vertical plane and the other surface, supported by the boom directed parallel to the plane of the rotor disc, is inactive since it is in a horizontal position. The machine, which is illustrated diagrammatically in Fig. 7.5, is furled by reversing the orientation of the two surfaces. Furling is initiated by the upward movement of a float in a plenum tank, fed by the outflow of the centrifugal pump, the water level within which rises under strong

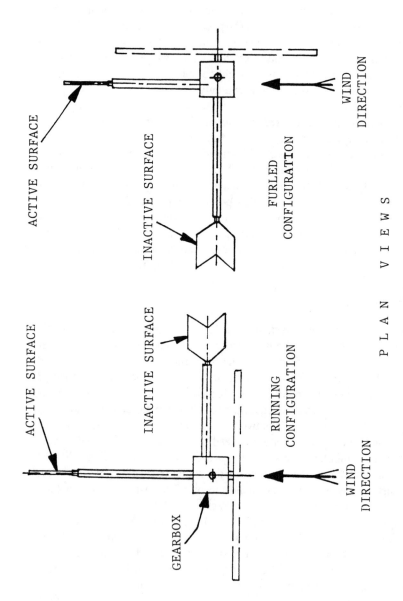

Figure 7.5. Alternating tailvane arrangement (diagrammatic).

wind conditions resulting, ultimately, in furling the rotor and, therefore, stopping the pump. During normal operation, in weak or moderate winds, the flow delivery rate from an outlet pipe connected to the bottom of the plenum tank is sufficient to prevent the water level rising in the plenum tank and thereby initiating furling. Whilst this system seems to work well as a turbine-overspeed control device it would appear that a shortage of supply water, a condition that never seems to arise in practice, would result in a loss of turbine-overspeed control. The machine can be fully furled by shutting-off the plenum-tank discharge pipe.

7.1.5. Upward-Lifting Rotor

Another furling arrangement that is sometimes feasible is an upward-lifting rotor tilting about a horizontal axis. In the furled state the turbine shaft is orientated vertically with the plane of the rotor disc then lying above the machine. An advantage of such an arrangement is that a tail surface can be employed that is rigidly attached to the head assembly of the machine. It is only really possible, with direct-drive systems, to use an upward-lifting rotor if a worm and wheel, or some equivalent, is employed in the machine transmission with the worm, or equivalent, mounted on the turbine shaft. The axis of tilt of the upward-lifting motion must then be coincident with the axis of the worm-wheel or equivalent.

It is the general mechanical inconvenience caused by a lifting rotor in a direct-drive arrangement that inhibits the use of this furling system. However, lifting rotors are sometimes employed in small wind-electric units that could constitute the core of a wind-electric water pumper. When the lifting rotor concept is employed in wind-electric machines it is normal to tilt the alternator, or generator, integrally with the turbine rotor as a monolithic assembly. This, therefore, avoids difficulties with transmission connecting the wind-turbine and alternator, or generator, shafts. Figure 7.6 illustrates such an arrangement.

7.1.6. Variable-Pitch Blades

Another method of controlling wind-turbines is to employ variable-pitch blading. Since, for this scheme, each blade has to be hinged individually, along a radial axis, usually at the blade leading edge, an arrangement of this kind can lead to a very large number of moveable components on a rotor of the typical multibladed type. However if, say, elastomeric hinges are employed the severity of this problem is much reduced. It is important that the elastomeric hinges demonstrate a long operational life for their use to be practical. In addition to the individually moveable blades a

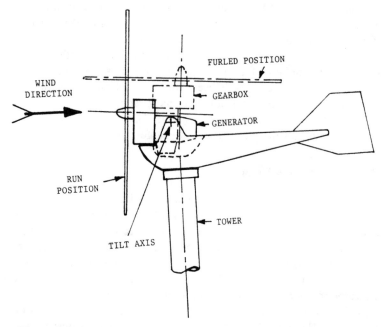

Figure 7.6. Small wind-electric machine with tilting rotor (diagrammatic).

coordinator ring, or some counterpart, is needed to connect the blades to the hand-operated pull-out system used for manual furling. It should be possible to arrange for automatic furling to occur, during operation of the turbine, due mainly to the aerodynamic loads acting on each turbine blade.

An advantage of variable-pitch blades in a water pumper environment relate to the resultant simplification of the tail assembly which is joined rigidly to the head structure. Other advantages are the elimination of gyroscopic moments associated with the rapid re-orientation, during furling, of the plane of rotation of rigid rotors and an expectation of a rapid response to sudden gusts. Variable-pitch blading is currently employed on a production water pumper equipped with a multibladed downwind rotor.

7.2. Downwind Machines

The initial, intuitive attraction of a downwind-rotor configuration lies in the possibility of eliminating the tail boom and tailvane normally required for autonomous upwind machines. It is noteworthy that large, upwind, non-autonomous, grid-connected, wind-electric machines rarely use a boom-supported tailvane. Instead reliance is placed on servo-type, vane-controlled, electric-motor-driven yaw systems. Even in the large wind-electric machine field some manufacturers prefer free-yaw downwind systems thereby eliminating the need for a yaw-control mechanism which, amongst other components, normally requires a large-diameter ring-gear attached to the tower top.

7.2.1. Folding Rotor and Variable-Pitch Blading

During the late nineteenth century and during the early part of this century a large number of small, downwind-type, water-pumping machines were produced in North America by several manufacturers. These machines were equipped with slatted, sectional-type rotors mostly of essentially timber construction (Baker, 1985).

Factors influencing the selection of sectional rotors have been studied previously, as reported in §7.1.1, in relation to upwind machines. Hence that discussion will not be repeated here. A machine of much more recent design features a multibladed downwind rotor with variable-pitch blades. This example was mentioned, and aspects of variable-pitch blading were discussed, in §7.1.6; hence there is also no need to repeat that material.

The incentives to use folding rotors or variable-pitch blades were formerly much greater due to the lack of alternatives, when downwind rotors were considered than was the case for upwind units where there are several well-known, practical, alternative control strategies available. However, quite recently a relatively simple, canard-type, tilting vane furling system has been applied, successfully, to a downwind configuration of the rigid rotor type. A side view of this machine is presented in Fig. 6.2.

7.2.2. Canard Flap

The downwind configuration shown in Fig. 6.2 features a rigid Mark 3 delta-turbine rotor with furling controlled by means of a single upwind wing, or canard, surface. The canard surface, or foreplane, is, during normal operation of the machine, inclined slightly to a horizontal position such that some aerodynamic lift is generated but little drag. Hence the canard generates only a small wake. When the wind speed reaches the furling value the canard, which is pivoted, close to the trailing edge, to the forward-directed canard support boom, generates sufficient aerodynamic lift to swing into an essentially vertical plane.

Due to the geometry of the installation, on the machine, a plan view of which is presented in Fig. 7.7, the essentially vertical canard surface has the effect of causing a yawing movement such that the turbine takes up a stable position substantially edgewise to the wind direction. This, therefore, stops the rotor.

Once parked in the furled position it has been shown, from wind-tunnel tests of a model system, that the wind speed must drop to about 60% of the furling value before the machine will unfurl and resume normal operation. It can be seen, from the enlarged portion of Fig. 7.7, that the canard surface is canted, spanwise, such that the tip closest to the rotor is a little lower than the opposite tip. This vectors the canard lift such that the drag asymmetry of the system is cancelled out by the lateral component of lift resulting in the turbine axis, viewed in plan, aligning with the wind direction.

It was found, from wind-tunnel tests of the model, that a damper was required to restrict the rapidity of both the raising and lowering of the canard surface. This had the important effect of reducing, very substantially, the rate of precession of the machine during both furling and unfurling. It also prevented the canard returning, prematurely, to the running position during any transient overshooting, or deflection, beyond the stable, furled, position of the machine.

The dampers of the prototype machines, which employed turbines of 2.44 m diameter, were automotive shock absorbers. The pull-out system serves to elevate the canard surface from the running to the furled position by means of a simple cable. This also allows the operation of the dampers to be verified, from ground level on a calm day, by noting the time required to raise the canard when subjected to a prescribed load and, subsequently, the time required for it to return to the run position when the pull-out is released. More details of this downwind machine, including performance data, are available (Kentfield, 1992(b)).

7.3. Additional Considerations

It should be noted that there is a preferred direction of turbine-rotor rotation for all edgewise-furling systems. The preferred rotational direction serves to minimise the gross bending moment on the turbine rotor shaft during furling. This is accomplished by setting the gyroscopic moment in opposition to that acting on the turbine shaft due to gravity. This consideration leads to the conclusion that for a furling movement in a clockwise direction, when viewed from above, the turbine rotor should be arranged to rotate in a clockwise direction when the upwind face is viewed by an observer looking downwind. Similarly for a machine designed for an anti-clockwise furling motion the preferred direction of rotation of the turbine rotor is also anti-clockwise.

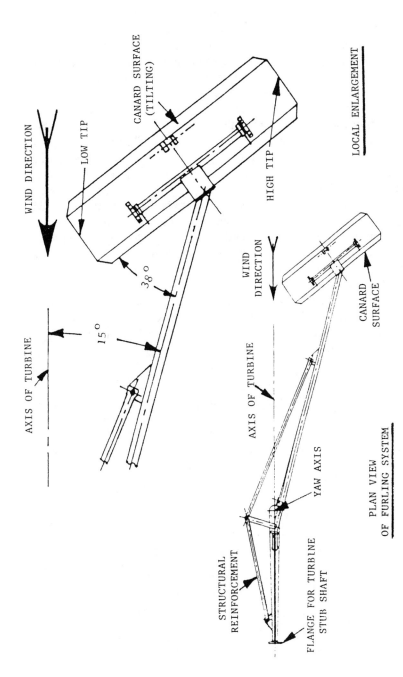

WIND DIRECTION

CANARD SURFACE
(TILTING)

LOW TIP

HIGH TIP

38°

15°

AXIS OF TURBINE

LOCAL ENLARGEMENT

WIND
DIRECTION

CANARD
SURFACE

AXIS OF TURBINE

YAW AXIS

STRUCTURAL
REINFORCEMENT

FLANGE FOR TURBINE
STUB SHAFT

PLAN VIEW
OF FURLING SYSTEM

Figure 7.7. Plan view of canard furling vane of machine illustrated in Fig. 6.2.

In each case the gyroscopic moment is additive to the gravitational moment during unfurling. However, unfurling occurs at a lower wind speed than that for furling and, furthermore, the rotor is normally not rotating at the commencement of the unfurling process. Thus unfurling is perceived as a generally less demanding process than furling and hence one that gives rise to smaller gyroscopic moments.

Many, but not all, wind-pumps incorporate a rotor-brake that is activated only by the act of furling the machine. In the writer's view this refinement is desirable but not one that is essential. The spokes of a furled rotor can always be tied to the tower structure before maintenance work is undertaken. This will ensure that the turbine cannot rotate. For brakeless machines shut down for extended periods, say a winter shutdown in regions with very cold climates, the pump transmission can be disconnected, at ground level, after furling the unit. This will ensure that water cannot be brought to the surface, where it can freeze, due to repeated small movements of, say, a reciprocating pump due to oscillation, or very slow turning of the turbine rotor.

Descriptions are available of a centrifugal-governor-actuated turbine rotor speed controller and also a specialized, countermass-actuated, gravity type furling system (Kentfield, 1980). Neither of these items are described in this chapter since they are both of rather a specialized nature.

CHAPTER 8

Pumps

The choice of pump type can influence radically the remainder of the design of a wind water pumper. For example, the transmission requirements are very different for rotary versus reciprocating pumps. The pump type selected will also influence, strongly, the type of turbine rotor employed. For example, the selection of a perimeter-bladed rotor can often be justified if a traditional reciprocating pump is used but not if the pump is of the high-speed rotor-dynamic, or turbo, type.

The rate of work input into an ideal, loss free, pump, $\dot{W}_{IDEAL}$, is given by:

$$\dot{W}_{IDEAL} = \Delta P \dot{Q} \qquad (8.1)$$

where ΔP is the pressure differential corresponding to the lift h and $\dot{Q}$ is the flow rate of water, or indeed oil or other incompressible fluid, delivered. The pressure differential ΔP is expressed more conveniently in terms of the head, or lift of the pump, a variable that must be known in order to proceed further.

With reference to Fig. 8.1(a) where z is a vertically upward directed coordinate and ρ_L is the invariant liquid density:

$$\delta P = \rho_L g(Z - z - \delta z) - \rho_L g(Z - z)$$

thus:

$$dP/dz = -\rho_L g$$

or, since $h = Z - z$ where h is a depth coordinate:

$$dh = -dz$$

hence:

$$dP/dh = \rho_L g$$

and thus integrating between stations 1 and 2:

$$\int_1^2 dP = \rho_L g \int_1^2 dh$$

Thus:

$$P_2 - P_1 = \rho_L g (h_2 - h_1) \tag{8.2}$$

It is, perhaps, worth noting that the same results can also be established from Bernoulli's equation, keeping in mind the relationship between z and h, when the flow velocities are equal at stations 1 and 2.

When station 1 is located at the pump delivery level and station 2 at the level of the water table, $h_1 = 0$ and h_2 can be identified simply as h the depth of the water table below the pump delivery point and hence the required pump lift. Also noting that $P_2 - P_1$ is identified as ΔP substitution in equation (8.2) gives:

$$\Delta P = \rho_L g h \tag{8.3}$$

Substitution in equation (8.1) from (8.3) gives an expression for $\dot{W}_{IDEAL}$ in terms of the pump lift h:

$$\dot{W}_{IDEAL} = \rho_L g h \dot{Q} \tag{8.4}$$

When account is taken of losses in the pump and associated system the actual rate of work input to the pump, $\dot{W}$, is given by:

$$\dot{W} = \rho_L g h \dot{Q} / \eta \tag{8.5}$$

where η is termed the pump efficiency.

The pump efficiency, η, takes into account the additional work input required to overcome flow entry and exit losses, any other fluid-flow pressure losses within the pump due to, say, internal leakage or fluid friction, mechanical friction, fluid-flow pressure losses in the riser main and the irrecoverable, usually small, kinetic energy given to the fluid to maintain flow through the system. Additionally, if the hydraulic work actually done by the pump is expressed as a fraction of the work input to the pump as deduced from knowledge of the turbine shaft-power output then η also takes into account the pump-drive transmission losses.

Yet another factor that can have an apparent influence on pump efficiency is the draw-down of the water-table level in the vicinity of the pump due to pumping action. In reality this should be accounted for by using a value of h larger than the nominal value based only on the vertical distance between the undisturbed level of the water table and that of the pump delivery. However, if the draw-down is not known, and is not allowed for by using an appropriately adjusted value of h, then by implication the pump is debited with the additional work required to raise the water (or the pumped liquid) by the increment Δh shown in Fig. 8.1(b). Clearly the latter situation is "unfair" to the pump designer since the draw-down is a property of the permeability of the ground and does not represent a deficiency of the pump system due to poor design or some other defect. In some circumstances, for example, when the water source is a river or lake, the draw-down is usually negligible. When the pump lift, h, is very small the otherwise insignificant additional elevation of the pump delivery above the level at which the water will be utilised can constitute a significant, but perhaps unavoidable, loss of potential performance for a pumping system.

Another parameter of relevance to the performance of positive-displacement pumps is the volumetric efficiency, η_V. This simply expresses the actual flow rate, $\dot{Q}$, divided by the theoretical value, $\dot{Q}_T$, based on the nominal swept volume of the pump and the operational speed or frequency, ie.,

$$\eta_V = \dot{Q}/\dot{Q}_T \tag{8.6}$$

It might be expected that due, in particular, to inflow pressure losses η_V would always be less than unity. In practice η_V can vary from zero for the slow-speed operation of positive-displacement pumps with very high internal, or short-circuit, leakages to values slightly greater than unity when favourable dynamic influences are active in pumps with negligible internal leakages. Substituting, for positive-displacement pumps, from equation (8.6) in equation (8.5):

$$\dot{W} = \rho_L gh\eta_V \dot{Q}_T/\eta \tag{8.7}$$

It can be seen from equation (8.7) that for pumps in which the ratio η_V/η is invariant $\dot{W}$ is directly proportional to the rotational speed, or frequency, of the pump. However the power output of a wind-turbine operating at a prescribed power coefficient is directly proportional to the cube of the wind speed whilst the corresponding tip-speed ratio is invariant implying that the turbine rotor speed is directly proportional to the wind speed. This conclusion can be confirmed from equation (2.8), the

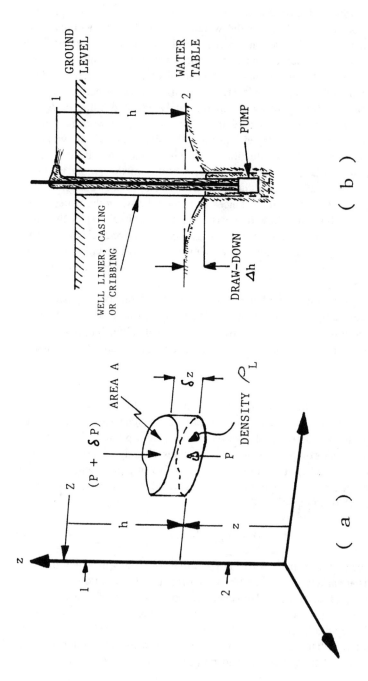

Figure 8.1. Well fundamentals: a) derivation of pressure, depth and lift relationships; b) illustration of water table draw-down.

definition of the power coefficient, in conjunction with the inspection of a typical turbine performance characteristic, say, that presented in Fig. 5.18.

This shows that if, for example, at a prescribed wind speed the load on a turbine, due to a pump with invariant η_V/η, is such that the turbine driving it is operating at peak power coefficient an increase in the wind speed will also cause the turbine tip-speed ratio to increase. This will result in a reduction in the power coefficient hence reducing the fraction of the available energy that can be converted into useful pumping work. If, on the other hand, the wind speed were to drop below that corresponding to operation at the maximum power coefficient the tip-speed ratio would be reduced, as would the power coefficient until, finally, the turbine stops. The wind speed at which that occurs represents the minimum operational wind speed of the system. This may be equal to, but is often less than, the wind speed required to start the machine from rest. The latter is termed the cut-in wind speed.

One inherent problem with general water-pumping applications is that a broad range of pump sizes is required for a prescribed wind-turbine prime mover. This situation is due to the wide range of depths from which water must be raised. Generally the value of h will be uniquely related to the proposed pumping site and, as can be seen from equation (8.5), $\dot{Q}$ is inversely proportional to h for a given pump efficiency. Furthermore the required water flow rate depends upon both the needs of the user and a maximum flow rate that the well can supply without sustaining damage. In practice many manufacturers offer a range of, say, four machine sizes in conjunction with a large range of pump throughputs thereby covering most situations. In many cases the pump is not manufactured by the same company that builds the remainder of the wind water pumper.

For some types of pump, for example, rotor-dynamic pumps and those based on the so-called progressive-cavity principle, the input torque is fairly uniform for one complete rotation of the pump drive shaft. This is not, however, true for traditional, single-cylinder, reciprocating lift pumps commonly employed on wind water pumpers, without the use of some other artifact to serve, specifically, as a torque-smoothing device.

8.1. Reciprocating Pumps

Reciprocating lift pumps are the type most commonly used, currently, on wind water pumpers. They have the advantage of being able to achieve a high pump efficiency, usually in the range of 70% to 80% inclusive of riser-main and transmission losses, but exclusive of draw-down effects, over a wide speed range. Generally the lower efficiency value is associated with low lifts, less than about 2 m. Reciprocating pumps also have the advantage of great mechanical simplicity and are relatively easily maintained in the field. The piston, or plunger, seal is usually in the form of a thick-walled, flexible, leather cup, or bucket. In some cases a more durable, and modern, material than leather is employed. A replacement leather plunger-bucket can usually be made locally, even in rural areas, as can leather, or rubber-canvas, valve discs. Provided the bore of the riser main, to the lower end of which the pump cylinder barrel is attached, is greater than that of the pump cylinder the pump plunger can be withdrawn for servicing, complete with the pump delivery valve, by means of the pull, or sucker, rod. In some deep-well pumps the pump head, containing the inlet valve, is also removeable through the riser main. An illustration of a pump of this latter type is available elsewhere (Fraenkel et al., 1993). Yet another possibility is to make the entire pump removeable, as a complete unit, through the bore of the riser main. An arrangement of this type makes pump servicing easier at the expense of a larger-diameter riser, and hence also well casing, than would otherwise be needed. For complete servicing of the pump it is normally necessary to extract it from the well by means of withdrawing, and dismantling in sections, the riser main. Pump cylinders, or barrels, are usually of bronze or stainless steel or at least have liners of these materials. In some cases plastic, or plastic-lined, barrels are employed. The component normally subject to the greatest wear rate is the soft, water-lubricated, plunger seal. Because of this frequently two, or more, plunger seals are arranged in series.

The lower portion of Fig. 8.2 shows, in cross-section, a simple lift-type pump. This unit, provided with only a single piston-sealing cup, is intended for fairly low-lift applications. Each valve is arranged in the form of a thick, annular disc cut from canvas-reinforced rubber sheet in such a way that water can flow past both the inner and outer edges of each valve when in the open position. Accordingly the valves are provided with both an inner and an outer seat-ring. All the seat rings are very narrow. This ensures that only a small pressure differential is needed to open a valve since the area subjected to back pressure, tending to retain the valve in the seated position, is only slightly greater than that on the opposite face tending to open the valve. The faces of the metal seat-rings, whilst narrow, are radiused to minimise any tendency to cut the rubber ~ canvas valves. In some pumps, particularly those intended for high lifts, ball-type non-return valves are employed. It is important that the maximum lift of ball-type non-return valves be restricted to approximately 1/4 to 1/3 of the diameter of the adjacent valve port. This ensures prompt reseating of the valve when the flow is reversed but does not throttle the flow significantly when the valve is open.

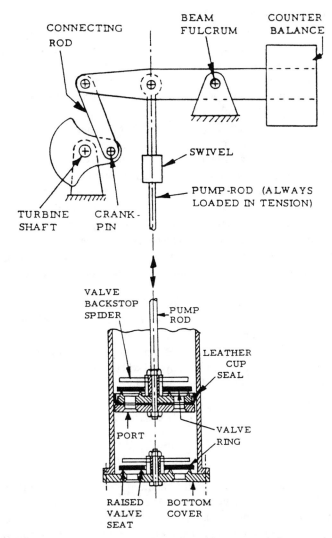

Figure 8.2. A simple reciprocating pump with a counter-balance-equipped drive.

The pump-rod of a reciprocating pump must always be loaded in tension since it is, for all practical purposes, too long and slender to accept compression loads without buckling. Hence it is normal practice to rely upon gravity to return the pump plunger on the downward stroke. The resultant imbalance on the wind-turbine mechanism, giving rise to a very uneven torque load on the turbine, can be overcome, at least in part, in three ways. One method is to employ a significantly buoyant pump-rod of wood or sealed, joined, metal tubes. However this technique is, in a sense, counter-productive with respect to the downward movement of the plunger since the buoyancy force serves to oppose that due to gravity although it clearly assists the upward, pumping, stroke. A second alternative is to utilise strong springs to pull upward on the upper end of the pump-rod. A third alternative, preferred by the writer, is to employ a counter-mass.

An arrangement incorporating a counter-mass is shown in the upper portion of Fig. 8.2. Because the maximum permissible acceleration of the pump-rod is low the acceleration and deceleration of the counter-mass does not constitute a problem even at the highest speed of the machine. The counter-mass should, ideally, balance all the mechanical load, less the small pump-rod and plunger inherent buoyancy force, plus half the pumping load. The greatest significance of the counter-mass occurs at start-up where, it will be shown, it serves to reduce the cut-in wind speed by a nominal factor of $1/\sqrt{2}$ compared with that of the same unit without the counter-mass.

An evaluation of the cut-in wind speed of a wind water pumper equipped with a reciprocating pump can be made based on equating the work done on the pump during one pump cycle to that generated by the turbine at $\lambda \rightarrow 0$. Assuming a value of η at start-up, the work input, W_u, required to implement one pumping cycle, where A_{PUMP} is the area of the pump bore and ℓ is the stroke, is given by:

$$W_u = \Delta P\, A_{PUMP}\, \ell/\eta$$

hence:

$$W_u = \rho_L\, gh\, A_{PUMP}\, \ell/\eta \tag{8.8}$$

This can be equated, for a perfectly balanced system, to the work done by the turbine. Hence, where n_G is the gear ratio, the turbine completes n_G revolutions per pump cycle, and from the definition of the torque coefficient C_T, as presented in equation (2.9) adapted to a horizontal-axis rotor and also invoking equation (8.8) gives, for a steady wind situation:

$$(\rho_L gh A_{PUMP}\ell/\eta) = 2\pi \left\{ n_G C_{T(\lambda=0)}\rho_\infty U_\infty^2 \pi D^3/16 \right\}$$

Hence the steady, cut-in wind speed is:

$$U_\infty = \left\{ \frac{8\rho_L gh A_{PUMP}\ell}{\eta n_G C_{T(\lambda=0)}\rho_\infty \pi^2 D^3} \right\}^{1/2} \tag{8.9}$$

When no counter-balance mass is used then, to a first approximation, the pumping work has to be performed during only half of one complete cycle of the pump. Thus for such a case it can be shown that the corresponding relationship to equation (8.9) is:

$$U_\infty = \left\{ \frac{16\rho_L ghA_{PUMP}\ell}{\eta n_G C_{T(\lambda=0)}\rho_\infty \pi^2 D^3} \right\}^{1/2} \quad (8.10)$$

Comparison of equations (8.9) and (8.10) shows that by removing the counter-balance mass the cut-in wind speed is increased by a factor of $\sqrt{2}$ or, conversely, the cut-in wind speed is reduced by a factor of $1/\sqrt{2}$ by adding a counter-balance mass.

In practice it is very difficult to incorporate a counter-balance mass on a classically designed, geared machine because of the presence of the oil bath, pitman and mechanism cover. It is, however, easy to add a counter-balance mass to a direct drive, gearless arrangement as indicated in the upper portion of Fig. 8.2. At least one commercial machine employing an unusual, worm type reduction gear box uses a counter-balance mass mounted externally to the gear box. Worm-drive reduction gearing is not, normally, noted for achieving a high mechanical efficiency.

8.1.1. Inertia Problems

Whilst the problem of the imposition of a maximum pump-rod acceleration has been mentioned previously, elsewhere in addition to this chapter, it is not merely the important problem of the pump-plunger return stroke that is critical. A high pump-rod acceleration on the upward, or pumping, stroke can lead to very high dynamic loads within the hydraulic system and hence also in the pump-rod and the pump drive train. On the assumption of simple harmonic motion the nominal maximum, and minimum, pump-rod accelerations occur at the ends of the strokes and can be shown to have magnitudes of $\pm 2\ell\pi^2 f^2$, where f is the operational frequency of the pump. In terms of the turbine angular velocity, ω, the magnitudes of the maximum and minimum accelerations of the pump-rod are $\pm\ell\omega^2/(2n_G^2)$.

Since, on the most simple basis, it is only necessary, in order to avoid the risk of pump-rod buckling, for the modulus of the peak accelerations to be less than that due to gravity that condition corresponds to:

$$g \geq 2\ell\pi^2 f^2 \quad (8.11)$$

or

$$g \geq \ell\omega^2/(2n_G^2) \quad (8.12)$$

However, the derivations of (8.11) and (8.12) make no allowances for the action, during the plunger downstroke, of the hydraulic, flow pressure loss across the plunger-mounted delivery valve, mechanical friction within the pump and the pump-rod gland-seal (if any) and the buoyancy of the pump-plunger and pump-rod. Referring to practical results, presented in Fig. 8.3, in an attempt to establish the maximum safe value for the modulus of the pump-rod acceleration, or deceleration, it appears that it should not exceed $0.3g$; a safer practice is to try not to exceed half of this value, a feasible target on the basis of actual demonstrated performances.

8.1.2. Inflow and Outflow Losses

There are, due to the automatic inlet and outlet valves of reciprocating pumps, pressure losses caused by the flow through these valves. The valve pressure losses have the general effect of reducing pump efficiency. They can be minimised by arranging for the largest possible flow-passage areas and by bellmouthing the entries to unavoidable contractions in flow cross-sectional areas. The pump illustrated in the lower portion of Fig. 8.2 incorporates all these features. An attempt was also made, by employing narrow valve seats, to minimise the area differences between the upstream and downstream active faces of each valve to reduce to a minimum the overpressure required to precipitate valve opening. Generally valve pressure losses are relatively more significant with low-lift pumping than for applications involving high lifts.

Employing a large pump diameter in conjunction with a short stroke is a way of minimising valve-passage flow velocities. It can be shown that for a prescribed maximum pump-rod acceleration the average pump-plunger speed is proportional to $\sqrt{\ell}$, where ℓ is the pump stroke. Hence since the flow velocity through the valve ports is, in general, proportional to pump-plunger speed a short stroke can lead to a reduction in valve pressure losses. However there are three reasons why the selection of a very short pump stroke is not usually a good design choice.

A large bore pump with a short stroke is a configuration giving rise to large forces active on the machine during the pumping stroke. Also a large bore pump is generally more difficult to accommodate, due to the need for a correspondingly large-diameter well casing, particularly in deep wells, than an alternative pump of larger stroke and smaller bore. Lastly a short-stroke pump means that for a prescribed stress level in the pump-rod the elastic stretching of the pump-rod can become a significant proportion of the nominal stroke in short-stroke systems applied to deep wells. As an example, with a small pump-stroke of 50 mm ($\simeq$ 2 in) and with a realistic pump-rod stress level of 35 MPa ($\simeq 2.5t/\text{in}^2$) the elastic stretch

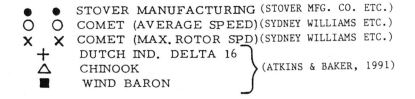

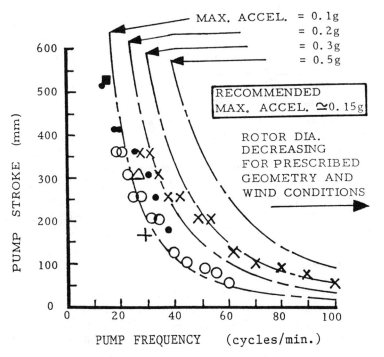

Figure 8.3. Pump-stroke versus pump frequency with parameters of constant acceleration.

of a mild-steel pump-rod will equal half the stroke at a lift, h, of about 130 m ($\simeq 430'$).

8.1.3. Pump Unloading

The Netherlands-based CWD organisation, described previously in §4 of Chapter 5, carried out development work on reciprocating pumps with the objective of obtaining easier start-up conditions, by means of load reduction, for their specially designed, relatively light-weight, low-solidity, turbine rotors. A general characteristic of the CWD rotors was a relatively low torque coefficient at low tip-speed ratios as indicated in Fig. 5.2.1.

Two approaches were studied both theoretically and experimentally. The first involved incorporating a small, deliberately created, bypass or "short-circuit" leakage passage drilled through the pump plunger. The purpose of this was to allow the turbine to commence rotation, and hence build up a sufficiently high tip-speed ratio corresponding to a high torque coefficient, before significant water delivery occurred.

The second approach focussed on an alternative, and more sophisticated, development of a pump incorporating a floating, or buoyant, delivery valve. The aim was similar to that of the pump bypass approach, by allowing the turbine rotor to achieve, in the substantially unloaded state, a speed sufficient for pumping to occur before the floating delivery valve commenced to work in the manner of a conventional delivery valve.

Due, essentially, to the floating valve being closed even earlier in the pumping stroke as the turbine speed increased the transition from operation with the floating delivery-valve permanently fully open to a mode of operation corresponding to that of a conventional pump-delivery valve was a smooth function of increasing turbine speed. The CWD experiments, and analysis, showed that both systems worked in the intended manner with the best results being obtained from the floating delivery-valve arrangement (Cleijne et al., 1986).

8.1.4. Flow Control

For water-pumping turbines delivering into a reservoir of finite capacity, a means, preferably automatic, is required to prevent over-filling and spillage. There are a number of possibilities. One is, for example, to employ a float system to furl the turbine when the reservoir becomes filled. However solutions of this kind tend to be complicated. An ingenious and very simple procedure adopted by at least one commercial manufacturer is to return the excess water back to the well via the annular gap between the outer surface of the riser pipe and the inner surface of the well casing. An arrangement of this type is illustrated, diagrammatically, in Fig. 8.4(a). Care should be taken to ensure, by the use of flow restrictors if need be, that the returning water does not damage the well and that contamination is not transported back into the water if it is for drinking purposes. The latter consideration should not prove to be a problem under normal operating conditions but care will be needed with this, or any other, potable water system when the well is opened for pump withdrawal and servicing.

Another restriction is that the water flow rate must not exceed some permissible maximum value without risking damage to the well and pump

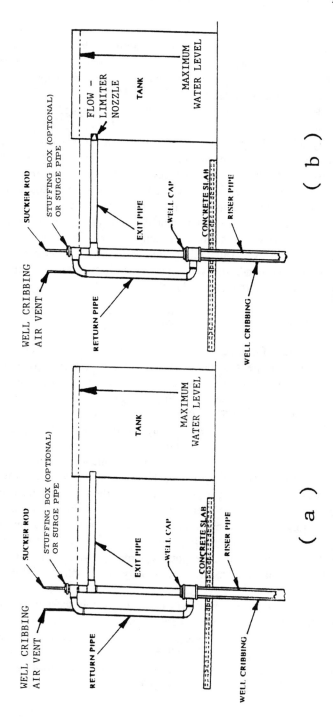

Figure 8.4. Water-return system of Dutch Industries Ltd.: a) basic arrangement; b) with a maximum flow rate control orifice.

by drawing silt into the pump and, alternatively or additionally, running the well dry and subsequently damaging the pump due to dry operation. It is fairly conventional practice to meet the well maximum flow rate restriction by adjusting, appropriately, the turbine furling wind speed and also by selecting a suitably sized pump.

A simple alternative to adjusting the furling wind speed, etc., is to provide, in a system of the type shown in Fig. 8.4(a) a throttle, such as a carefully adjusted valve or an orifice plate, in the discharge pipe communicating with the storage tank, or reservoir, as shown in Fig. 8.4(b). This will ensure, regardless of the water level in the storage system, that pumping at too great a rate to be sustained by the well will not occur since excess water will be returned, immediately, to the well. Another advantage of the restrictor concept is that the well can quite safely be equipped with a slightly over-sized wind pump without the attendent risk of well and pump damage. This will provide an increased water delivery rate under weak-wind conditions and hence assist in maintaining a more uniform water delivery rate than would otherwise be the case.

8.1.5. Test Data Using Reciprocating Pumps

Numerous sets of data from the field testing of various wind water pumpers have been obtained at the Alberta Renewable Energy Test Site (ARETS) currently located at Pincher Creek, formerly at Lethbridge, Alberta, Canada. Four sets of such data are presented in Figs. 8.5 to 8.8 inclusive. In each case the water lift, h, was 5.5 m. Because of the differing diameters of the turbines tested the pumping data are presented per unit of rotor-disc projected area. All the machines employed simple reciprocating pumps. The data of Figs. 8.5 and 8.6 are for systems with reduction gearing, those of Figs. 8.7 and 8.8 are for direct-drive machines. The performance shown in Fig. 8.8 was obtained using a pump exactly of the type illustrated in Fig. 8.2 driven by a perimeter-bladed turbine having a solidity, σ', of 0.34. The turbine rotors of the remaining machines were of the classical multi-bladed type with solidities, σ', ranging from approximately 0.6 to 0.8. In each case the monthly, cumulative, total volumes of water pumped are based on Rayleigh distributions of wind velocity and months of 30 days duration.

The ratio $1/\sigma'$ referred to in each figure caption is the number by which the ordinate values of the diagrams should be multiplied when the performances are to be expressed per unit of rotor-blade surface area rather than per unit of turbine disc projected area. The specific pumping performances based on rotor disc projected area are all relatively comparable with the best results being those of the Chinook 7.5 m diameter

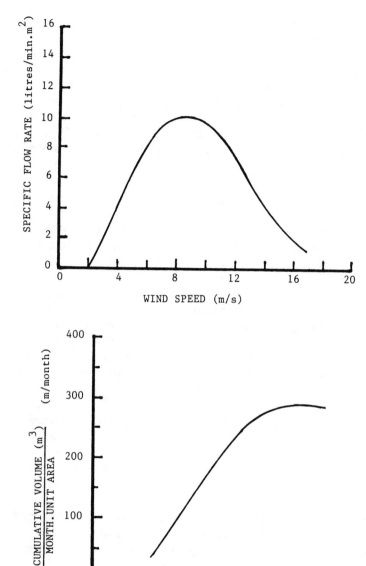

Figure 8.5. Aeromotor pumping performance. Geared reciprocating pump, gear ratio 3.29:1, rotor diameter 2.44 m, Pump bore 102 mm, stroke 185 mm, lift 5.5 m. From ARETS field-test data ($1/\sigma' \approx 1.3$).

machine the performance of which is presented in Fig. 8.7. When the ranking is based on the pumping performance per unit of rotor blade area the most effective machine is the Dutch Industries Delta 16, 4.88 m diameter, perimeter-bladed unit with the Chinook 7.5 m diameter wind water pumper in second place. It is noteworthy that for each of the ARETS-generated data sets the water-flow delivery rate was essentially directly proportional to the corresponding turbine rotor speed. This observation indicates that, to a first approximation, the volumetric efficiency of a well-designed reciprocating pump is a constant independent of the pump operating frequency.

8.2. Progressive-Cavity Pumps

Although the term "progressive-cavity pump" seems to be relatively new there is a class of pumps, suitable for incompressible fluids, that can be described, accurately by that umbrella term.

The commonalities between the various forms are:
   a) Cavities, such as a series of bucket-like containers or spaces of constant volume bounded by moving and fixed surfaces of the pump, conveying the liquid being pumped progressing from the inlet to the discharge end of the device.
   b) No valves as such are employed. Progressive-cavity pumps are designed in such a way that the boundaries of each progressing cavity substitute for the valves of traditional reciprocating pumps.
   c) The mechanical input motions are continuous with pseudo-continuous inflows and outflows of the pumped liquid.

The origin of the design of some forms of progressive-cavity pump appear to be lost in antiquity, for example, the scoop-wheel, in essence a reversed water wheel, and the Archimedean-screw pump, whilst other concepts are much newer. Because of the need for a continuous input motion progressive-cavity pumps require a power input delivered by a rotating shaft. This implies, therefore, a very different transmission system between the turbine and the pump to that used for reciprocating type pumps.

Only the most recently developed versions of the progressive-cavity type of pump, namely the Mono or Moyno pump, and also, possibly, the Imo pump are really suitable for deep-well pumping. The remaining versions can, however, be used effectively, in suitable circumstances, for relatively efficient low-head pumping duties. A possible exception are pumps of the external, or internal, gear-wheel type; these are also of the progressive-cavity class. Gear pumps can pump against a substantial

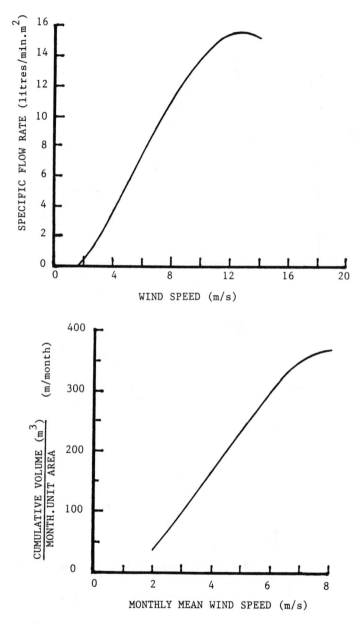

Figure 8.6. Wind Baron Softwind 21 pumping performance. Geared reciprocating pump, gear ratio 3.25:1, rotor diameter 6.4 m, pump bore 305 mm, stroke 518 mm, lift 5.5 m. From ARETS field-test data ($1/\sigma' \approx$ 1.3).

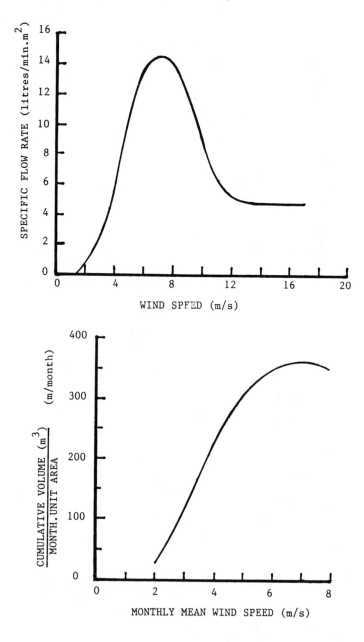

Figure 8.7. Pumping performance of Chinook 7.5 (derived from an IT power design). Direct drive non-geared reciprocating pump, rotor diameter, 7.5 m, pump bore 305 mm, stroke 305 mm, lift 5.5 m. From ARETS field-test data $(1/\sigma' \approx 1.7)$.

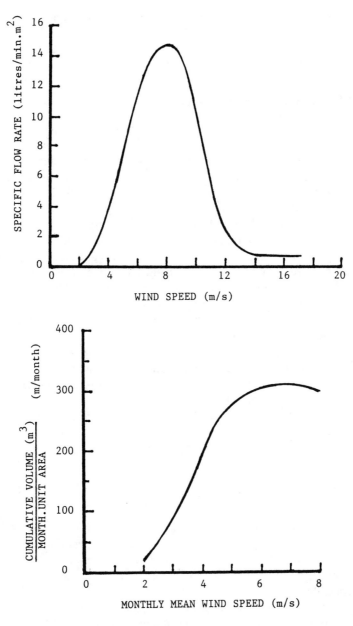

Figure 8.8. Dutch Delta 16 pumping performance. Direct drive non-geared reciprocating pump, rotor diameter 4.88 m, pump bore 264 mm, stroke 165 mm, lift 5.5 m. From ARETS field-test data $(1/\sigma' \approx 2.9)$.

pressure difference but, because of their external shape, are not suitable for most deep-well applications. However they can, in principle, be used in shallow wells, rivers or lakes, when a large lift is required, for example, to feed a tower-mounted storage tank.

8.2.1. Archimedean-Screw Pumps

An Archimedean-screw pump consists, essentially, of a single or multiple-start, coarse, screw thread cut on, or attached to, the outside of a relatively large-diameter core, the whole arranged inside a close-fitting tubular casing. The pump is installed with the axis inclined with the lower end submerged below the water level as indicated in Fig. 8.9. The submerged end of the pump constitutes the pump inlet; the pumped water is discharged from the raised end of the device. Pumping occurs when the Archimedean screw is rotated about the centre-line of the device in, for the arrangement depicted in Fig. 8.9, a clockwise direction when viewed by an observer looking into the discharge end of the pump.

It is essential that such a pump be inclined, which effectively inhibits deep-well applications, such that water fills only the lower sector of the apparatus. The depth of filling achieved is self-regulating since excess water flows back through the helix. Because of the self-regulating partial-filling property the upper sector of the tubular casing is not essential and can be removed without loss of pumping effectiveness. The active loss mechanisms are: water back-flow in the vicinity of the inlet, leakage between the outer edge of the helix and the lower portion of the tubular casing, mechanical friction mainly between the helix and the tubular casing and water carry-over on the wetted surfaces of the helix and core. The last two considerations in particular imply the desirability of a low operational speed.

8.2.2. "Conveyor-Belt" Pumps

A particular class of progressive-cavity pump employs what can be termed the "conveyor-belt" principle. There are many variants of this concept a couple of which will be discussed here. In "conveyor-belt" pumps the pumping action is due to a series of containers, attached to a chain, belt or rope, that each fill with water as they dip below the level of the water source and discharge the water at, or close to, the uppermost portion of their travel. Two pumps of this type are illustrated in Fig. 8.10(a) and (b). These concepts which, in common with the Archimedean-screw pump, are of great antiquity have been employed frequently in the past.

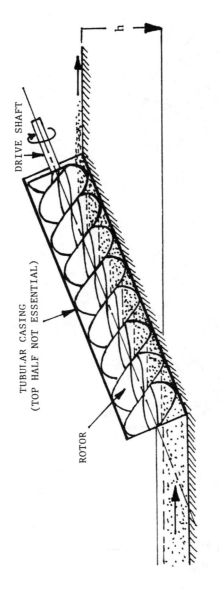

Figure 8.9. Archimedean-screw pump, diagrammatic.

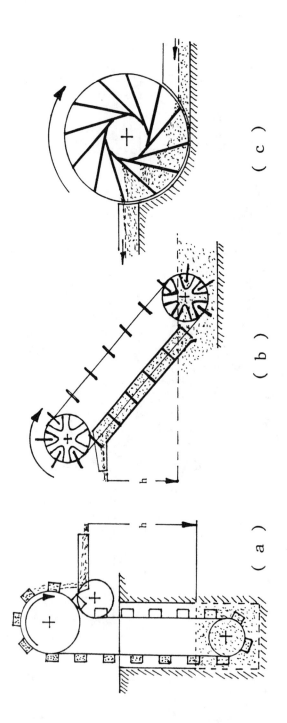

Figure 8.10. "Conveyor belt" style pumps: a) bucket-chain system; b) discs-on-chain system; c) scoop-wheel.

The device shown, diagrammatically, in Fig. 8.10(a) is currently incorporated in some hand-, and foot-, driven low-lift pumps but could, of course, be wind-driven if need be. It would appear that, in order to minimise losses during both filling and emptying, a low operating speed is desirable. A problem effectively inhibiting deep-well pumping uses is the large well-bore required. Nevertheless the device can be regarded as suitable for shallow, wide wells and for pumping from rivers and lakes suggesting irrigation-type applications. Since leakage is not a problem it would appear that a uniformly relatively high efficiency can be expected over a wide speed range provided the maximum speed is kept low.

The pump shown in Fig. 8.10(b) consists, essentially, of a series of disks, or pistons, attached to a rope, or chain, running over pulleys at each end of the pump. Pumps of this type have been employed in the past, in a vertical rather than an inclined form, as manually operated bilge-pumps for sailing ships. Fairly recently the aid organisation Volunteers in Technical Assistance, based in Arlington, Virginia, USA, developed a wind-driven irrigation pump, for use in Thailand, employing an inclined chain-and-disc-type pump. It would appear that filling losses should be less than for the pump of Fig. 8.10(a) thereby permitting efficient operation up to a higher chain speed. The inherent difficulties with this concept relate to leakage past the discs and also mechanical friction losses due to the discs sliding in the inducer tube.

Although not quite a "conveyor-belt" pump the simple scoop-wheel, Fig. 8.10(c), has seen much use in the past, in The Netherlands in particular, as a low-head, wind-turbine-driven, drainage pump. Pumps of the Archimedean-screw type have also been employed for such duties. Scoop-wheel losses are due, essentially, to the blades impacting the water at the entry side of the device, back leakage and carry-over much in the manner of the paddles of paddle-ships.

8.2.3. Rotary Positive-Displacement Pumps

Of the many types of pump that can be described as the rotary positive-displacement type it would appear that, so far, only two kinds have lent themselves to deep-well wind water-pumping. In both cases the pumps are of relatively small overall diameter, and hence cross-sectional area, in relation to the flow throughput area. In one application the pump was of the proprietary Imo meshing-rotor type which was used, at least experimentally, by an Australian manufacturer of wind water pumpers.

The Imo meshing rotor concept can be described, somewhat crudely, as in effect a twin, counter-rotating, rotor Archimedean-screw pump with the parallely mounted, meshing rotors each serving to block, mutually, the back-flow that would otherwise occur through the continuous helical flow path of each Archimedean screw. Because of this arrangement an Imo pump can be used in the vertical position with both rotors running full in contrast to the inclined, and only partially filled, single rotor of the Archimedean-screw pump described in §8.2.1. If an Imo pump is made with sufficiently small internal clearances it can sustain, with minimal internal leakage, pressure differentials typical of deep-well pumping. In some Imo type pumps more than two meshing rotors are employed. Normally Imo pumps involve close-clearance metal components and would therefore, it seems, be sensitive to grit entrained in the flowing fluid. The meshing, helical rotors of Imo pumps have, to ensure proper leakage-free engagement, male and female thread forms.

Another type of rotary positive-displacement pump that has been used with success in the wind water pumper field is the single rotor Mono or Moyno pump. This device, illustrated diagrammatically in Fig. 8.11, is usually identified in Europe by the first name and elsewhere by the second name. Pumps of this kind are manufactured by a number of companies. In this type of pump a metal rotor, somewhat reminiscent of a large corkscrew, runs in an elastomeric stator retained in a metal housing. The rotor is normally case hardened or, alternatively chromium plated to provide both a hard and corrosion-resistant surface.

In effect the rotor of a Mono or Moyno pump displaces, with a helical motion leading from the pump inlet to the outlet, water-filled cavities, or pockets, formed between the rotor and the stator surfaces. Hence instead of employing a continuous linear motion derived from a rotary input, as is the case for the system of Fig. 8.10(b), the Mono or Moyno type pump screws feature discrete pockets of water from the inlet to the outlet of the pump with the axis of the rotor making a resultant orbital motion as it rotates. This type of pump has a good reputation for durability earned, primarily, in the oil industry where devices of this type operating in reverse, using drilling mud as the working fluid, are sometimes employed as hydraulic turbines for driving drilling bits. The theory associated with the long durability with particulates suspended in the working fluid appears to be based on the hypothesis that particles that become indented in the elastomeric stator spring out, and return to the flow, without harm to either the rotor or stator, once the rotor/stator contact area has moved on.

Whilst Mono, or Moyno, pumps are ultra-simple from the mechanical viewpoint it is necessary, because of the flexibility of the stator, to load the rotor and stator components together by employing an interference fit to obtain substantially leak-free operation. This results in a high initial torque being required to overcome the static resistance due to the interference fit. Alternatively without an interference fit there is heavy internal, short-circuiting, leakage at start-up. In some cases this can be sufficient to result in a volumetric efficiency of zero, thus there is no delivery of fluid until a threshold pump-rotor speed has been exceeded. Normally multiple pump-stages are used, a stage being defined as the minimum length of rotor and stator needed to prevent direct communication occurring between the pump inlet and outlet. Hence even low-lift pumps are not likely to have less than one and a half stages. The number of stages required to minimise internal leakage increases with increasing pump delivery head.

It should be noted that because of the nature of the equipment involved it is not normally possible to repair, or recondition, in the field components of rotary pumps, component replacement being the only realistic possibility. However, a compensation is that the inertia problems of reciprocating pumps are removed permitting furling of the turbine driving a rotary pump to be postponed to a higher wind speed than would generally be acceptable for a classical reciprocating pump. This, therefore, permits rotary pumps to achieve greater maximum pumping rates than otherwise comparable reciprocating pumps.

The measured field performances of two Mono, or Moyno, pumps, each driven by a Mark 3 delta-turbine, are presented in Figs. 8.12 and 8.13. Figure 8.12 presents data, obtained at the ARETS facility, for a lift of 5.5 m. Hence this diagram can, therefore, be compared with the corresponding data presented in Figs. 8.5 to 8.8 inclusive for wind-driven reciprocating pumps. It was found, for the case presented in Fig. 8.12, that the water flow rate was, to a first approximation, directly proportional to the rotational speed of the driving turbine. This implied that the pump volumetric efficiency behaved in a similar manner to that of a reciprocating pump. Figure 8.13 was established for a lift of 15.25 m employing a pump with a relatively small internal interference. It can be seen that for that case the turbine rotation commenced at a lower wind speed than that required to initiate water delivery.

Whilst it can be shown that the peak combined pump and transmission efficiency for the case presented in Fig. 8.12, employing what appears to be a somewhat undersized pump, was approximately 0.8, it can be seen, from Fig. 8.13, that the maximum value applicable to the more appropriately sized pump with the relatively small internal interference was a little less than half that amount. Hence, because of the apparent sensitivity of Mono, or Moyno, pumps to the appropriate selection of the internal details of the pump, an irrelevant consideration for a reciprocating pump with normal leak-free valves and piston seals, it is suggested, in the absence of superior information, that, for system design purposes, it be assumed that the peak efficiency of a Mono, or Moyno, pump be taken as 0.6 in place of the 0.8

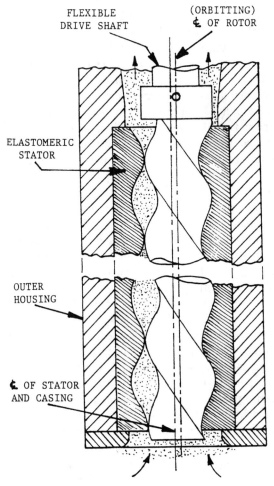

Figure 8.11. Diagrammatic illustration of a Mono or Moyno pumpconfiguration.

value recommended for reciprocating piston pumps. The choice of a 0.6
value is intended to provide a margin of conservatism.

8.3. Rotor-Dynamic Pumps

Rotor-dynamic pumps, usually of the centrifugal type, are sometimes employed in wind water pumpers. The most common applications are in

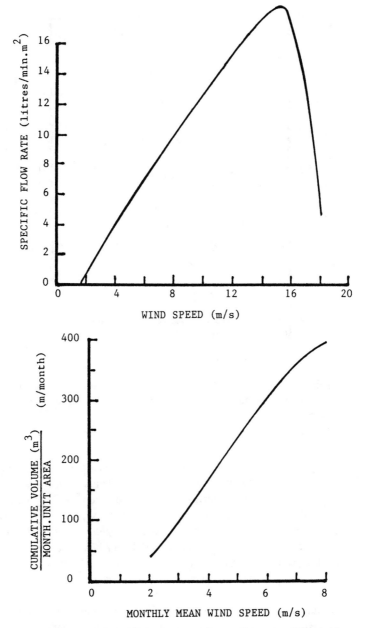

Figure 8.12. Maverick Windmotor pumping performance. Direct drive non-geared Mono or Moyno pump, rotor diameter 2.44 m, lift 5.5 m. From ARETS field-test data.

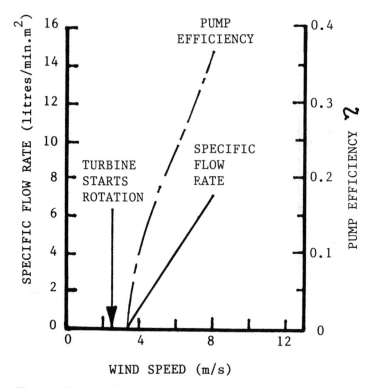

Figure 8.13. Maverick Windmotor preliminary pumping performance. Direct drive non-geared Mono or Moyno pump with small rotor-to-stator interference, lift 15.25 m.

conjunction with wind-electric pumping but at least one commercial machine, a low-lift drainage unit built in The Netherlands, employs a mechanically driven single-stage centrifugal pump. For deep-well applications it is usually necessary to provide more than a single stage in which case an appropriate number of centrifugal pumps are ganged together, in series, on a common shaft to generate the required delivery head. For wind-electric systems the pump is normally driven by a submerged electric motor upon the extended output shaft of which are mounted the series-connected pump rotors.

A major difference in pump performance characteristics between rotor-dynamic and, say, conventional positive-displacement pumps is that a rotor dynamic pump can be run stalled, that is, the rotor can rotate, and develop a corresponding head, with zero throughput. Essentially, because of this property, the throughput instead of being directly proportional to pump speed, as is the case for typical reciprocating pumps, increases, for a prescribed lift h, much faster than the rate of increase of rotor speed. Another major difference is that instead of the pump efficiency, η, being substantially independent of throughput for a prescribed delivery head, as is the case for most conventional reciprocating pumps, it is strongly dependent upon throughput.

Figure 8.14 attempts to illustrate these differences by means of a performance map typical of an efficient centrifugal pump. The values assigned to the efficiency contours show that the peak efficiency of approximately 85%, which occurs at about 65% of the maximum flow rate, is excellent. However the efficiency drops off substantially, for a prescribed value of h, as the flow rate is increased above, or reduced below, that corresponding to the maximum efficiency point resulting in an average efficiency of approximately 70%. The efficiencies shown in Fig. 8.14 do not include allowances for losses in the transmission, electrical or mechanical, connecting the wind-turbine to the pump.

The pump characteristics presented in Fig. 8.14 represent those of a pump with not only a well-designed rotor but also one incorporating an effective, radially disposed diffuser. For deep-well pumps, usually of the multi-stage type, somewhat lower efficiencies can be expected than those of Fig. 8.14 due to the usual need to restrict the outside diameter of the diffusers in order to allow the pump to be accommodated within the well casing or cribbing. Due to the relatively high rotational speeds involved erosion can also be a problem when gritty particulates are entrained in the pumped liquid. Advantage of rotor-dynamic pumps relative to other types of mechanical pumps are the absence of valves and the elimination of close fitting, and close tolerance, components. An additional advantage is that a wide range of components are mass-produced by a number of firms specialising in rotor-dynamic pumps. This makes it relatively easy to find components, or combinations of components, to suit a wide range of applications.

More detailed material on rotor-dynamic pumps in general, and the centrifugal type in particular, can be obtained from most works on fluid mechanics and from more specialised material, for example, the work of Gasch et al. (Gasch et al., 1987) and also that of Burton (Burton, 1988). Smulders et al. (Smulders et al., 1991) studied the feasibility of substituting a regenerative pump for a directly driven centrifugal pump in a wind water pumper and concluded that the main advantage related to a reduction in the speed-increasing gear ratio required.

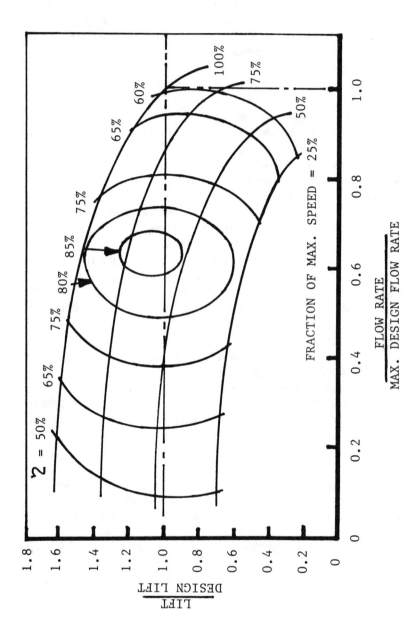

Figure 8.14. Performance characteristics of a typical centrifugal pump.

8.4. Air-Lift Pumps

In a simple air-lift pumping system the wind-turbine drives an air compressor which supplies an air-lift pump submerged in the well, or water source. Since a simple air-lift pump does not contain any moving parts an advantage is that all the moving parts of the system are above ground level and are easily accessible for servicing and maintenance. Because the wind-turbine-driven compressor is connected to the submerged air-lift pump only by means of a single compressed air hose it is, therefore, possible to locate the turbine/compressor unit remotely from the well site. Hence this feature may allow a turbine/compressor to be positioned in a superior wind regime, and also possibly more conveniently, than would otherwise be the case had it been confined to the well site.

The principle of a simple air-lift pump can be described with reference to Fig. 8.15 which show, diagrammatically, a typical installation. The essential requirement is that the hydrostatic head corresponding to the submergence, S_B, is equal to or slightly greater than, that due to the height $(S_B + \Delta h + h)$ of the eduction column. The eduction tube contains a mixture of air and water. Labelling the effective average density as ρ_M then:

$$\rho_L S_B \geq \rho_M (S_B + \Delta h + h) \qquad (8.13)$$

Hence it can be seen, from (8.13), that for frugal use of the air supply S_B must be a significant fraction of the total lift $(h + \Delta h)$.

It is fairly easy to show by analytical means that when fluid friction losses, etc., are ignored air-lift pumping is, given ideal isothermal compression, a loss-free process and hence is comparable with any other ideal water-pumping process. However it has been found in practice, as reported by Stepanoff (Stepanoff, 1966), that energy losses within the air-lift pump itself result in peak efficiencies of only 60%, or less, based on ideal isothermal compression of the air supplied to the pump. The loss mechanism is rather complex but it appears that, on the basis of flow visualisation experiments, a major contribution is a consequence of gravitational influences that tend to allow water to separate from the ascending flow in the eduction tube and run back down the tube inner wall only to become subsequently re-entrained and re-elevated. Experimental results reported by Stepanoff (Stepanoff, 1966) and Aziz et al. (Aziz et al., 1976) generally correlate with a slug-flow mode in the water/air column as indicated in Fig. 8.15.

A typical air-lift pump performance characteristic, based on the work of Stepanoff (Stepanoff, 1966), is presented in Fig. 8.16. It can be seen from that diagram that a water flow rate variation in the region of 3:1 is all that can be tolerated if the pump efficiency is not to fall below

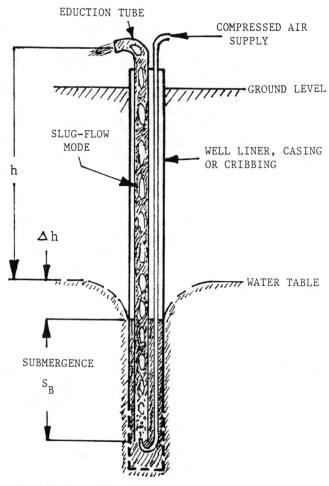

Figure 8.15. Diagrammatic illustration of an air-lift pump.

about 50%. The submergence is also another critical variable. For the data presented in Fig. 8.16 it has been shown (Stepanoff, 1966) that the optimum submergence, S_B, expressed as a percentage of the total lift, $(h + \Delta h)$, was 80%. More generally it has been found in practice that the optimum submergence as a fraction of the total lift is given by:

$$(1/2) \leq S_B/(h + \Delta h) \leq 1 \tag{8.14}$$

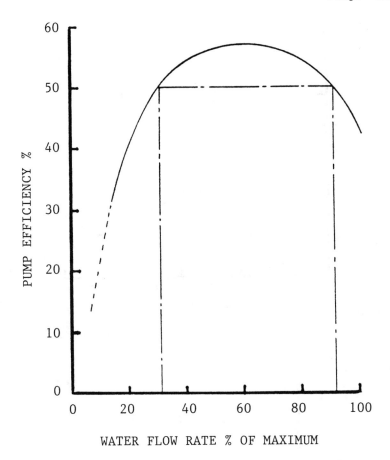

Figure 8.16. Typical performance characteristic of an air-lift pump.

the particular value depending upon details of the pump geometry, etc. Thus (8.14) confirms the comment made with respect to (8.13) relating to the magnitude of the submergence required. The need to bore the well substantially deeper than would be necessary for any other type of pump is a particular disadvantage of simple air-lift pumps.

In addition to the losses experienced in the air-lift pump itself account must also be taken of losses, due to irreversibilities, within the wind-turbine-driven air compressor. Assuming that a compressor isothermal efficiency of 80% can be achieved, a value representative of an efficient low-speed reciprocating compressor, the overall efficiency of air-lift pumping cannot, therefore, be expected to exceed about 40% or about half

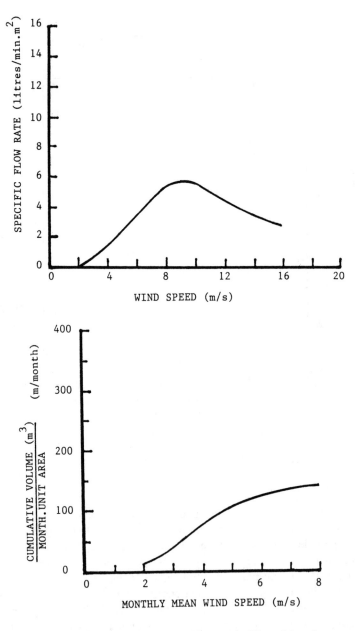

Figure 8.17. Praire PD8-6 pumping performance. Direct drive air compressor supplying an air-lift pump. Rotor diameter 2.24 m, lift 5.5 m. From ARETS field-test data.

that of a well-designed reciprocating pump. The pumping performance of a small air-lift system is presented in Fig. 8.17. From a comparison of these results with those of Figs. 8.5–8.8 inclusive it can be seen that the specific pumping performance of the air-lift system is, for equal lifts, about half that of positive-displacement reciprocating pumps.

The potential for obtaining a somewhat better overall pumping efficiency, perhaps up to 50–60%, using air-lift pumping can, it is hypothesised, be realised if the simple air-lift pump without moving parts is replaced by a more sophisticated, and complex, arrangement in which an air expander is employed to operate a hydraulic pump. A particular advantage of a simple air-lift pump is that it can be run dry without risk of damage. This is of particular advantage when pumping from a drainage sump where the ability to pump the sump dry is an asset. The wind-turbine-driven compressor unit of an air-lift pump can also be used to aerate lakes or rivers to improve water quality or for other purposes requiring compressed air.

Detailed analyses that can assist in obtaining a more detailed understanding of air-lift pumps and their oil industry counterparts, gaslift pumps, are available. Apazidis (Apazidis, 1985) presents a study of the functioning, and stability, of air-lift pumps. Lopes and Dukler (Lopes and Dukler, 1987) consider two-phase, gas/liquid, flows at high gas flow rates in vertical pipes.

CHAPTER 9

Variable-Delivery Pumps

As can be seen from the previous chapter, for example from Figs. 8.5–8.8 inclusive, most wind water pumpers cut-in, and hence commence to deliver water, at a wind speed of approximately 2 m/s. Also from the performance characteristics of a typical high-solidity turbine of the classical multibladed type, say those shown in Fig. 5.18, it can be seen that the torque coefficient, C_T, is essentially proportional to $(\lambda_{MAX} - \lambda)$. Furthermore it can also be seen that the peak power coefficient of the turbine occurs when λ is approximately half that of the runaway value corresponding, therefore, to a value of C_T of around half that at cut-in. Thus keeping in mind the relationship between torque and wind speed, U_∞, represented by equation (2.9) it becomes apparent that for the substantially constant torque load of a positive-displacement water pump with an invariant lift, h, the peak power coefficient occurs at a wind speed of about $\sqrt{2}$ times that at cut-in.

Hence for a 2 m/s cut-in wind speed the peak power coefficient is reached, typically, at a wind speed of less than 3 m/s! When the wind speed is twice the cut-in value, or 4 m/s, the torque coefficient has dropped to about 25% of the cut-in value and for a wind speed 4 times that at cut-in, ie., about 8 m/s, the torque coefficient is only 1/16 of the cut-in value and hence is almost negligible, implying that the turbine fast approaches the runaway condition with increasing wind speed. It is clear, therefore, that from the viewpoint of the utilisation of the energy available in the wind such a mode of operation is relatively inefficient. Further thought also reveals the sensitivity of the pumping rate to the choice of the cut-in wind speed. To a first approximation a turbine equipped with a pump sized for a 3 m/s cut-in wind speed can be expected to pump, over a significant wind-speed range, at nearly four times the rate achievable had the pump been sized to allow cut-in to occur at a wind speed of only 1.5 m/s.

If it were feasible to adjust the lift, h, of a positive-displacement pump in proportion to the square of the wind speed then the torque coefficient, and hence also the power coefficient and rotor tip-speed ratio, λ, would all remain invariant. An optimal choice of variables would, therefore, ensure that the power coefficient remained, over the effective operating wind-speed range, at the peak value and consequently the power input to the pump would always be the maximum possible. An application of wind water-pumping in which the optimum condition can be achieved quite easily is one in which the pump discharge is forced to flow through a nozzle of fixed exit area. For such a case the pressure rise due to the pump which, as can be confirmed by reference to equation (8.3) is directly proportional to lift h, will vary with the square of the flow velocity through the nozzle exit. The latter is, for a leak-free positive-displacement pump in particular, directly proportional to the pump speed, which for invariant λ is, in turn, directly proportional to the wind speed. At the fundamental level a wind-turbine-driven water-jet type marine propulsion unit constitutes a system of this kind at least for cases where the speed of the craft is low relative to the wind speed and the water is at rest. It is not, of course, essential to refer, specifically, to a jet-propulsion unit based on a positive-displacement pump. A system employing any other type of pump having suitable, comparable performance characteristics could be employed. A marine propeller geared to the wind-turbine is yet another possible version of the concept.

For most water-pumping situations the lift, h, is invariant and hence if operation at maximum C_P is to be sustained over a range of wind speeds another method must be found for adjusting the pump load, as a function of wind speed, to achieve this result. The possibilities are to employ pumps of variable capacity or to adjust, suitably, the speed of the pump relative to that of the wind-turbine. Generally, the introduction of a variable-speed drive between the turbine output shaft and the pump appears to be the most appropriate technique when rotary pumps are employed whereas the application of a variable-stroke mechanism is usually more convenient for reciprocating positive-displacement pumps. A variable-stroke pump is a single-cylinder, reciprocating pump having an adjustable swept volume or capacity.

9.1. Variable Speed-Ratio Concept

For a typical wind speed range of, say, 4:1 between cut-in and the commencement of furling, that is, between wind speeds of 2–3 m/s up to 8–12 m/s, then a speed ratio range of 4^2 (= 16) is the nominal requirement to permit C_P, C_T and λ to remain constant based on the assumption that the input torque to the pump remains invariant for a constant pump lift h. In fact a speed range of 16:1 is a very severe demand to impose upon a single continuously variable-ratio-drive mechanism. Two, typical, commercially available, variable-speed drives arranged in series could, no doubt, handle a 16:1 speed ratio range but this level of complexity seems hardly justifiable. Hence, if a variable speed-ratio drive is to be employed that makes use of a single, continuously variable-ratio, commercially available unit the user should be prepared to accept a realistic speed-ratio range of, say, 4 or 5:1, or possibly less. This will still be a speed-ratio range sufficient to yield a significant increase in pump output compared with a single direct-drive, invariant speed-ratio transmission, between the wind-turbine output shaft and the pump input shaft.

A critical aspect of any variable pump-delivery device, such as a variable speed-ratio mechanism, is the control technique employed. Clearly some form of electrical controller is a possibility. However for stand-alone, or isolated, systems an electrical controller can represent a reliability problem. For an isolated system with an electrical speed-ratio controller the controller would be battery powered. The battery would, in turn, be charged by means of an auxiliary generator driven by the wind-turbine. The reliability of such a control system is, therefore, largely dependent upon providing proper battery servicing and maintenance.

The battery maintenance requirement of an electrical control system can be eliminated if a simple hydro-mechanical controller is used. Figure 9.1(a) shows, diagrammatically, a simple system based on the supposition that the position of the continuously variable-ratio-drive mechanism control lever is directly proportional to the active speed ratio of the device. The system of Fig. 9.1(a) features a small, positive-displacement, hydraulic pump, driven by the wind-turbine, charging a hydraulic actuator cylinder. The hydraulic fluid leaves the cylinder by means of a nozzle and returns to the sump of the hydraulic circuit to be recirculated. The pressure drop across the nozzle equals that across the piston of the hydraulic actuator. When the controller is in equilibrium the force acting on the piston of the hydraulic actuator is balanced by that generated by the tension spring shown in the diagram. Alternately a compression spring located, for example, within the empty portion of the hydraulic cylinder can be substituted for the tension spring.

The control lever of the continuously variable-ratio-drive mechanism is connected to the rod-end connection of the hydraulic actuator. Under equilibrium conditions the displacement of the piston, and hence the

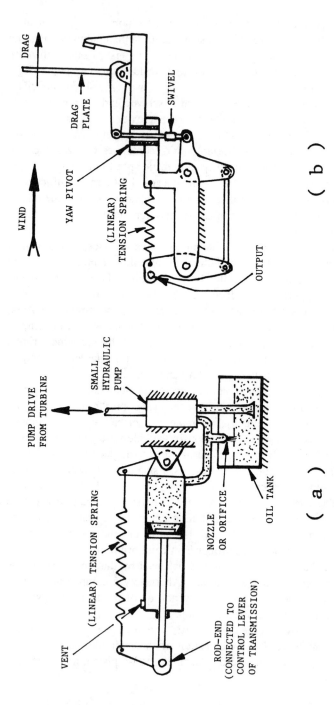

Figure 9.1. Non-electric controller systems (diagrammatic): a) hydro-mechanical system; b) aero-mechanical system.

rod-end connection, of the controller shown in Fig. 9.1(a) is directly proportional to the square of the turbine rotor speed. This is the condition
necessary to maintain constant C_P, C_T and λ as a consequence of mod-
ulating, appropriately, the water pump load and hence the torque reaction
to this acting on the turbine shaft.

Another version of the controller in which the hydraulic circuit is
eliminated is shown in Fig. 9.1(b). Here a drag plate is employed to
generate a force directly proportional to the square of the wind speed.
The system of Fig. 9.1(b) is functionally similar to that of Fig. 9.1(a) but
has the disadvantage that it does not monitor, directly, the turbine rotor
speed.

Since both the systems of Fig. 9.1 are of the force-balancing type
they have the disadvantage that at the equilibrium condition the net force
generated is zero. This implies that controllers of this type should be
constructed in a manner such that a relatively small displacement from
the equilibrium position gives rise to a large restoring force. The spring
employed in each of the systems shown in Fig. 9.1 ensures that a sudden
drop in wind speed results in the controller returning automatically, to the
minimum speed-increase-ratio position, the control lever of the continuously variable-ratio-drive mechanism. It would appear that the types of
rotary pump best suited to the use of a variable speed-ratio drive are of
the Mono, or Moyno, progressive-cavity kind since these will tolerate a
large range of operating speeds.

9.2. Variable-Stroke Reciprocating Pumps

Ideally the stroke range needed to cope with an operational wind-speed
range of 4:1 is 16:1 corresponding to the previously deduced speed range
for variable-speed pumps. The stroke-range ratio required ideally can
be accommodated quite easily by most variable-stroke mechanisms since
these can be designed for a minimum stroke of zero and hence the ratio
of the maximum-to-minimum stroke can, therefore, be infinite, if desired,
based on a finite maximum stroke. However a practical problem arises
with very high stroke ratios due to the relatively large pump-cylinder bore
required for a prescribed maximum pump-stroke. This, consequently,
gives rise to large pumping loads. Hence maximum-to-minimum stroke
ratios from, say, 4 to 8:1, are realistic practical limits for variable-stroke
mechanisms.

Usually, for reciprocating pumps, the variable-stroke mechanism is
located in the wind-turbine tower and hence the power input is normally
of a reciprocating nature. Variable-stroke mechanisms of the required
type usually have to be designed and fabricated especially for wind water

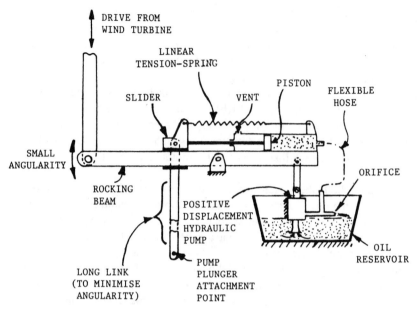

Figure 9.2. Ultra-simple variable-stroke mechanism due to Kennell (Kennell, 1984) (diagrammatic).

pumpers. Several systems have been built and tried in practice. One very simple arrangement employs the same controller shown in Fig. 9.1(a). This apparatus, due to Kennell (Kennell, 1984), is illustrated diagrammatically in Fig. 9.2. A weakness of Kennell's concept is that the comparatively large forces associated with the pumping action of the machine would tend to take charge of the slider and move it along the rocking beam. To inhibit such unwanted slider movements Kennell arranged for the maximum angularity of the rocking beam to be severely restricted and also a long link, to minimise angularity, was provided to connect the slider to the pump-rod.

   Another system, slightly more complex in nature, due to Avery (Avery, 1983) avoids the problem of unwanted movement of the slider unit by making ingenious use of a hydraulic cylinder not as an actuator but as a lock-up device to prevent unwanted movement of the slider. The principle involved in Avery's variable stroke mechanism is shown, diagrammatically, in Fig. 9.3. The Avery mechanism employs a control unit of the type shown in Fig. 9.1(b) to operate hydraulic valves that permit the piston of the hydraulic cylinder to move in one direction only, that

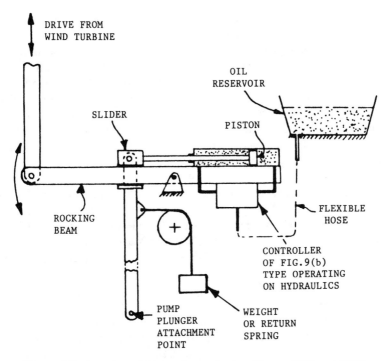

Figure 9.3. Avery's variable-stroke mechanism (Avery, 1983 and 1984) (diagrammatic).

required to adjust, correctly, the stroke, by blocking movement in the opposite direction. Forces generated due to pumping action are relied upon to move the slider along the rocking beam and therefore to adjust the pump stroke. When the optimum stroke has been achieved all the hydraulic valves actuated by the controller close to lock the piston of the hydraulic cylinder in a fixed position in the cylinder and, consequently, fix the position of the slider along the rocking beam.

Avery (Avery, 1984) carried out field testing of a classical multi-bladed Dempster 2.44 m (8′) diameter wind water pumper equipped with his variable-stroke mechanism which had a maximum-to-minimum stroke ratio of approximately 5.3:1. Compared with the performance of the same machine in a standard configuration, recommended by the manufacturer, the water flow rate at a wind speed of 3.6 m/s was unaltered whilst at a wind speed of 6 m/s the water flow rate was increased by about 50% due to employing the variable-stroke system. At wind speeds of 7, 8 and 9 m/s the flow rates were increased by approximately 96%, 144% and

141%, respectively, due to the use of the variable-stroke system. A wind speed of 9 m/s appeared to represent the furling condition of the machine.

On the basis of the stroke ratio employed the results obtained by Avery appear to be in line with expectations. A maximum water flow rate of 2.44 times that achieved without the variable-stroke mechanism is just under half the maximum-to-minimum pump swept-volume, or stroke, ratio of 5.3 implying a reduction of turbine rotor speed, due to the increased pumping load, of just over 50%. This, in turn, suggests that the turbine rotor speed settled at a tip-speed ratio a little less than that corresponding to the peak power coefficient, a situation quite close to the targeted operating condition.

Yet another variable-stroke mechanism prevents unwanted excursions of the pump-link slider by moving the slider by means of a leadscrew rather in the manner by which the saddle of lathe is moved along the lathe bed. In this system, originally developed for a very large water-pumping turbine of 16 m rotor diameter, the slider travels along a track on a rocking beam as indicated in Fig. 9.4.

The stroke-controller can be thought of as two interactive systems: a hydraulic signal generator, or control module, and a mechanical drive train, or actuator module, which serves to implement a load-pump stroke increase or decrease as appropriate. Whether a stroke increase or decrease is called for is "decided" within the control module. This in turn receives intelligence from the wind-turbine rotor. A tendency for the rotor to speed up, at a fixed wind speed, is interpreted as a need for a stroke increase; the opposite is the case for a decrease of rotor speed. A diagram representing the stroke controller as a control module interacting with an actuator module is presented in Fig. 9.5.

The contents of the control module/actuator containment shown in Fig. 9.4 is illustrated, diagrammatically, in detail in Fig. 9.6. A reciprocating input is provided, by the wind-turbine, to lever L2. This input movement drives the differential piston hydraulic pump H and also, via elements 1 and 2, actuates lever 3 which provides the power input to the actuator module, or drive train, portion of the stroke controller. The hydraulic pump H draws oil from the base of the containment (Fig. 9.4) and discharges it via an orifice, shown in Fig. 9.6, back into the sump in the containment. The pressure in the hydraulic circuit varies, therefore, as the square of the rotational speed of the wind-turbine. This pressure is communicated to the clutch actuator cylinder C of the actuator module. The tension spring, located above cylinder C and attached to lever 4 is arranged to be extended in direct proportion to the load-pump stroke by means of pulley P2 and winding drum D.

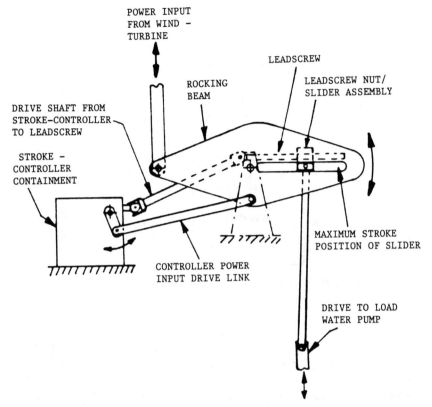

POWER INPUT
FROM WIND –
TURBINE

LEADSCREW

ROCKING
BEAM

LEADSCREW NUT/
SLIDER ASSEMBLY

DRIVE SHAFT FROM
STROKE–CONTROLLER
TO LEADSCREW

STROKE –
CONTROLLER
CONTAINMENT

CONTROLLER POWER
INPUT DRIVE LINK

MAXIMUM STROKE
POSITION OF SLIDER

DRIVE TO LOAD
WATER PUMP

Figure 9.4. Configuration of a screw-jack operated variable-stroke mechanism.

The clutch element Z is keyed to, but is free to slide axially on, input shaft 8. The input shaft 8 rotates, intermittently, in one direction only due to the sprag-clutch R incorporated in lever 3. Axial movement of Z engages either clutch element X or Y. When Z engages with X the stroke is increased: it is decreased when Z engages with Y. Pullies P1 and P3 and link 5 constitute a clutch override control to limit both the maximum and the minimum strokes of the load pump. The sprag clutch, labelled R, at the left-hand end of shaft 8 serves to prevent backward rotation of shaft 8. In fact it was found, from testing of a prototype model stroke-control system, that a small measure of backward rotation of shaft 8 was desirable in order to unload the clutch teeth. This facilitated easier and more precise operation of the clutch mechanism. The device provided to accomplish cyclic unloading of the clutch teeth is shown in Fig. 9.7.

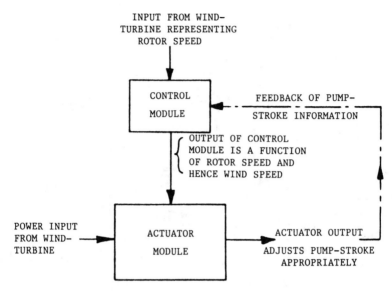

Figure 9.5. Diagrammatic illustration of the stroke-controller of Fig. 9.4 as a combination of a control and an actuator module.

The system illustrated in Figs. 9.4 to 9.7 inclusive was built in the form of a working model. No load pump was provided but a variable-speed electric motor was used to simulate the variable-speed wind-turbine power input source. A test result obtained from the model is presented in Fig. 9.8. The corresponding theoretical, predicted, performance curve is also shown. Subsequently a full-scale hydromechanical variable-stroke mechanism, of the same type was built and installed on the prototype 16 m diameter wind water pumper. Although the full-scale system was never tested over the full operational range it was, after some initial teething troubles had been overcome, operational when the full-scale wind-turbine performance test data presented in Fig. 5.27 were obtained yielding a very high system power coefficient of approximately 0.32. The system power coefficient is the product of the turbine power coefficient, C_P, multiplied by the pump efficiency, η. More details of this and other variable-stroke mechanisms are available elsewhere (Kentfield and Vardi, 1985(a), 1985(b)).

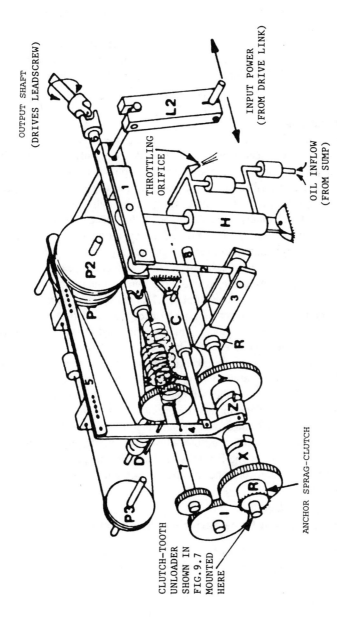

Figure 9.6. Diagrammatic representation of the contents of the stroke-controller containment of Fig. 9.4.

9.3. Variable-Delivery Air-Lift Compressors

The compressor of an air-lift pump can, of course, be made into a variable-delivery system by introducing either a variable-speed transmission or, for a dedicated special-purpose reciprocating compressor, arranging for a variable-stroke capability. There is, however, the additional possibility, for a multi-cylinder reciprocating compressor, of arranging to lift the inlet valves of some of the cylinders sequentially in such a way that the system starts up employing only a small number of cylinders due to the inlet valves being raised off their seats, and therefore rendered nonfunctional, on the remaining cylinders.

Examining this concept a little further, if a specially built compressor with, say, four cylinders is employed then at cut-in only two of the four cylinders will be used, these operating in antiphase, thereby eliminating the need for a countermass, or any other measure, to smooth torque peaks at start-up. As the wind speed increases the third cylinder can be brought into operation and finally, at a yet higher wind speed, the inlet valve of the fourth cylinder will be lowered into an operational position and that cylinder will commence to deliver compressed air. It is not necessary, or desirable, with such a compressor for all the cylinders to be of equal swept volume. It seems reasonable to make the two cylinders permanently on line small and of equal swept volumes. The next cylinder to come online would, ideally, have a swept volume greater than that of the combined swept volumes of the two small cylinders employed at start-up. The last cylinder to become operative would have the largest swept volume of all. In this way cognizance can be taken of the square law relationship, for a prescribed value of λ, between wind speed and turbine torque.

It seems likely that either of the controllers illustrated in Fig. 9.1 could be adapted to perform the compressor inlet-valve lifting function. In view of the rather limited operational range of an air-lift pump it may prove desirable to employ multiple, clustered, air-lift pumps with only one or two cylinders of the compressor delivering to each air-lift pump. Clustered air-lift pumps can be installed in a common well, or sump, if need be.

9.4. Consequences of Using Variable-Delivery Pumps

There are a number of consequences, some favourable others unfavourable, arising from the employment of variable-delivery pumps. The most obvious favourable result of a variable-delivery system is the much enhanced water flow rate. This benefit generally increases in magnitude with increasing wind speed. Clearly no advantage can be expected from a variable-delivery pump at the operating point, which normally occurs at a low wind

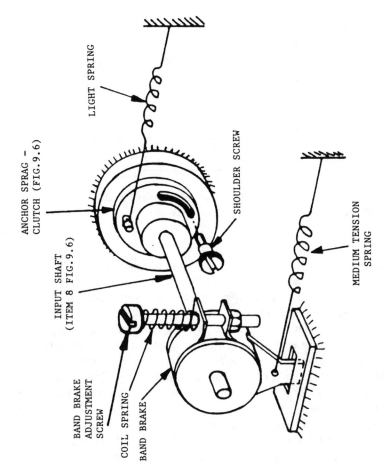

Figure 9.7. Clutch-tooth unloader incorporated in the mechanism shown in Fig. 9.6.

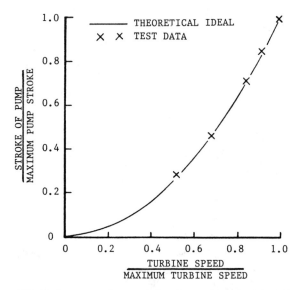

Figure 9.8. Performance characteristic of a working model of the variable-stroke mechanism of Figs. 9.4–9.7 inclusive.

speed, where the rotor power coefficient is a maximum of a corresponding machine not provided with a variable-delivery pump.

It is also inherently possible, at least with variable-stroke reciprocating pumps, to reduce the cut-in wind speed below that feasible for a conventional version of the machine. This is, however, a relatively minor advantage since the energy available is very small at low wind speeds. A benefit of academic interest, due to employing variable-delivery pumps, is the superior utilisation of the available wind energy. This is, however, of little practical interest to equipment operators concerned with plant cost-effectiveness.

An unfavourable aspect of the potential for an increased water delivery rate is that the water flow rate variation with wind speed is increased when a variable-delivery system is employed. This may, in some cases, imply a requirement for a larger storage capacity to cope with the relatively infrequent and irregular strong winds. A wind water pumper with a variable-delivery pump also implies that there is a greater risk of exceeding the permissible maximum flow rate when used in conjunction with a well as distinct from what can be regarded as an infinite water source such as a river or lake.

Because of the need for an increased pump bore when employing a variable-stroke reciprocating pump, due to the limitation on the maximum permissible pump-rod acceleration imposing, in turn, a limit on the maximum permissible stroke, an effective variable-stroke pump can create, when used in a narrow well an installational problem. It would appear that such installational problems are minimised when the pump used is a Mono or Moyno type, progressive-cavity, rotary unit driven via a variable speed-ratio transmission.

A variable-delivery pump implies additional complexity and first costs not only due to the speed, or stroke, control apparatus itself but also as a consequence of the increased loads acting on the wind water pumper, particularly in the drive train but also elsewhere, requiring that a stronger, and hence more costly, structure be employed. The likely severity of a structural strengthening requirement can be appreciated by means of an example involving a variable-stroke reciprocating pump the maximum stroke of which is here assumed to be prescribed due to a pump-rod maximum acceleration limitation. Since the use of a variable-stroke pump permits the quantity of water delivered per stroke to be increased relative to that of a conventional fixed-stroke pump then, due to the maximum stroke restriction, the additional water quantity must be accommodated by means of an enlargement of the bore of the pump cylinder. This will, therefore, increase proportionally the load in the pump-rod and drive train.

Since the quantity of water delivered per stroke of the pump could easily be increased, due to using a variable-stroke pump, say by a factor of 8, this also represents the magnitude of the increase in the pumping force to be handled by the wind water pumper leading to much larger transient forces not only in the transmission but also, for example, in the tower. One means suggested for minimising tower transient loadings due to pumping action is to hang the riser pipe from the tower top. This solution is only practical for installations with relatively short, light, riser pipes.

Actually, provided extreme confidence is placed in the combined reliability of the variable-stroke mechanism, pump and well water-supply, a longer stroke can be used with an operative variable-stroke system than with a conventional fixed-stroke pump. This is because the maximum speed of the turbine rotor is lower, using a variable-stroke pump, thereby permitting a longer stroke before exceeding the permissible maximum pump-rod acceleration. This can, therefore, help to alleviate the load increase problem.

9.5. An Alternative to a Variable-Delivery Pump

An alternative to an application of a variable-delivery pump is to employ more than one conventional wind water pumper operating in parallel. The use of multiple units as an alternative may, in many cases, be feasible since, as pointed out in §9.4, variable-delivery pumps are not, for various reasons, usually attractive for deep-well applications and for pumping from lakes or rivers multiple, conventional, wind water pumper installations are usually feasible. Two similar, conventional machines would provide the advantage of doubling the flow at low wind speeds, where each machine operates optimally, compared to the low-wind performance of a single unit provided with a variable-delivery pump. Thus the variation of the water flow rate with wind speed will be much less than that of a single unit provided with a variable-delivery pump.

If a greater water flow rate is needed from the two equally sized machines one unit can be provided with a larger pump delaying cut-in to a wind speed about 50% higher than that of the other. Typically the cut-in wind speeds would be, say, 2 m/s and 3 m/s. The latter unit will deliver approximately twice the flow rate of the former making the total flow rate about three times that of a single machine with a cut-in wind speed of 2 m/s. It will be necessary to increase the counter-mass, if any, of the unit with the 3 m/s cut-in to about twice that needed for a 2 m/s cut-in machine. Also the pump loads of the machine with the greater cut-in wind speed will be about twice those of the unit with the lower cut-in wind speed. Clearly other permutations are possible than those suggested here. Questions relating to the cost- effectiveness of a multiple array of machines compared with that of a more complicated machine equipped with a variable-stroke mechanism depend upon many factors related to scale of production, installational costs, etc. These topics are beyond the scope of the material covered here.

CHAPTER 10

Flapping Vane, Savonius and Drag-Type Machines

There are a number of types of wind-driven water pumpers not in common use but which offer the advantage of a particularly simple, easy to fabricate design. Three concepts in this category are described here. A disadvantage, in each case, is that these machines are not particularly efficient and hence they make relatively poor use of the materials, particularly with respect to blade surface area, from which they are fabricated. This factor is, however, of diminished importance for very small machines where material costs tend to be low compared with labor costs.

Ironically the most efficient of the three concepts, the Savonius rotor, presents the greatest difficulties with respect to the provision of storm protection. Only two of the three concepts dealt with can be described as turbines, in fact vertical-axis turbines, the remaining concept incorporates a non-rotating, oscillating system. The oscillating motion makes it particularly easy to couple a reciprocating pump to the machine without having to first convert from rotary to reciprocating motion. The oscillating, or flapping-vane, pumper is, due to the absence of a rotor, particularly easy to fabricate when only limited workshop facilities are available.

10.1. Flapping-Vane Pumpers

It appears that the original concept of a flapping-vane driven wind water pumper, or aeolian pumpjack, is due to an Argentinian, J. Albisú of Saladillo, Argentina (Anon, 1920). Albisú's machine, and subsequent machines of that type, featured a single lifting surface, sometimes in the form of a cloth-covered frame pivoted, aft of the centre-of-pressure, about

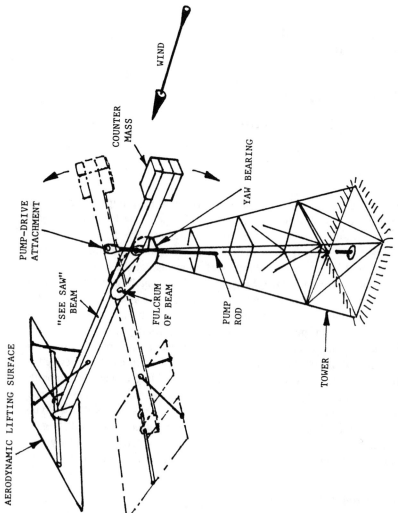

Figure 10.1. Diagrammatic illustration of a simple flapping-vane pumper or aeolian pumpjack.

a horizontal axis at the downwind end of a "see-saw"-like beam. During normal operation of the device the "see-saw" beam, which is supported on top of a tower and about the vertical axis of which it is free to yaw, is aligned such that the longitudinal axis of the beam lies on a vertical plane parallel to the wind direction. Since the pivot of the lifting surface is aft of the centre-of-pressure the lifting surface is, when balanced about the pivot and in the horizontal position parallel to the ground, unstable and if provided with a freedom to tilt can "flip" upwards or downwards. Stops, usually ropes secured to the leading edge of the lifting surface and also to the "see-saw" beam, limit the magnitude of the "flip" motion to, say, ±25°.

Thus during operation of the device if, for example, the downwind end of the "see-saw" beam is in the low position and, as a result, the lifting surface "flips", such that the leading edge is raised upwards at an angle of +25° relative to the beam, aerodynamic lift and drag forces are generated acting to raise the downwind end of the "see-saw" beam. When the downwind end of the beam has been raised sufficiently for the lifting surface to "flip" to the opposite position, that is to an angle of −25° relative to the beam, the downwind end of the beam is then driven downwards leading, ultimately, to a repetition of the cycle. It can be seen, therefore, that a system of this nature sets the beam into an oscillating motion with the inertia of the moving beam and attached components being relied upon to carry the lifting surface beyond the horizontal position, and hence initiate a "flip-over", at the end of each stroke. A pumping action can be achieved by connecting the oscillating beam, via a pump-rod, to a reciprocating pump located in a well, or sump, under the tower. A simple system of this type is illustrated, diagrammatically, in Fig. 10.1.

Further study of the cycle just described reveals that the positive, or negative lift force, assisted by drag, is of greatest magnitude immediately following a "flip" motion and then decays to essentially zero as the lifting surface approaches the horizontal position only to be maximised again, but acting in the opposite direction, after the subsequent "flip" and so on. A weakness of this system is that under low wind conditions a stoppage can occur when the aerodynamic forces acting on the lifting surface are insufficient to complete a stroke and the inertia of the system is consequently too small to initiate a "flip-over" of the lifting surface.

It was to overcome the problem of involuntary stoppages that a modified version of the machine was developed by the writer, at the University of Calgary. The solution adopted, whilst maintaining the inherent simplicity of the flapping-vane pumper, was not of particularly great efficiency. It involved attaching rigidly to the "see-saw", upwind of the beam pivot,

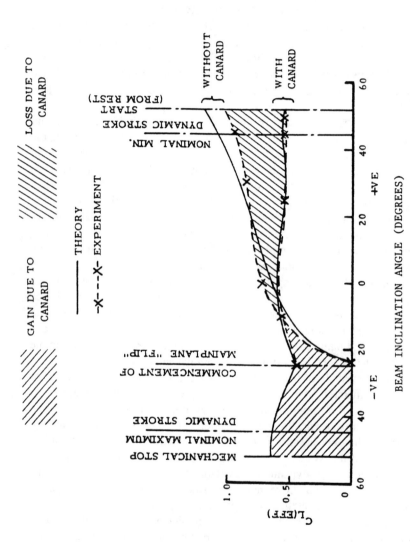

Figure 10.2. Effective lift coefficient of model canard-equipped flapping-vane pumper versus inclination of "see-saw" beam.

a small foreplane, or canard, aerodynamic surface. Whilst the canard sur-face opposes the motion due to the main, downwind, lifting surface at the commencement of a stroke it assists that motion towards the end of the stroke. The canard helps, therefore, to smooth out, and make relatively independent of the angle of inclination of the "see-saw" beam, the com-bined aerodynamic moment generated by the main and canard surfaces acting jointly.

The functioning of the canard is illustrated quantitatively in Fig. 10.2 for a 25° "flip" angle. The abscissa of the diagram represents the angle of inclination of the beam relative to the horizontal. The lift has been expressed in terms of an effective lift coefficient based on the planform area of the mainplane. The situation depicted in Fig. 10.2 refers to the "see-saw" beam starting from rest with the downwind end of the beam at the lowest position corresponding, for the particular case shown, to an inclination angle of the beam of +54°, with motion assumed to continue, without any further contribution from the mainplane, beyond the nominal mainplane flip angle of –25° until the beam reaches the opposite travel stop with the mainplane in the highest position at a beam inclination angle of –54°. Under normal operating conditions the beam does not contact the motion stops due to mainplane "flipping" having occurred sufficiently early to prevent this. Symmetry indicates that a similar, but reversed, diagram to Fig. 10.2 applies to the downwards movement of the mainplane. The experimental data added to Fig. 10.2 were obtained by means of wind-tunnel tests. The solid lines were based on individual airfoil characteristics also obtained experimentally.

Figure 10.3 shows the geometry found, on the basis of the wind-tunnel test data presented in Fig. 10.2, to be optimum for the canard-equipped machine. The airfoil surfaces of the model were made from thin corrugated sheet metal with, in order to simplify the structure, the corrugations running spanwise. This was shown, on the basis of other wind-tunnel tests, to have only a relatively small adverse influence on the performances of the nominally flat aerodynamic surfaces due, it seems, to their very low aspect ratios leading to significant regions of separated flow coupled with gentle stalling. The chordwise slot in the middle of the mainplane is to provide clearance for the single, central, oscillating beam.

The performance of a pump-equipped working, wind-tunnel model is shown in Fig. 10.4. It is noteworthy that once operation has com-menced the operating frequency is, in large measure, directly proportional to wind speed. A true linear relationship between operating frequency and wind speed is to be expected, and was demonstrated experimentally, with the pump drive disconnected. The apparatus was arranged to be out of balance such that half of the pumping load, which corresponded to the

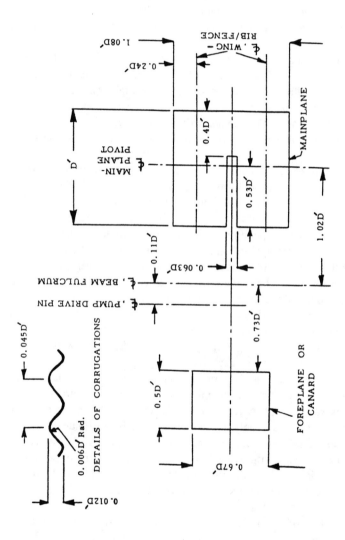

Figure 10.3. Optimised configuration of canard-equipped flapping-vane pumper employing transversely corrugated aerodynamic surfaces.

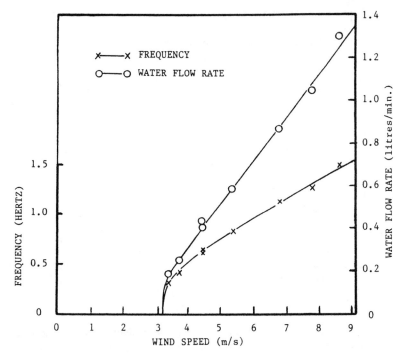

Figure 10.4. Pumping performance of twin-surface flapping-vane unit tested in wind-tunnel.

downward movement of the mainplane and the upward movement of the pump piston, was provided by gravity. This meant that equal work outputs were extracted from the system on both the upward and downward movements of the mainplane, the upward stroke increasing the system potential energy which was subsequently recovered on the pumping stroke as the mainplane descended. The yaw motion of the beam was due to a combination of the tailvane-like action of chordwise structural reinforcing surfaces attached to the mainplane plus the lift and drag forces acting on the mainplane.

Figure 10.5 presents the performance obtained from a full-scale version of the prototype with aerodynamic surfaces of 28 gauge corrugated steel sheet, a material commonly used for house roofing, etc., in many developing nations. The cord of the mainplane, D', was 2.26 m compared with the 203 mm of the working scale model. The water lift of the full-scale machine was 3.05 m using a pump cylinder of 102 mm bore. When the pumping performance shown in Fig. 10.5 is compared with that

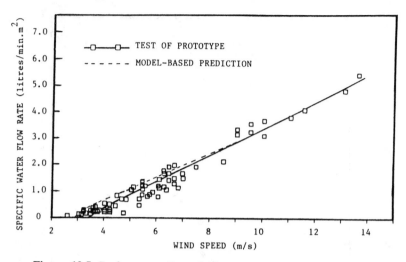

Figure 10.5. Performance, from field test, of full-scale twin-surface, flapping-vane pumper.

of, say, an Aermotor turbine (Fig. 8.5) with allowance made for the head difference between the two cases, the performance of the flapping-vane unit is only about 15% of that of the Aermotor at a wind speed of 8.5 m/s. Both machines have approximately equal performances at a wind speed of 14 m/s. The dotted line in Fig. 10.5 was the result of a performance prediction based on the model test results of Fig. 10.4. The scale-up laws applicable to establish the predicted performance of the full-scale machine from the model performance can be shown to be given, for a prescribed value of U_∞ by:

$$\frac{\text{Aerodynamic force (full-scale)}}{\text{Aerodynamic force (model)}} = (S')^2 \qquad (10.1)$$

$$\frac{\text{Frequency (full-scale)}}{\text{Frequency (model)}} = 1/(S'\sqrt{M'}) \qquad (10.2)$$

where S' is the linear dimensional scale factor; thus:

$$S' \equiv \frac{\text{Full-scale dimension}}{\text{Corresponding dimension of model}}$$

and where M' is termed the mass-ratio factor representing the mass of the full-scale component to that of the corresponding model component,

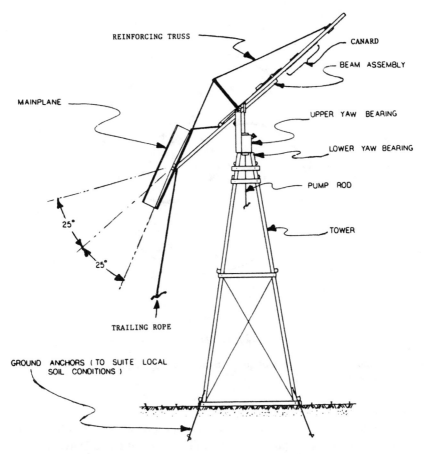

Figure 10.6. Side view of full-scale, prototype, flapping-vane pumper.

which may be made of a material of different density to that of the full-scale counterpart component, multiplied by the cube of the scale factor S' hence:

$$M' = \frac{\text{Mass (full-scale)}}{\text{Mass (model) } S'^3}$$

or alternatively based on a unit surface area;

$$M' \equiv \frac{\text{Mass per unit area (full-scale)}}{\text{Mass per unit area (model) } S'}$$

A better performance was obtained than that shown in Fig. 10.5 when the 28 gauge corrugated sheet-steel mainplane was replaced by a

END PLATE, DIAMETER D

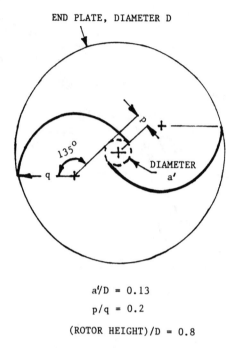

$a'/D = 0.13$

$p/q = 0.2$

(ROTOR HEIGHT)$/D = 0.8$

Figure 10.7. Plan view of quasi-optimised configuration of a Bach-style Savonius rotor.

corrugated aluminum surface of similar thickness. Figure 10.6 is a side view of the full-scale prototype unit built and tested at the University of Calgary. It was found to be necessary to add a simple air damper cylinder to eliminate the severe "snatch" associated with the "flipping" action of the mainplane. Whilst this device represented an irreversibility incorporated into the system this was deemed to be of minor importance relative to the smoother and less damaging mode of operation obtained.

The prototype was not equipped with any automatic furling mechanism but could be stopped, manually, by snagging the trailing rope attached to the downwind end of the oscillating beam to a convenient tower ground-anchor. A better and more comprehensive protection system would be to then clamp the leading edge of the mainplane to the beam, such that the "flipping" action became inhibited, with the mainplane surface parallel to the beam. Subsequent release of the ground anchor rope would then result in minimum wind loading on the structure with the mainplane and beam "floating", in the limit, at zero angle of incidence relative to the

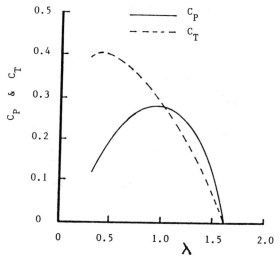

Figure 10.8. Performance projection, based on test data, of Savonius rotor configuration presented in Fig. 10.7.

oncoming wind. More information on the flapping-vane water pumper concept is available (Kentfield et al., 1986; Kentfield, 1986(b); Kentfield and Horsley, 1987).

10.2. Savonius Rotor Machines

A number of workers have attempted to optimise the geometry of Savonius rotors, a vertical-axis turbine concept introduced in Chapter 3, §3.9. An inherent difficulty in interpreting the results of earlier attempts to optimise, by experimental means, the geometries of Savonius rotors hinges on the degree of contradiction contained in the various reports available. A fundamental, simple, theoretical technique for establishing the ideal performance of a Savonius rotor is not yet available, although some theoretical work on performance prediction has been carried out (Fernando and Modi, 1989; Schwitzer, 1991); hence most available information is, therefore, based on experimentation. Whilst a wide range of geometrical variation is possible, as implied in Fig. 3.11, most workers have concentrated on rotors based on semi-cylinders as indicated in Fig. 3.11(a) and (b) or rotors of the so-called Bach type (Bach, 1931) illustrated in Fig. 3.11(c). At least two teams of researchers have found the Bach rotor geometry to be more promising than that of the semi-cylindrical class (Modi

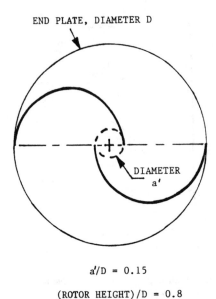

END PLATE, DIAMETER D

DIAMETER
a'

a'/D = 0.15

(ROTOR HEIGHT)/D = 0.8

Figure 10.9. Plan view of quasi-optimised Savonius rotor configuration with semi-cylindrical blades.

et al., 1982, 1985, 1990; Ushiyama et al., 1982). Part of the difficulty of interpreting rotor performances established from wind-tunnel tests appears to be associated with the apparent sensitivity of Savonius rotors to Reynolds number (Newman, 1974; Ushiyama et al., 1982). Another test difficulty appears to be correcting, appropriately, for the influence of tunnel blockage on rotor performance this topic having been studied by Modi et al. (Modi et al., 1985).

Figure 10.7 depicts what purports to be something approaching the optimum geometry of a Bach-style Savonius rotor. The geometry shown was based upon a composite of the results reported by Modi et al. (Modi et al., 1982, 1985, 1990) and by Ushiyama et al. (Ushiyama et al., 1982). Figure 10.8 shows the expected performance of the rotor of Fig. 10.7 based on test data due to the same workers. Generally the peak power coefficient is rather high relative to other results available in the technical literature for Savonius rotors.

Figure 10.9 presents what appears to be, or at least is close to, the optimum geometry for rotors composed of semi-cylinders. The practical importance of this configuration relates to the possibility of building the rotor of a small Savonius machine from, say, the two halves of an oil

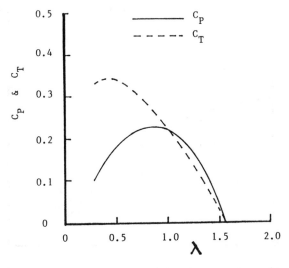

Figure 10.10. Performance projection, based on test data, of Savonius rotor configuration presented in Fig. 10.9.

drum cut longitudinally. The expected performance of such a machine, based once again on the results of the workers already quoted with respect to the Bach style rotor, is presented in Fig. 10.10. It can be seen from Fig. 10.10 that the peak power coefficient is lower than that shown in Fig. 10.8 for the Bach style rotor.

Both the groups of workers referred to previously found, based on tests of single-element rotors, that the optimum aspect ratio of Savonius rotors, defined as the axial height of the rotor divided by the diameter, was approximately 0.8. It also appears that, from the practical viewpoint, it is quite satisfactory to fill, completely, with a central rotor support tube the central space between the two blades. This is particularly convenient from the structural viewpoint since it makes rotor construction easier and eliminates the need to employ only a very slender central shaft, or to omit the central shaft entirely, an implication of the original concept in which the flow through the gap between the two blades was expected to have a beneficial influence. The anticipated action of flow passing through the gap between the blades is illustrated, diagrammatically, in Fig. 3.11(b) and (c). Apparently, in accordance with test data, this effect is of minor significance.

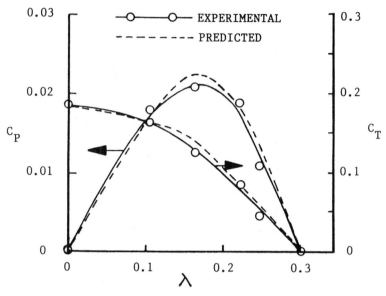

Figure 10.11. Experimentally obtained and theoretically predicted performances of a three-cup drag-type wind-turbine.

Nevertheless the aerodynamic performance of Savonius rotors is much superior to that expected from pure drag-type turbines, the optimum performance of which was predicted analytically in Chapter 3, §3.8. Hence, for Savonius rotors, aerodynamic lift must be a major contributor to performance and it is probably variations in both lift and drag that tend to make Savonius rotors somewhat sensitive to Reynolds number. The curves shown in Figs. 10.8 and 10.10 are expected to be realistic for small Savonius machines with rotor diameters in the region of, say, 1 m to 2 m operating in typical winds.

An inherent problem with Savonius rotors is the variability of rotor torque, at starting conditions, with rotor angular position. For most configurations the torque is zero, or slightly negative, at discrete angular positions of the rotor relative to the wind direction. It is because of this that most Savonius machines employ stacked rotors with a minimum of two single rotors, or elements, set at a mutual angle of 90° to each other. The elements of stacked rotors are normally delineated by circular disc-type separators with similar disc-type end plates at the top and bottom of the rotor stack. The solidity of Savonius rotors based on the rotor projected area is particularly high, normally in the region of 3.8 for a single element when the area of the end plates, or discs, is also included. The

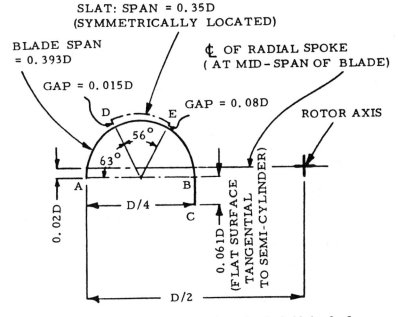

SLAT: SPAN = 0.35D
(SYMMETRICALLY LOCATED)

BLADE SPAN
= 0.393D

₵ OF RADIAL SPOKE
(AT MID-SPAN OF BLADE)

GAP = 0.015D

GAP = 0.08D

ROTOR AXIS

D   E

56°

63°

A   B

D/4

C

0.02D

0.061D
(FLAT SURFACE
TANGENTIAL
TO SEMI-CYLINDER)

D/2

Figure 10.12. Geometries of three versions of a single blade of a five-bladed drag-type turbine.

solidity is somewhat less, about 3.3, for a pair of rotors stacked to reduce starting-torque problems.

Another difficulty with Savonius rotors is making adequate provision for the control of rotor speed under storm conditions. With a runaway tip-speed ratio in the region of 1.5 it is very difficult to arrange to construct continuously operational Savonius rotors sufficiently robustly to withstand storm conditions without incurring excessive costs. Several suggestions have been made to overcome the runaway problem including the use of a strong brake to simply overcome the rotor torque and stop the machine. Another suggestion was to allow the two rotor blades, when each is hinged to the end plates at their outer extremities, to move, due to centrifugal force, towards an inoperative position. Strong springs were to be used to control the blade motion relative to the rotor end plates and hence to restore the blades to their normal operative position when the wind weakened. Other suggestions involve the use of a retractable tubular sheath to shroud the rotor or the provision of a hinged tower by means of which the rotor is withdrawn from the flow. With the exception of the last proposal all systems fail to avoid the generation of very large drag forces

Table 10.1

Typical Drag Data for Isolated Blades (extracted from data presented by Hoerner (Hoerner, 1965))

Description of shape	C_{DD}	C_{DU}	C_{DU}/C_{DD}
Hollow, axisymmetric, hemispherical cup	1.42	0.38	0.27
Hollow, axisymmetric, domed cup, length ≈ 30% of diameter	1.38	0.50	0.36
Hollow cone, 60° included angle	1.36	0.54	0.40
Hollow cone, 90° included angle	1.33	0.72	0.54
(2 dim.) hollow semi-cylinder	2.30	1.20	0.52
(2 dim.) 60° included angle hollow wedge	2.32	1.26	0.54
(2 dim.) 90° included angle hollow wedge	2.26	1.46	0.65

C_{DD} ≡ drag coefficient of an isolated blade moving downwind. C_{DU} ≡ drag coefficient of an isolated blade moving upwind.

during storm conditions. All the methods introduce major complications in an otherwise very simple machine.

10.3. Drag-Type Units

The most sophisticated of drag-type wind-turbines involve retraction of the advancing blades, that is retraction of the blades moving upwind. A configuration of this type was, it seems, developed in the distant past in China. However, even when the complication of blade retraction is incorporated the idealised performance prediction presented in Chapter 3, §3.8, showed that the maximum power coefficient achievable is not likely to exceed 0.07 or 7%. Hence consideration here will only be given to ultra-simple drag-type turbines that do not involve blade articulation or shields, to reduce the drag of the advancing blades, since shields must be provided with a yaw capability.

What might be termed a classical drag-type wind-turbine, in very common use, is the cup-anemometer. Using wind-turbine terminology the cup-anemometer always operates at the runaway (no load) condition. Cup-anemometers must be designed to withstand the strongest winds without

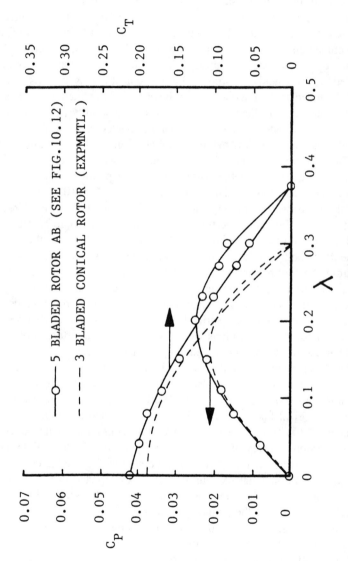

Figure 10.13. Wind-tunnel performance of a five-bladed drag-type turbine employing simple semi-cylindrical blades.

the provision of any furling mechanism. It is the possibility of completely eliminating the complexity of a furling mechanism that is one of the few, but not the only, fundamentally attractive features of simple drag-type turbines. A wind-tunnel-based study of the performance of simple drag-type turbines has been carried out, by the writer, at the University of Calgary and subsequently reported in the technical literature (Kentfield, 1990). The study included cup-anemometer-like turbines and other configurations.

The cup-anemometer-like turbine the performance of which was investigated experimentally incorporated three conical blades, or cups, each of 96.7° included angle, the diameter of the open end of which was a quarter of the rotor overall diameter, D, giving a rotor solidity (total surface area of the cups divided by the rotor frontal projected area) of about 1.5. The configuration tested was based upon that of an available commercial unit. The performance established, by means of wind-tunnel testing, is presented in Fig. 10.11 together with a theoretical prediction of the performance. The rotor torque characteristic revealed in Fig. 10.11 confirms the suitability for water pumping and similar applications of simple drag-type rotors. The theoretical performance prediction procedure employed to establish the dotted curves of Fig. 10.11 took into account the drag coefficients of both the advancing and retreating cups, these data being taken from the fourth line of Table 10.1, in addition to both a general acceleration, due to rotor blockage, of the flow passing around the rotor and also a circulation about the axis of the rotor induced by rotor rotation. The prediction procedure is described in full detail elsewhere (Kentfield, 1990). Other rotor configurations were investigated in an effort to obtain a smoother starting-torque and a generally improved performance.

This developmental activity resulted in the evolution of a five-bladed rotor with semi-cylindrical type blades. The geometries of three versions of this rotor are shown in Fig. 10.12. The basic version employed only the semi-cylindrical blades, AB in Fig. 10.12, and had a solidity of approximately 2. A further development of this configuration introduced the flat extension surfaces BC the optimum dimension of which, $0.061D$, was established experimentally. The final version of the five-bladed rotor incorporated additional slat-like surfaces DE also depicted in Fig. 10.12. A comparison of the performance obtained using only the semi-cylindrical blades, AB, with that of the conically bladed rotor, described previously, is presented in Fig. 10.13. Figure 10.14 compares, on the C_P and C_T versus λ planes, the performances of all three versions of the five-bladed rotor. Figure 10.15 compares the performances, in terms of power output and torque, of the conically bladed rotor and the three versions of the five-bladed rotor for invariant ambient density, wind speed and rotor diameter.

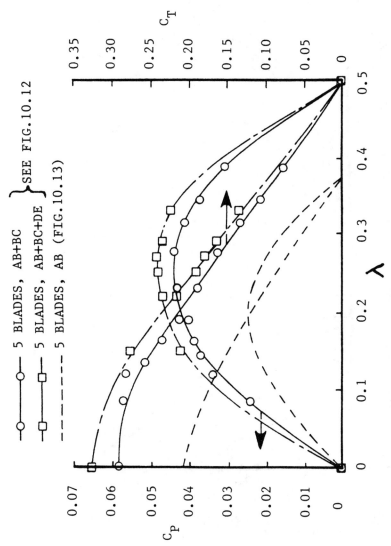

Figure 10.14. Wind-tunnel performances of the five-bladed rotor of Fig. 10.12 with blade extensions BC and slats DE.

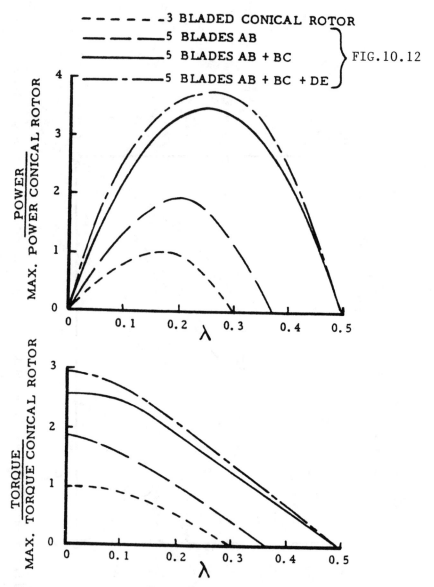

Figure 10.15. Performance comparisons of drag-type rotors for invariant air density, wind speed and rotor diameter.

A suggested mechanical design for the five-bladed rotor is presented in Fig. 10.16. This design, which permits easy dismantling for packaging

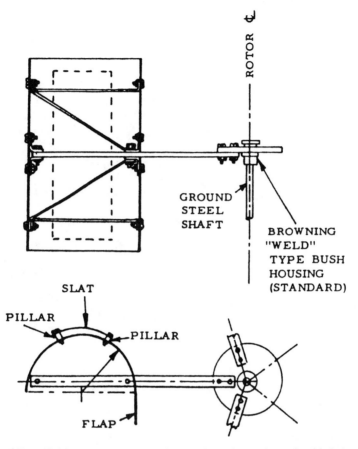

Figure 10.16. Suggested mechanical design scheme for a five-bladed drag-type rotor.

and transportation, avoids the generation of major shaft bending moments under storm conditions, the main shaft loading being due, predominantly, to shear. Due to the low runaway tip speed ratio of $\lambda \approx 0.5$ the maximum angular velocity of a 2 m diameter rotor in a wind of, say, 50 m/s is only about 240 revolutions per minute. Rather limited potential uses for small drag-type rotors appear to lie in the area of low flow-rate air-lift pumping, low-head direct pumping, pond aeration, pond agitation and the agitation of anaerobic digesters, etc. The very poor use of the blade area provided effectively inhibits the application of large drag-type turbines.

CHAPTER 11

Structural Design

Numerous factors influence the design of wind-driven water pumpers. Many of these factors differ either fundamentally, or at least in emphasis, from considerations influencing the design of wind-electric machines. For example, it is often feasible, with wind-electric machines, to employ a tower design that has a fundamental resonant sway frequency lower than the normal rotational speed, or frequency, of the machine during operation. Such a design can be acceptable for a wind-electric unit since the rotor frequency only coincides with the tower sway frequency very briefly during a run-up to the operating condition or, of course, when the machine is stopping. For a water pumper the running speed can reside anywhere in the range from zero to a predetermined maximum value at which furling occurs. Hence any important structural resonance lying within the operating speed range can represent a serious problem.

Another area in which design considerations differ very considerably between most wind water pumpers and typical, large, wind-electric machines relates to the use of a crane for assisting with the erection process. Whilst the cost, per unit time, of hiring a crane to erect a small water pumper will usually be much less than that required for the erection of a large wind-electric machine costing, say, 50 to 100 times more than the wind-driven water pumper, the crane-hire cost as a fraction of the capital value of the machine will usually be much greater for the small water-pumping unit. This factor can be further aggravated when consideration is given to a typical circumstance in which only a single water-pumping unit is to be installed at a particular site when, on the other hand, multiple wind-electric turbines are to be erected adjacent to each other at, say, a wind-farm location.

11.1. Portability

Clearly any wind-turbine must be dismantable into sufficiently small components to permit easy, and low-cost, transportation from the manufacturer to their installation site. However for small water pumpers these requirements are often more stringent than for large wind-electric units especially with respect to a possible need to hand-carry components from the delivery vehicle to the erection site if no vehicle access is possible. This consideration would not usually apply to a location selected as suitable for a large wind-electric machine since an access road, or path, for a mobile crane, and hence also a delivery vehicle, would normally be a mandatory requirement.

This suggests, therefore, that the maximum size and weight of the largest single component of a wind water pumper should not exceed the carrying capacity of a single person, or at most that of two people. Since transportation charges are, for low-density items, usually based on the volume of the crate or container in which they are packed it is also very desirable that at least some attention be paid, during the design process, to arranging, where possible, for the nesting, or stacking, of suitably compatible components, for example, rotor blades or lengths of steel angle-section material used for, say, the construction of a lattice type tower.

11.2. Erection Methods

The most common procedure for erecting conventional wind water pumpers is to assemble the tower, which is usually of the lattice space-frame type, from the ground upwards on a pre-prepared foundation. The tower assembly task does not normally require the use of a crane since individual tower components are light and each bay, or stage, of the tower is of a height that allows the assemblers to reach the next stage from a suitable platform of planks resting on the top of the previously completed stage. When the tower is fully assembled the head, rotor and tail components, each of which has been preassembled at ground level, are hoisted to the tower top and installed in position to complete the machine.

For very small machines the hoisting process usually consists of merely lifting the individual tower-top components, manually, by means of a rope. For relatively large machines a temporary tower-extension derrick is secured to the tower-top to support a block-and-tackle type hoist allowing a worker at ground level to raise the tower-top mounted components, one by one, to other workers stationed at the tower top. These procedures have been used for many years and, in the hands of skilled and experienced wind-turbine assemblers, function well. However, if due care is not taken at all stages of the hoisting and subsequent tower-top-located assembly tasks there is a much increased risk of an accident occurring. The risk of such an accident can be diminished greatly if a mobile crane is available to assist with the final stages of the assembly work.

11.2.1. Crane Erection

A wind water pumper designed for manual assembly is also generally suitable for crane-assisted assembly. The main difference in the assembly sequence would be that in order to minimise high risk tower-top assembly tasks the head-rotor-tail system would be assembled, as an integral unit, at ground level, complete with the yaw post, before being lifted, by the crane, into position over the tower top. At this time the lower flange of the yaw post would be bolted to the tower top. The crane would, during this operation, remain in position attached to the head-rotor-tail assembly until the lower flange of the yaw post has finally been fully secured to the tower top. It is also important, during such an assembly process, to prevent rotation of the turbine and also to secure the tail boom to the head to inhibit involuntary furling type movements of the tail relative to the head and rotor. If need be the head-rotor-tail assembly can be steadied, to eliminate unwanted wind-induced movements, by means of attached ropes, the opposite ends of which are handled by workers at ground level.

An inherent problem is that of the cost of mobile-crane hire. Even though the amount of lifting involved would likely not be such as to occupy much crane time, crane charges normally cover not only the time on site but also, at the same hourly hire rate, the time occupied by both the outboard and return journeys of the crane from, and back to, the base location of the vehicle. The travel-induced portion of the crane cost can obviously be considerable if the wind-turbine site is a substantial distance from the operating base of the crane. As mentioned previously crane-hire charges can be equivalent to a significant fraction of the capital value of a relatively low-cost wind water pumper. Furthermore the use of a crane implies that the crane has road access to the wind-turbine site, a situation that may not always be the case. Crane-hire problems can be avoided if a so-called self-erecting system is employed.

11.2.2. Self-Erecting Systems

It is usually possible to incorporate a so-called self-erecting capability, with but little increase in capital cost, into the design of a wind water pumper. Most self-erecting systems fall, essentially, into one of two categories. In one category a tilt-up tower arrangement is employed in which the machine is provided with a tower hinged at the base, enabling the tower, and tower-top machinery, to be assembled at ground level prior to pulling the complete machine into the upright position. In the second category the tower is built-up, vertically, from ground level in the traditional manner of the towers of conventional, manually erected, wind water pumpers; however, in this case, the machinery assembly takes place substantially at ground level. The complete head-rotor-tail assembly is subsequently slid up the tower, with the help of a winch, and secured to the tower top.

The two alternative concepts yield somewhat different results in terms of the fundamental forces involved. Figure 11.1 shows, diagrammatically, a tilt-up tower. It is assumed, in the diagram that the tower itself is weightless but carries a concentrated load, W, at the top. Figure 11.2 presents the cable tension F, as a fraction of load W, required to raise the tower as a function of the tower inclination angle ψ. Typical forces prevailing in such a system at $\psi = 0°$ are listed, as multiples of the dead load W, in Table 11.1. Generally the loadings incurred in a gin-pole tilt-up system of the type illustrated in Fig. 11.1 are considerably greater than those for a system of the second category employing the inclined-plane principle. An inclined plane system is illustrated in Fig. 11.3. The load W is hauled, with the aid of a winch, to the tower top. The closest approach of the load W of Fig. 11.3 to ground level depends upon the dimensions y', x' and angle δ. The smaller the angle δ the shorter is y'. A possible arrangement of a relatively tall inclined tower for which δ is relatively large is presented in Fig. 11.4, which shows an extension of y', y_a, that folds onto the ground to allow the tower-top platform to approach the ground much more closely than would otherwise be the case. More details of both gin-pole and inclined plane-type towers are available elsewhere (Kentfield, 1989(b)). Both the gin-pole and inclined plane tower concepts have been applied, successfully, to commercially available wind water pumpers.

11.3. Fatigue Considerations

A typical, fairly small, wind water pumper, without reduction gearing, will complete during a 30-year life span about 300 million pumping cycles with a similar, but much larger, machine accumulating about half that number of pumping cycles. By comparison each cylinder of a typical four-stroke car engine will also accumulate about 300 million cycles during a 10-year life span running for an average of one hour per day.

Hence it is apparent that it is very important, when designing a wind water pumper, to take into account the risks of incurring fatigue failures during the expected, useful, operational life of the machine. The potential

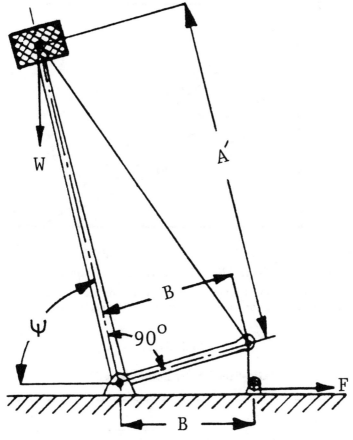

Figure 11.1. Arrangement of a hinged, tilt-up or gin-pole, wind-turbine tower.

for causing fatigue failures is not necessarily represented only by a count of the number of pumping cycles completed but also by other influences, for example, by wind gusts, yaw motions and furling. Since significant gusts can occur every few seconds, and these are often accompanied by corresponding yaw realignments, the counting of such events, primarily affecting the rotor blades and their support structure, is likely to lead to sums roughly equal in number to the accumulated pumping cycle count. Thus in the region of 2×10^8 gust events can be expected with, say, several thousand full-furling events per year leading to, perhaps, 10^5 furlings over a 30-year life span.

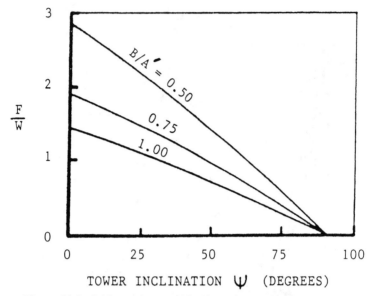

Figure 11.2. Cable tension, as a fraction of tower load, versus the inclination angle ψ for tilt-up towers (tower weight neglected).

Table 11.1

Gin-Pole Tower Loads ($\psi = 0°$)

	B/A'		
Nature of load	0.50	0.75	1.00
Compressive load in gin-pole	3W	2.33W	2W
Compressive load in tower	2W	1.33W	W
Shear load in tower base	4W	2.67W	2W

Fatigue failures should not occur in structural steel components provided maximum stress range levels do not exceed that corresponding to the horizontal portion of the stress-range versus the number-of-cycles-completed relationship for the particular steel being considered. However if the maximum stress range in a structural steel component exceeds

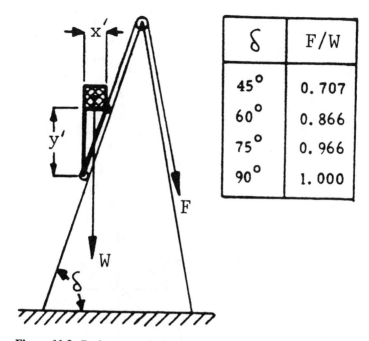

δ	F/W
45°	0.707
60°	0.866
75°	0.966
90°	1.000

Figure 11.3. Basic geometrical arrangement of a simple inclined-plane tower with a table of ratio of cable tension, F, to load W, as a function of δ.

the fatigue limit the number of cycles expected prior to failure can be read from the negative slope portion of the log log stress-range versus number-of-cycles diagram. Unfortunately no definite fatigue limits exist for welded structural steel components, light alloys or fiber-glass materials. Also great care should be taken in the design of bolted joints in structural steel assemblies to ensure that fatigue failures are not likely to occur in otherwise satisfactorily designed components.

11.3.1. Welded Joints

The use of welded joints in wind water pumpers is particularly convenient, from a production viewpoint since, unlike, say, a typical, small, internal combustion engine in which it is usually possible to avoid welded joints entirely, wind water pumpers are usually produced only in fairly small numbers. Further, some of the components they incorporate do not lend themselves to production methods such as forging, casting or machining

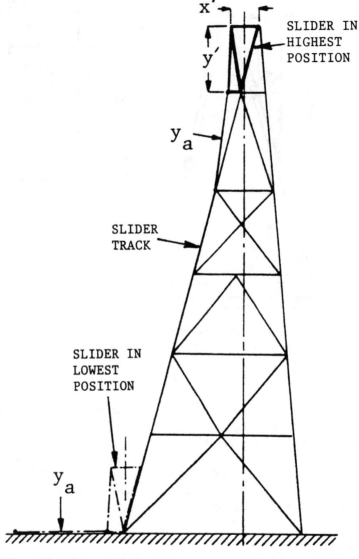

Figure 11.4. Advanced inclined-plane tower employing a steeper inclination angle, δ, than the conceptual arrangement of Fig. 11.3.

from the solid since such processes are often either not cost-effective, due
to the nature of the component, or are simply impractical.

The inherent problem when employing welds in a fatigue-inducing environment with a life expectancy corresponding to a very large, accumulated, number of cycles is, generally, the very low stress range permitted under such circumstances. This situation is illustrated, qualitatively, in Fig. 11.5. The class of weld indicated in Fig. 11.5 refers to details of the welding process employed and subsequent post-weld processing such as joint dressing by grinding, etc. Usually, for most welded components likely to be incorporated in a wind water pumper, significant post-weld processing is frequently regarded as non cost-effective. Keeping this in mind the maximum permissible joint stress range in order to achieve about 2×10^8 cycles is, for joints immersed in air, in the region of 16 MPa, for typical structural steels, with a corresponding statistical risk of failure of about 2.3%. A justification for accepting a 16 MPa maximum stress range, together with many more details relating to the properties of welded joints in structural steel, has been given by Gurney (Gurney, 1976).

Although a stress range of 16 MPa appears, at first glance, to be cripplingly low it is, in fact, in some cases approximately representative of the safe load range of a typical comparable bolted joint. Usually, provided a permanent welded joint is acceptable from the transportation and erection viewpoints, the welded joint is likely to be of lower cost than the bolted counterpart. The use, and welding, of light alloys is not discussed here because of the generally low fatigue resistance of these materials. The use of more exotic steels than structural steels is also not considered because they appear to be unlikely to find application in essentially low-cost equipment like wind water pumpers.

11.3.2. Bolted Joints

Fatigue problems can arise with bolted joints if proper allowances are not made for the local stress concentration factors applicable to both the bolt holes and, due to their threaded portions, the bolts themselves. A potential relief from the first problem can be obtained, for bolts loaded in tension, by passing the bolts not through the structural members but, instead, through thick walled tubes welded, over their entire length, to the structural members to be joined. This technique is particularly useful for joining, end-on-end, tubular structural members. A solution of this kind has been applied in practice to the joints between the sections of the tower of at least one type of commercially manufactured, dismantable, tall, construction-site crane.

An additional possibility to relieve potential problems related to bolt fatigue is to employ long bolts with waisted sections similar to the big-end bolts often used in internal combustion engines giving much increased bolt

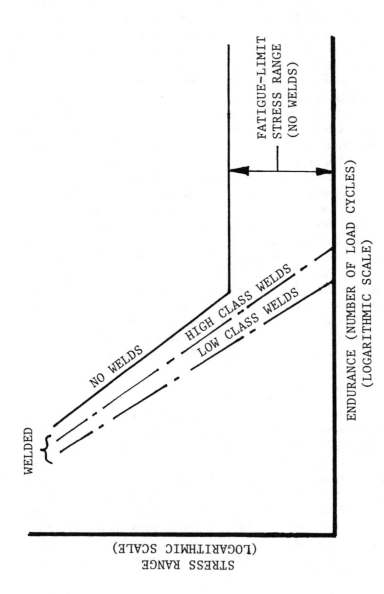

Figure 11.5. Conceptual diagram showing influence of welded joints on the fatigue properties of a typical structural steel.

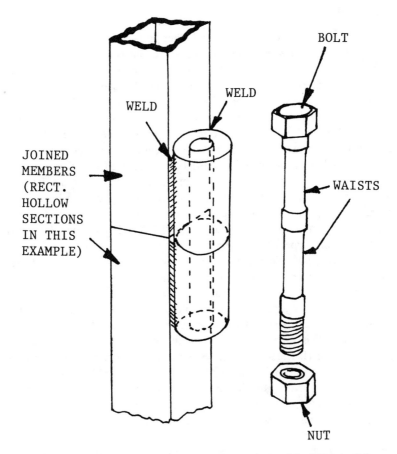

Figure 11.6. Sophisticated arrangement to minimise risk of fatigue failure at a bolted joint.

elasticity and hence yielding reduced stress ranges in bolts subjected to fatigue-inducing loadings. The bolt-receiving tube solution for the bolt-hole problem is, of course compatible with the use of the long special, waisted bolts as indicated in Fig. 11.6. It seems unlikely that either of the suggested solutions to bolt, and bolt-hole problems are likely to be adopted fairly generally in wind water pumpers for cost reasons. Most of the towers of current wind water pumpers employ ordinary, standard, engineering bolts, loaded in single shear, passed through holes drilled or punched directly through steel-angle structural members.

11.3.3. Fiber-Glass

Although research into the fatigue and other properties of various forms of fiber-glass is still ongoing it appears that these materials do not exhibit any definite fatigue limit. To attain 2×10^8 cycles the maximum permissible stress range varies from about 10 to about 70 MPa depending upon details of the material tested. The variabilities in the material include, for hybrid composites, the ratio of glass fiber to carbon fiber, lay-up sequence, the directionality of the fibers and the resin employed. Hence the subject is, at least in so far as hybrid materials are concerned, rather complex.

Whilst fiber-glass materials have been little used in water-pumping wind-turbines, fiber-glass is now the preferred material for the fabrication of the blades of large wind-electric machines. The most likely, and promising, application of fiber-glass materials in water-pumping turbines appears to be as a blade material or for tailvane fabrication. For such duties it would appear that a relatively simple and straightforward glass-reinforced material, identified as E-glass, would be preferred. Great mechanical strength and stiffness are not normally required for the blades, or the tailvane, of relatively slow running water-pumping turbines.

For fiber-glass surfaces exposed to the atmosphere it is conventional practice to use a material known as gel-coat for the outer layer of the component. This provides a very smooth external finish, important for aerodynamic surfaces such as blades, since it does not contain coarse fibrous material and provides a measure of protection against UV radiation and weathering. Normally, for moulded components, gel-coat is applied within the mould before adding the fiber-glass matting and resin that subsequently provide the required mechanical strength.

It is pure fiber-glass (E-glass) material that gives rise to the lowest maximum fatigue-stress range referred to previously. Generally the substitution of layers of carbon fibers yields, in a properly designed material, an increase in the maximum fatigue-stress range and an increase in material stiffness at the cost of embrittlement. Thus materials with a high carbon content tend to fail catastrophically when failure occurs and to have a lower impact resistance than that of E-glass, or the somewhat similar, but more chemically resistant, S-glass material. The substitution of carbon layers allows components for which the loading is prescribed to be constructed more lightly, with thinner walls, than when pure E-glass is employed. However care must be taken to ensure that failure due to buckling does not become a problem with the lighter component. More complete information is available on fiber composite hybrid materials (Hancox, 1981).

11.4. Dynamic Considerations

Because a water-pumping wind-turbine can operate at any rotor speed between zero and a maximum value, limited by the furling arrangements provided, it is unwise, or at the very least risky, to build such a machine with major structural resonant frequencies lying within the operating speed range. This, therefore, implies the use of an inherently stiff structure. However, due to the relatively low rotational speed in relation to machine size of most water-pumping turbines it is not, in general, difficult to achieve the required result. Furthermore, the desirability of using the wind-turbine tower as a derrick by means of which the pump can be withdrawn from the well, an operation which in most cases implies withdrawal of the riser pipe, requires, in many instances, a heavier tower construction than that otherwise necessary. This consideration tends, therefore, to support the stiff tower hypothesis.

It is important to ensure that structural resonances do not occur within the operating speed range of a machine, to evaluate the natural frequencies of the tower when supporting the tower-top mass due to the turbine, etc., and the natural frequencies of the tower components. Other natural frequencies likely to be of concern are those of the rotor structure, although for most water-pumping machines the rotor blade support frame is relatively stiff, and the frequencies of bending and torsional oscillations in the tail-support structure. All the required results can be obtained using suitable, existing computer software. For example, the necessary natural frequencies of the large-scale, 16 m rotor diameter, delta-wing-bladed turbine referred to in Chapter 5, §5.5, were established, for the writer, using the Control Data Corporation Stardyne code.

Minor resonances of, say, tower cross-braces lying within the operating speed range of a machine are generally not of a critical nature, depending upon the magnitude of the inherent aerodynamic and mechanical damping, and can often be accepted without attempting detuning. Detuning usually involves adding mass, to reduce the frequency, or increasing the local structural stiffness in an attempt to increase the frequency and hence push it outside the operating speed range of the machine. Generally computerised predictions of structural natural frequencies decrease in accuracy with increasing harmonics.

11.5. Bearing Selection

Bearings used in wind water pumpers range from simple, split, wood-bearing blocks bolted to the machine, in which run elementary shafts made of steel pipe, to conventional plain bearings, ball and roller races some of the last two types being of the self-aligning kind. Very simple bearings made from blocks of wood are sometimes found on agricultural machines supporting drive shafts to auxiliary equipment, etc. Bearings of this type were employed on the prototype flapping vane pumper, or aeolian pumpjack, illustrated in Fig. 10.6. In keeping with the ultra-simple construction of that machine the bearing blocks were made from oil-soaked soft wood. Superior, oil-soaked, fully machined hardwood bushes have been used for many years, with great success, as the main bearing surfaces of the Australian Comet series of water-pumping turbines made by Sydney Williams and Company.

Most water-pumping wind-turbines employ either plain bronze bushing-type bearings push-fitted into bores machined, accurately, in a head casting, which usually also serves as an oil reservoir, or ball or roller races similarly mounted. An alternative arrangement when a head coasting is not employed, and a minimally machined welded head structure is substituted, is to install standard, sealed, self-aligning, grease-lubricated, ball or roller races supplied in standard pillow-block or flange-mounted housings. It is, for most cases, advisable to choose steel or malleable-iron housings instead of the cast iron type. The self-aligning feature implies that provided the mounting faces for the bearing housings are flat it is not essential for a pair of such bearings supporting a shaft to be in exact alignment with each other. Normally sealed bearings will operate for at least a year between applications of grease from a grease gun. The expected life of such bearings can be ascertained from data supplied by the manufacturer. Generally, for a prescribed bearing, the lighter the loading the longer the life.

A cost-avoidance procedure associated with bearing selection is to use, with ball or roller-race type bearings, shafting made from standard, bright-finished, bar stock. This avoids the need for major machining of a shaft to provide seats for the bearings. In such cases the bearings are secured to the shaft by means of built-in collets supplied as an integral part of the bearing assembly. Practical experience has demonstrated that alternative, commercially available, systems employing grub-screws to secure the inner races of bearings to shafts are inadequate for duty in water-pumping wind-turbines. At least one maker of commercial water-pumping wind-turbines employs, successfully, a collet-secured, self-aligning, sealed, grease-lubricated bearing system in conjunction with a built-up, welded, head assembly.

Ball, or roller, yaw bearings are generally preferred to plain yaw bearings since they permit greater yaw sensitivity although many machines employ plain type yaw bearings. It appears to be worthwhile, in order to prevent damage to ball or roller type main bearings, to install an earthing brush contacting the rotor shaft to discharge, to ground, static electricity generated by the turbine rotor thereby avoiding such discharges through the shaft bearings. This technique was pioneered many years ago, in the United States, by Jacobs in order to protect the bearings of wind-electric machines.

11.6. Towers

Many types of tower have been used in conjunction with wind water pumpers. Small machines were, in the past, commonly equipped with nut-and-bolt assembled timber lattice towers. Although timber can be protected by means of creosote this is, today, not a preferred timber preservation technique because of some adverse environmental concerns. However, modern, pressure-impregnated, timber could be used for a present day timber tower. Wood has the disadvantage that it is generally, for a given load-carrying ability, more bulky than steel and hence is at a disadvantage from the packaging and transportation viewpoints.

The majority of current wind water pumpers employ simple lattice-type towers built up from pre-cut, and drilled, lengths of galvanised steel angle section bolted together on site. Inherent advantages of this concept are compactness for transportation, durability and efficient use of material. Most lattice towers employ a rectangular planform since this suits, particularly well, standard steel angle sections. Some towers use tubular, rather than angle-type, corner posts and yet others employ three rather than four uprights and hence are triangular in planform. The lattice, or space-frame, tower concepts lend themselves to serve as a derrick when withdrawing, or reinstalling, a pump located under the tower vertical centre-line.

Many towers have fairly narrow bases thereby economising in the steel incorporated in horizontal and bracing members but making greater demands upon the stability of the foundations than is the case for towers with wider bases. Towers with wide bases are necessary when a wind water pumper is to be installed over a typical manually dug well. A wide tower base also lends itself to incorporating a simple slide-up-type self-erection system such as that suggested in Fig. 11.3 for a fairly short tower, or in Fig. 11.4 for a taller tower. Figure 11.7 shows both side and plan views of a three-bay relatively short, wide-base slide-up type tower. A tower of this type is incorporated in a commercially produced water-pumping wind-turbine employing a perimeter-bladed rotor.

In some cases, as a cost- and weight-saving measure, galvanised-wire diagonal braces are employed in the bays of some space-frame towers. The wires are normally tensioned by twisting them together, in pairs, by means of a special clip which also serves to prevent untwisting and hence loss of

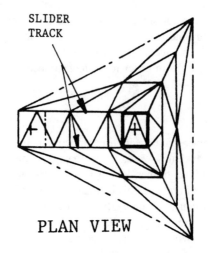

SLIDER
TRACK

PLAN VIEW

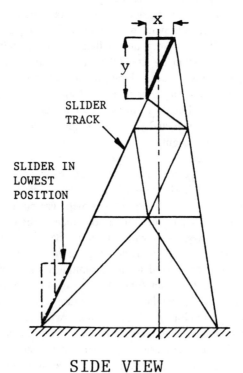

x

y

SLIDER
TRACK

SLIDER IN
LOWEST
POSITION

SIDE VIEW

Figure 11.7. Example of a simple, three-bay, tower of the slide-up type.

tension. A system of this type does, however, impose a compressive load on the horizontal members of the tower structure and also on the corner posts. The corner post loads due to the tensioned, wire cross-braces is additional to the compressive loads otherwise imposed due to gravity plus pump operation, wind loading and gyroscopically generated loads due to yaw action. A critical consideration in the design of space-frame towers is to take proper account of the compressive loads acting on the corner posts in order to avoid failure due to buckling. It is a relatively high resistance to buckling loads that makes tubular steel attractive for use in tower corner posts. An inherent disadvantage of tubes is the relative complexity, and cost, of implementing satisfactory, dismantable, joints using fishplates, flanges or, perhaps, by means of the system shown in Fig. 11.6. Some provision, possibly by galvanising, is also needed to inhibit internal corrosion of the tubes.

Other tower types used are tubular towers, often made from steel pipe, and narrow lattice-work towers. In both cases some form of guying or staying is normally required. There is, with such tower types, a problem in using the tower as a derrick for pump servicing when the pump is installed on the tower centre-line. An offset reciprocating pump unless driven, via linkage, by means of a pump or sucker rod installed on the tower centre-line generates cyclic bending moments in the tower. Furthermore guy cables can cause problems if large animals are able to use them as "back scratchers". The "back scratching" activity can increase, transiently, guy cable tension substantially leading, ultimately, to damage. "Back scratching" can be prevented by fencing-off the guy cables or by using very steep cables that serve to prevent large animals stepping between the guy cables, or rods, and the machine tower. One of the most successful applications of a narrow tubular tower in conjunction with a reciprocating pump was that employed by CWD on their Model 2000 machine.

Light, relatively large-diameter, free-standing, tubular, towers commonly used for large wind-electric machines do not appear to have been adapted for use with reciprocating water pumpers due, no doubt, to transportation and pump access problems. An example of a small system employing a tubular tilt-up tower, the design of which was adapted from that of a lamp post, is illustrated in Fig. 6.2. The machine shown in Fig. 6.2 was equipped with a rotary, progressive cavity pump.

11.7. Rotors

The rotors of horizontal-axis water-pumping wind-turbines are subjected, during normal operation, to five major loading modes. The five modes can be identified, subjectively, as loads that tend to:

i) burst the rotor apart in a radial direction due to centrifugal action. Hence centripetal forces have to be provided, via the rotor spokes, to resist centrifugal action,

ii) bend the rotor spokes in a downwind direction due to wind forces acting on the rotor primarily on the blade surfaces,

iii) bend the rotor spokes forward, in the direction of rotor rotation, due to the resistive torque generated by the pump load,

iv) buckle the rotor about a diameter due to the gyroscopic moments associated with yawing,

v) bend the spokes cyclically, at the rotor rotational frequency, due to gravity acting on each blade and spoke.

If the machine furls by turning edgewise to the wind an additional loading mode, loading mode (vi), comes into play after furling. In this mode the spokes of the upper and lower segments of the stationary, or very slowly rotating, rotor tend to be bent, due to aerodynamic loads active on the blade surfaces, in a downwind direction in both segments with the spokes in one segment simultaneously being bent to the right and in the other segment to the left.

In principle all the foregoing loads can be resisted using a rotor design in which each blade is supported by means of an individual spoke cantilevered from the rotor hub. However this can require relatively large-diameter, heavy, spokes if stress levels are not to exceed the fatigue limit of the spoke material at the location where bending moments are greatest, that is, in the vicinity where the spokes join the hub. This problem can be aggravated greatly, due to the poor fatigue resistance of welds, if the spokes are welded to, say, attachment plates for bolting to a convenient disc-type hub. Simple radial spokes are most effective in resisting the radial loading mode, (i), tending to burst the rotor. Typically, for a small water-pumping wind-turbine with a relatively high runaway tip-speed ratio of 3 the centrifugal loading, or tension, is in the region of 100 to 200 times that due to gravity action alone, that is, the load acting on a spoke of a stationary rotor when the spoke, and attached blade, are directed towards the ground.

Improved resistance to loading modes (ii) and (iv) can be obtained by bracing each spoke to an upwind-directed extension of the rotor shaft, somewhat after the style of the Cretian rotor illustrated in Fig. 5.1, although adequate support can normally be obtained without the bracing extending to the full radius of each spoke. Sufficient resistance to loading mode (iii) can, for most cases, be incorporated, quite easily, in radially oriented spokes. However for relatively large-diameter rotors of light construction, for example, the perimeter-bladed rotors shown in Fig. 5.30, added resistance to loading mode (iii) can be obtained by attaching the spokes tangentially to one hub disc of a twin-disc hub assembly. The other disc supports a second set of spokes, also attached tangentially, that serves to brace the first set of spokes to improve resistance to loading mode (ii) as described previously. A hub-spoke system of this type, used in a production perimeter-bladed wind water pumper, is illustrated, diagrammatically, in Fig. 11.8.

Improved resistance to loading modes (v) and (vi) can be obtained by connecting adjacent rotor spokes in a circumferential direction. Reinforcement of this kind is inherent, as part of the blade support structure, in the rotors of conventional multibladed turbines, illustrated in Fig. 5.13, and perimeter-bladed rotors, as shown diagrammatically in Figs. 5.30 and 11.8. Such bracing has also been applied to delta-wing-bladed rotors in the form of tie-bars connecting adjacent spokes. It is essential for all but the very smallest of diameters that turbine rotors be dismantable into small components for ease of shipment and handling.

It should be kept in mind that a conventional rotor shaft supporting a horizontal-axis turbine is also subject to fatigue-inducing direct and shear loading due to the overhung way in which the rotor is carried. The cyclic frequency of the application of the loading experienced by a point in such a shaft equals the rotor rotational speed. Additional transient direct stresses in a rotor shaft are due to gyroscopic effects resulting from yawing motions and also furling if the turbine is of the kind in which furling involves turning the rotor edgewise to the wind. Yet another load source is due to gale force winds impinging on an edgewise-furled rotor giving rise to both direct and shear stresses in the rotor shaft. Additional shear stresses in the shaft of a turbine are due to the torque transmitted from the turbine rotor to the load.

Cyclically induced direct and shear stresses in a rotor shaft can be avoided if the rotor rotates, on suitable bearings, around the outer surface of a fixed shaft. Arrangements of this kind are commonly used in motor vehicles. A fixed, non-rotating shaft supporting a wind-turbine rotor will normally be hollow to permit an inner, torque transmittal, shaft, one end of which is attached to the upwind face of the turbine, to pass through the fixed shaft. An example of a turbine with such an arrangement is the machine illustrated in Fig. 6.2. The unit shown in Fig. 6.2 employs a flexible shaft to couple the turbine rotor to the submerged progressive-cavity pump located in the well below the tower.

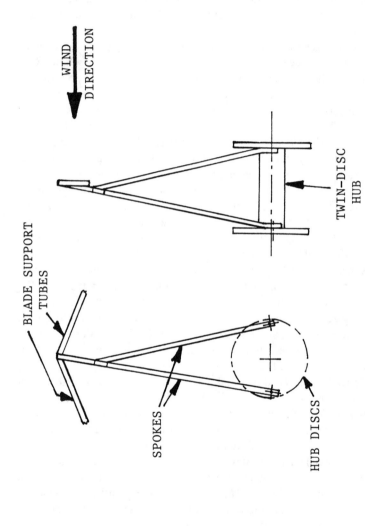

Figure 11.8. Frame of a light, perimeter-bladed rotor with two sets of joined spokes each spoke attached tangentially to a hub disc (diagrammatic).

11.8. Head Assemblies

A major function of a head assembly is, in general, to retain in their correct relative position, and provide support for, the turbine rotor, pump drive transmission and tail assembly. In many of the machines designed some years ago the head is in the form of a casting that accommodates, via suitable bored holes in which bearings are mounted, the rotor shaft, reduction gearing if any, yaw bearing and tail-pivot support bearings. This arrangement is particularly compact and convenient for oil-lubricated machines equipped with plain bearings. The same, or a similar, arrangement can also be used when oil-lubricated ball, or roller, race bearings are substituted for plain bearings.

In at least one recently produced machine a standard worm-drive gear box is employed as a speed reducer the cast casing of which constitutes the necessary oil bath. The remainder of the head structure is built up; hence the system represents a composite of a casting containing the reduction gearing and associated bearings in conjunction with a built-up head structure. When reduction gearing is not employed and sealed, self-aligning, grease-lubricated, ball race or roller race bearings are employed, it is, of course, still possible to utilise a head casting with much reduced machining. It is, however, also possible in such circumstances to use a built-up, welded, head assembly also involving only minimal machining or, if the mounting pads for bearings remain adequately flat after welding, involving no machining other than the drilling of bolt holes, etc.

An important factor related to head design involves the provision of a support for the tail-pivot system for machines with edgewise-furling rotors. The choice here, for systems with a lifting tail, usually involves angling the tail pivot such that a rigid tail assembly rises the correct amount, due to furling, to provide the desired restoring torque to prevent either premature or delayed furling and to subsequently return the rotor to the operational position. Alternatively a more easily arranged vertical tail pivot can be provided the raising of the tail being due, in this case, to a chain, or tie bar, connecting the tail boom to a higher point on the head structure eccentric to the tail-pivot axis.

Systems of these two types are illustrated in Fig. 7.3. The writer tends to favour the system with the vertical tail pivot and chain or tie bar because it is more easily adjusted to trim the furling wind speed and to accommodate changes, or departures from design, in the weight of the tail assembly. A disadvantage of the vertical-pivot, lifting-tail arrangement is the need for an additional pivot, with a horizontal axis, incorporated in the tail boom. The tail-pivot bushes of simple machines should be made from material that does not require lubrication. In some older designs of existing "up-market" oil-lubricated machines the tail-pivot bearings are lubricated, automatically, from the oil reservoir. Additional factors impacting the design of the head are the provision of a manually activated furling arrangement, operated from ground level to override the automatic system and the provision of an anchor pivot location, if needed, for a furling damper to prevent violent automatic furling, or unfurling motions.

11.9. Tail Assemblies

A tail assembly used in conjunction with a conventionally arranged upwind horizontal-axis turbine is connected to the head assembly by means of a vertical, or in some cases an inclined, axis hinge when the furling process involves the turbine rotor orientating edgewise to the wind direction. For other systems, for example, those in which the rotor blades are pitched, collectively, to give zero lift in the furled mode, the tail assembly is attached rigidly to the head assembly.

Structural concerns to which attention must be paid relate to supporting adequately, and stiffening suitably, the tailvane surface. Whilst the tailvane should not, under normal circumstances, become orientated broadside to the wind direction it may well be angled to the flow direction sufficiently, particularly under transient conditions, to generate relatively high lift coefficients. Hence some stiffening will be required if the tailvane surface is made from, for example, thin sheet metal. The necessary stiffening can, of course, be accomplished in a number of ways. An increased tailvane drag due to the use of stiffeners need not be regarded as a serious penalty. The drag, while contributing to the bending moment imposed on the tower due to wind loading, also assists the steering function of the tailvane. Thin sheet-metal tailvanes can be stiffened in one direction by using corrugations. Hence if the corrugations run in a chordwise, or streamwise, direction the tailvane need only be stiffened with additional structure in the spanwise direction. If the corrugations run spanwise the tail boom itself may provide sufficient stiffening in the chordwise direction.

The writer has found that, without resorting to expensive construction techniques, the tail assembly usually more than balances the turbine giving rise to a moment on the tower that is additive to that due to wind loading acting on the entire machine. A lack of balance between the rotor, head and tail assemblies is also undesirable in that unless the yaw axis is completely vertical the machine tends to position itself, in the yaw mode, with the centre of gravity at the lowest point, an unwanted input into the yaw-guidance system.

Because the tail assembly has to be constructed relatively lightly care must be taken to ensure that it is not a candidate for resonance problems by checking that the fundamental bending mode and torsional mode natural frequencies do not coincide with a turbine running speed. An occupational hazard of the tailvane boom is the risk of sustaining damage due to receiving impacts from the head assembly because of occasional sudden, or violent furling movements when an edgewise-furling rotor is used. The tail boom can, of course, be strengthened in an attempt to minimise such damage. A better solution is to employ a simple damper, preferably of the air-filled cylinder type, connected between the head and tail assemblies. The use of such a damper was referred to previously in Chapter 7, §7.1.2., and again, in the previous section of this chapter. A damper used in the manner suggested will not only reduce head-on-tail assembly impacts but will also limit the rate of precession of the head and hence also the gyroscopically induced loads imposed on the rotor.

The provision of a ground-operated manual furling system interacts with the design of the tail assembly by virtue of the need, in most cases, to provide an anchor location for a cable the tensioning of which implements a furling movement. In most commercially produced machines the cable, or chain, of the manual pull-out, or furling, system passes down the hollow yaw-pivot post, in close proximity to the pump-rod, to a small hand-operated winch, attached to the tower, accessible from ground level. A much simpler system, only suitable for fairly short towers, incorporates a small winch attached, by an outrigger bracket, to the head assembly. The winch is engaged, from ground level, by means of a removable extension-shaft-type handle much in the manner in which building sun-blinds or skylights are sometimes operated remotely. A system of this type is in use on a commercially produced water-pumping wind-turbine. A possible variant of the scheme, suitable for both tall and short towers, would employ an endless rope, or chain, to operate a head-mounted, worm-drive winch. Although a strong wind may blow the endless rope or chain out of reach temporarily, this will not be a serious problem since, under such conditions, the machine will have furled automatically.

References

Abbott, I.H. and von Doenhoff, A.E., 1959, "The Theory of Wing Sections", Dover Publications.

Alberta Energy Scientific and Engineering Services, 1987, "Development of Delta-Blade Wind Turbines", Government of Alberta, Pacific Plaza, 10909, Jasper Avenue, Edmonton, Alberta, Canada.

Anon, 1920, "A Seesaw Windmill", Literary Digest, December 18.

Apazidis, N., 1985, "Influence of Bubble Expansion and Relative Velocity on the Performance and Stability of an Airlift Pump", International Journal of Multiphase Flow, Vol. 11, No. 4, pp. 459–479, Pergamon/Elsevier.

Atkins, R.P. and Baker, D.R., 1991, "Lethbridge Wind Research Test Site, Evaluation of Wind and Solar Pumping Systems, 1990 Final Report", Alberta Farm Machinery Research Centre, Alberta Agriculture, Lethbridge, Alberta, Canada, pp. 35–37.

Atkins, R.P. and Proctor, R.J., 1993, "Consumers Guide to Wind Powered Water Pumping", Report, Development Project DL0693, Alberta Farm Machinery Research Centre, Lethbridge, Alberta, Canada.

Avery, D.E., 1983, "Wind Water Pump Stroke Control", U.S. Patent No. 4,392,785 of July 12, US Patent Office.

Avery, D.E., 1984, "Some New Developments for Wind Powered Water Pumping", Proceedings, pp. 220–233, National Conference of the American Wind Energy Association, Washington, DC, USA.

Aziz, K., Gregory, G.A., Nicholson, M. and Kentfield, J.A.C., 1976, "Two-Phase-Flow Pipeline Test Facility", Proceedings, Symposium on Internal Flows, pp. L1–L9, National Research Council of Canada, Ottawa, Canada.

Bach, von G., 1931, "Untersuchungen über Savonius-Rotoren und verwandte Strömungsmaschinen", Forsch. auf dem Gebiete des Ingenierwesens, 2, pp. 218–231.

Bailey, B., 1993, (Chairman, Siting Committee, American Wind Energy Association), "Recommended Practice for the Siting of Wind Energy Conversion Systems", AWEA Standard 8.2, American Wind Energy Association, Washington, DC, USA.

Baker, D.R., 1986, "Performance Test Results of the Deltx WP50 Windpump Prototype", Report A/CERRF Project RP#46, Part III, Alberta Government Energy Scientific and Engineering Services, Pacific Plaza, 10909, Jasper Avenue, Edmonton, Alberta, Canada.

Baker, T. Lindsay, 1985, "A Field Guide to American Windmills", University of Oklahoma Press, Norman, Oklahoma.

Betz, A., 1920, "Eine Erweiterung der Schrauben-strahl-Theorie", ZFM.

Beurskens, H.J.M., Hageman, A.K., Hospers, G.D., Kragten, A. and Lysen, E.H., 1980, "Low Speed Water Pumping Windmills: Rotor Tests and Overall Performance", Proceedings Third International Symposium on Wind Energy Systems, Paper K2, pp. 501–520, BHRA Fluid Engineering, Cranfield, Bedford, MK43 OAJ, England.

Braay, C.P. and Tersteeg, J.L.J., 1990, "Windmills of Holland", van Mastrigt en Verhoeven, Arnhem, The Netherlands.

Burton, J.D., 1988, "The Mechanical Coupling of Wind Turbines to Low Lift Rotordynamic Water Pumps", Solar and Wind Energy Technology, Vol. 5, No. 3, pp. 207–214, Pergamon Press, U.K.

Cleijne, H., Smulders, P., Verheij, F. and Oldenkamp, H., 1986, "Pump Research by CWD: The Influence of Starting Torque of Single Acting Piston Pumps on Water Pumping Windmills", Report R815D, Technical University Eindhoven, The Netherlands, Faculty of Physics, Laboratory of Fluid Dynamics and Heat Transfer, (Note: also presented at the 6th European Wind Energy Conference, Rome).

de Vries, O., 1981, "General Introduction to Wind Energy Conversion", Paper presented at the VKI Lecture Series No. 9 Wind Energy Conversion Devices, June 1–5, Rhode-Saint-Genèse, Belgium, National Aerospace Laboratory NLR, The Netherlands, Document NLR MP 81014 U.

Eldridge, F.R., 1975, "Wind Machines", Report Published by the Mitre Corporation for the National Sciences Foundation, Washington, DC, p. 55.

Fernando, M.S.U.K. and Modi, V.J., 1989, "Performance and Unsteady Wake of the Savonius Rotor: A Numerical Investigation", Proceedings, Eighth ASME Wind Energy Symposium, pp. 51–58, American Society of Mechanical Engineers.

Fraenkel, P., Barlow, R., Crick, F., Derrick, A. and Bokalders, V., 1993, "Windpumps, A Guide for Development Workers", Intermediate Technology Publications Ltd., 103–105 Southampton Row, London WC1B 4HH, UK.

Fraenkel, P.L., 1994, "The Development of Wind-Pumps", International Journal of Solar Energy, Vol. 14, pp. 239–255, Harwood Academic Publishers.

Freris, L.L. (Editor), 1990, "Wind Energy Conversion Systems", Prentice-Hall.

Fuhs, S.E., Vanderplaats, G.N. and Fuhs, A.E., 1978, "Land Contouring to Optimize Wind Power", AIAA Paper 78-279, presented at the AIAA 16th Aerospace Sciences Meeting, Huntsville, Alabama, American Institute of Aeronautics and Astronautics, Washington, DC, USA.

Gasch, R., Kortenkamp, R. and Twele, J., 1987, "A Simple Method for Near Optimum Design of Wind Turbines with Centrifugal Pumps", Wind Engineering, Vol. 11, No. 5, pp. 293–312.

Glauert, H., 1948, "The Elements of Airfoil and Airscrew Theory", 2nd Edition, Cambridge University Press.

Golding, E.W., 1956, "Wind and Solar Energy", Proceedings, Fig. 1, p. 92, Symposium held in New Delhi, India, UNESCO publication.

Gurney, T.R., 1976, "Fatigue Design Rules for Welded Steel Joints", The Welding Institute Research Bulletin, Vol. 17, May, R124/5/76.

Hancox, N.L. (Ed.), 1981, "Fibre Composite Hybrid Materials", Scientific and Technical Books, MacMillan Publishing Co. Inc., New York, N.Y.

Hawthorne, W.R. (Ed.), 1964, "Aerodynamics of Turbines and Compressors", High Speed Aerodynamics and Jet Propulsion Series, Vol. X, Princeton University Press, Princeton, N.J., USA.

Hoerner, S.F., 1965, "Fluid Dynamic Drag", Hoerner Fluid Dynamics, P.O. Box 65283, Vancouver, WA 98665, USA.

Hoerner, S.F. and Borst, H.V., 1975, "Fluid-Dynamic Lift", Hoerner Fluid Dynamics, P.O. Box 65283, Vancouver, WA 98665, USA.

Jansen, W.A.M. and Smulders, P.T., 1977, "Rotor Design for Horizontal Axis Windmills", CWD Report 77-1, CWD, P.O. Box 85, 3800 AB, Amersfoort, The Netherlands.

Justus, C.G., 1978, "Winds and Wind System Performance", Franklin Institute Press, Philadelphia, PA, USA.

Kennell, E., 1984, "A Joint American-Mexican Variable-Stroke Water-Pumping Wind Turbine", Oral presentation at the American Wind Energy Association National Conference, Pasadena, California.

Kentfield, J.A.C. and Norrie, D.H., 1978, "An Axial-Flow Wind-Turbine with Delta-Wing Blades", Proceedings, 1st Miami International Conference on Alternative Energy Sources, Vol. 4, pp. 1615–1645, Hemisphere Publishing Corp.

Kentfield, J.A.C., 1979, "Tests in the NRC 30′ × 30′ Wind-Tunnel of a 130″ Diameter, Horizontal Axis, Delta-Wing Bladed Wind-Turbine", University of Calgary, Department of Mechanical Engineering Report No. 150.

Kentfield, J.A.C., 1980(a), "The Performance of Delta-Wing Bladed Wind-Turbines", Proceedings, 7th Australasian Hydraulics and Fluid Mechanics Conference, Brisbane, pp. 427–430, Institution of Engineers of Australia, Publication No. 80/4.

Kentfield, J.A.C., 1980(b), "The Characteristics of Two, Simple, Automatic Speed-Control Devices for Horizontal Axis Wind-Turbines", Proceedings, 2nd Miami International Conference on Alternative Energy Sources, Hemisphere Publishing Corporation, Vol. 4, pp. 1561–1580.

Kentfield, J.A.C., 1982, "A Performance Comparison of Various Wind-Turbine Types for Powering Water Pumps", Proceedings, 17th Intersociety Energy Conversion Engineering Conference, Vol. 4, pp. 2082–2088, Institute of Electrical and Electronic Engineers.

Kentfield, J.A.C., 1983, "The Performance of Simple Horizontal Axis Wind-Turbines for the Direct Drive of Water Pumps", Proceedings, 18th Intersociety Energy Conversion Engineering Conference, Vol. 3, pp. 1360–1366, American Institute of Chemical Engineers.

Kentfield, J.A.C. and Vardi, I., 1985(a), "A Hydro-Mechanical Variable-Stroke Mechanism for Water-Pumping Wind-Turbines", Proceedings, International Solar Energy Society Annual Meeting, Montreal, Canada.

Kentfield, J.A.C. and Vardi, I., 1985(b), "An Adaptive Load-Control Mechanism for Water-Pumping Wind-Turbines", Proceedings, 20th Intersociety Energy Conversion Engineering Conference, Vol. 3, pp. 656–662, Society of Automotive Engineers.

Kentfield, J.A.C., 1986(a), "Modification, Due to Gusting, of the Performance Characteristics of Wind-Turbines", Proceedings, 21st Intersociety Energy Conversion Engineering Conference, Vol. 2, pp. 1247–1252, American Chemical Society.

Kentfield, J.A.C., 1986(b), "The Performance of a Simple, Oscillating Beam Type, Wind-Driven Water Pumper", Proceedings, Wind Energy Expo, pp. 279–288, American Wind Energy Association.

Kentfield, J.A.C., Booth, M. and Horsley, D., 1986, "A Twin-Airfoil Type, Oscillating Beam, Wind-Driven Water Pumper", Proceedings of the Second National Conference of the Canadian Wind Energy Association, pp. 175–187, Canadian Wind Energy Association.

Kentfield, J.A.C. and Horsley, D., 1987, "Operational Experience with a Prototype, Full-Scale, Twin Airfoil Type, Oscillating-Beam Aeolian Pumpjack", Proceedings, Windpower '87, pp. 352–357, American Wind Energy Association.

Kentfield, J.A.C., 1987, "The Performance of Model and Full-Scale Delta-Wing Bladed Wind-Turbine Rotors", Proceedings, Windpower '87, pp. 226–233, American Wind Energy Association.

Kentfield, J.A.C., 1988(a), "Performance Criteria for Simple Water-Pumping Wind-Turbines", Proceedings, Canadian Wind Energy Association Annual Conference, pp. 323–333.

Kentfield, J.A.C., 1988(b), "The Influence of Vortex Flaps and Leading-Edge Snags on the Performance of Delta-Wing Bladed Wind-Turbines", Proceedings of the 3rd Annual (1987) Conference of the Canadian Wind Energy Association, pp. 119–128, Canadian Wind Energy Association, Ottawa, Canada.

Kentfield, J.A.C., 1988(c), "A Simple, Linear Wind-Turbine Wake-Model", Proceedings, 7th ASME Wind Energy Symposium, pp. 1–5, American Society of Mechanical Engineers.

Kentfield, J.A.C., 1988(d), "Perimeter Blading, a New Concept for Water-Pumping Wind-Turbines", Proceedings, 23rd Intersociety Energy Conversion Engineering Conference, Vol. 4, pp. 7–12, American Society of Mechanical Engineers

Kentfield, J.A.C. and Cruson, I., 1989, "A Prototype Canadian Water-Pumping Wind Turbine", Proceedings, 5th Annual National Conference of the Canadian Wind Energy Association, pp. 69–81, Canadian Wind Energy Association, Ottawa, Canada.

Kentfield, J.A.C., 1989(a), "A Prototype Water-Pumping Wind-Turbine Based on a New Design Philosophy", Proceedings, Windpower '89, pp. 291–297, American Wind Energy Association, Washington, DC.

Kentfield, J.A.C., 1989(b), "A Space-Frame Tower Concept for Small, Self-Erecting Wind Turbines", Proceedings, 24th Intersociety Energy Conversion Engineering Conference, Vol. 4, pp. 2015–2019, Institute of Electrical and Electronic Engineers.

Kentfield, J.A.C., 1990, "A Re-Examination of Drag-Type Rotors", Proceedings, Annual Conference of the Canadian Wind Energy Association, pp. 273–287, Canadian Wind Energy Association, Ottawa, Canada.

Kentfield, J.A.C., 1992(a), "The Delta-Wing Bladed Rotor Concept", Journal of Wind Engineering and Industrial Aerodynamics, Vol. 39, Nov. 1–3, pp. 405–416, Elsevier Science Publishers B.V., Amsterdam, The Netherlands.

Kentfield, J.A.C., 1992(b), "A Downwind Application of a Delta-Turbine Rotor to Water Pumping", Proceedings, Wind Energy '92, pp. 208–220, Canadian Wind Energy Association, Ottawa.

Kentfield, J.A.C. and Panek, M., 1993, "An Improved Perimeter-Bladed Rotor for Water-Pumping Wind Turbines", Proceedings, Wind Energy '93, pp. 231–244, Canadian Wind Energy Association, Ottawa, Canada.

Kragten, A., 1982, "The Hinged Side Vane as a Safety Mechanism for Windmills", CWD Internal Report R-515-D, Wind Energy Group, Laboratory of Fluid Dynamics and Heat Transfer, Department of Physics, Eindhoven University of Technology, Eindhoven, The Netherlands.

Kragten, A., 1985, "Windtunnel Measurements on a Scale Model of the WEU-I-4 Rotor to Determine $C_P \sim \lambda$ and $C_q \sim \lambda$ Curves", Report R-715-D, Wind Energy Group, Department of Physics, Laboratory of Fluid Dynamics and Heat Transfer, Eindhoven University of Technology, P.O. Box 513, 5600 MB, Eindhoven, The Netherlands.

Lopes, J.C.B. and Dukler, A.E., 1987, "Droplet Dynamics in Vertical Gas–Liquid Annular Flow", American Institute of Chemical Engineers Journal, Vol. 33, No. 6, pp. 1013–1024.

Major, J.K. and Watts, M., 1992, "Victorian and Edwardian Windmills and Watermills and Watermills from Old Photographs", Fitzhouse Books, London.

Meel, J.V., Smulders, P., Oldenkamp, H., Nat, A.V.D. and Lysen, E., 1986, "Field Testing of Water Pumping Windmills by CWD", CWD, P.O. Box 85, 3800 AB Amersfoort, The Netherlands.

Milborrow, D., 1994, "Grappling With Gusts", Wind Power Monthly, Vol. 10, No. 2, Feb., pp. 33–38, Wind Power Monthly, Vrinners Hoved, 8420 Knebel, Denmark.

Modi, V.J. and Roth, N.J., 1982, "Prototype Design of a Wind Energy Operated Irrigation System", Proceedings, 17th Intersociety Energy Conversion Engineering Conference, pp. 2089–2095, IEEE.

Modi, V.J., Fernando, M.S.U.K. and Roth, N.J., 1985, "A Prototype Design and Performance of the Savonius Rotor Based Irrigation System", Proceedings, Fourth ASME Wind Energy Symposium, pp. 245–256, American Society of Mechanical Engineers.

Modi, V.J., Fernando, M.S.U.K. and Roth, N.J., 1990, "Aerodynamics of the Savonius Rotor: Experiments and Analysis", Proceedings, 25th Intersociety Energy Conversion Engineering Conference, Vol. 4, pp. 213–218, American Institute of Chemical Engineers.

Newman, B.G., 1974, "Measurements on a Savonius Rotor with Variable Gap", Proceedings, Wind Energy: Achievements and Potential, pp. 116–136, Department of Mechanical Engineering, Faculty of Sciences, University of Sherbrooke, Sherbrooke, Canada.

Nierenberg, R., 1993, "Detailed Measurements on the Effects of Trees on Wind Speed, Energy, Vertical Shear and Turbulence", Proceedings, Windpower '93, pp. 218–225, American Wind Energy Association, Washington, DC, USA.

Park J., 1981, "The Wind Power Book", Cheshire Books, 514 Bryant Street, Palo Alto, CA 94301, USA.

Pennell, W.T. and Miller, A.H., 1982, "Procedures for Modelling Wind Turbine Performance from Site Wind Data", ASME Paper 82-Pet-7, American Society of Mechanical Engineers.

Perry, T.O., 1899, "Experiments With Windmills", United States Geological Survey, Government Printing Office, Washington, D.C.

Reynolds, J., 1970, "Windmills and Watermills", Hugh Evelyn Limited, 9 Fitzroy Square, London, W1P 5AH.

Rohatgi, J. and Nelson, V., 1994, "Wind Characteristics", Alternative Energy Institute, Box 248, Canyon, TX 79016-0001, USA.

Savonius, S.J., 1931, "The S-Rotor and Its Application", Mechanical Engineering, Vol. 53, No. 5, pp. 333–338.

Schwitzer, D., 1991, "Der Savonius-Rotor Entwicklung und Bauform", Wind Kraft Journal and Natürliche Energien, 4 Quartal, pp. 41–43, Verlag Natürliche Energie, Grevensberg, 24811 Brekendorf, Germany.

Smeaton, J., 1759, "On the Construction and Effects of Windmill Sails. An Experimental Study Concerning the Natural Powers of Water and Wind", Philosophical Transactions of the Royal Society of London, 51, Pt. 1, pp. 138–174.

Smulders, P.T., Kragten, A., Vaan, W., Logtenberg, A. and Leede, G. de, 1984, "Innovative Control and Safety Systems for Waterpumpers", Paper presented at, and published in the proceedings of, the European Wind Energy Conference (EWEC), Hamburg, 22–26 October.

Smulders, P.T. and Schermerhorn, R., 1984, "The Design of Fastrunning Waterpumping Windmills", Proceedings, Windpower '84, Pasadena, California, pp. 151–183, American Wind Energy Association, Washington, DC, USA.

Smulders, P.T., Alan, M.M. and Burton, J.D., 1991, "Wind Rotors and Rotordynamic Pumps", Proceedings, 1991 European Wind Energy Conference (EWEC '91), pp. 692–696, Elsevier Science Publishers B.V., The Netherlands.

Stepanoff, A.J., 1966, "Pumps and Blowers", John Wiley and Sons Inc., New York.

Stover Mfg. and Engine Co., "Samson Oil Rite Windmills and Ideal Towers", Catalog No. 41, Freeport, IL, USA.

Sydney Williams and Co. (Pty.) Ltd., "Windmill Pumping Plants", Catalogue No. 9, Constitution Road, Dulwich Hill, Sydney, Australia.

Ushiyama, I., Nagai, H. and Mino, M., 1982, "The Optimum Design Configurations of Savonius Wind Turbines", Proceedings, 17th Intersociety Energy Conversion Engineering Conference, pp. 2096–2101, IEEE.

Wilson, R.E., Lissaman, P.B.S. and Walker, S.N., 1976, "Aerodynamic Performance of Wind Turbines", US Energy Research and Development Authority Final Report ERDA/NSF/04014-76/1.

Author Index

Subject Index

pump servicing 172, 257
pumped-storage 7
pumping cycles 244

R

rate of precession 164
Rayleigh distribution 63, 66, 67, 180
reciprocating lift pumps 1
reciprocating positive-displacement
    pump 124
reduction gearing 5, 135, 244
regenerative pump 195
residual whirl 40, 41, 43
retractable tubular sheath 233
retracting tailvane 159
retreating cups 236
Reynolds number 31, 32, 36, 38,
    42, 81, 85, 101, 107, 110,
    119, 121, 230, 232
Reynolds number correction 94
rigid rotor type 163
riser main 171, 172
rising tail assembly concept 153
rocking beam 209, 210
roller races 253
rotary progressive cavity pump 257
rotary positive-displacement pumps
    1, 144
rotary, progressive cavity,
    positive-displacement pump 141
rotor aerodynamic performance 77
rotor aerodynamics 23
rotor angular position 232
rotor blade support frame 253
rotor blockage 236
rotor-brake 166
rotor-dynamic pumps 1, 192, 195
rotor frame 78
rotor peripheral speed 15
rotor shaft 259

rotors of equal blade area 134
rotor solidities 80
rotor/stator contact area 190
rotor tip-speed ratio 15, 18
rotor wakes 23, 42
rounded escarpment 61
runaway condition 203
runaway tip-speed ratio 48, 233

S

sail-cloth 3
sailing ships 189
San Gorgonio Pass 62
Savonius 3
Savonius rotor 23, 47, 48, 49,
    219, 229, 230, 232
scaling down 142
scaling up 142
scoop wheel 3, 144, 189
sealed bearings 254
seat rings 172
sectional rotor 137, 152
sectional-type rotors 163
see-saw beam 221
self-aligning races 254
self-erecting systems 243
semi-cylinders 229, 230
semi-cylindrical blades 236
separated flow 223
servo-rotor yaw control system 137
S-glass 252
shaft bending moments 239
sheet-metal blades 82
short-stroke pump 176
simple harmonic motion 175
simple lattice-type towers 255
simple lift-type pump 172
slatted rotors 94
slide-up-type self-erection 255